Thrift and Its Paradoxes

Max Planck Studies in Anthropology and Economy
Series editors:
Stephen Gudeman, University of Minnesota
Chris Hann, Max Planck Institute for Social Anthropology

Definitions of economy and society, and their proper relationship to each other, have been the perennial concerns of social philosophers. In the early decades of the twenty-first century these became and remain matters of urgent political debate. At the forefront of this series are the approaches to these connections by anthropologists, whose explorations of the local ideas and institutions underpinning social and economic relations illuminate large fields ignored in other disciplines.

Volume 10
Thrift and Its Paradoxes
From Domestic to Political Economy
Edited by Catherine Alexander and Daniel Sosna

Volume 9
Wine Is Our Bread
Labour and Value in Moldovan Winemaking
Daniela Ana

Volume 8
Moral Economy at Work
Ethnographic Investigations in Eurasia
Edited by Lale Yalçın-Heckmann

Volume 7
Work, Society, and the Ethical Self
Chimeras of Freedom in the Neoliberal Era
Edited by Chris Hann

Volume 6
Financialization
Relational Approaches
Edited by Chris Hann and Don Kalb

Volume 5
Market Frictions
Trade and Urbanization at the Vietnam–China Border
Kirsten W. Endres

Volume 4
Industrial Labor
Precarity, Class, and the Neoliberal Subject
Edited by Chris Hann and Jonathan Parry

Volume 3
When Things Become Property
Land Reform, Authority, and Value in Postsocialist Europe and Asia
Thomas Sikor, Stefan Dorondel, Johannes Stahl, and Phuc Xuan To

Volume 2
Oikos and Market
Explorations in Self-Sufficiency after Socialism
Edited by Stephen Gudeman and Chris Hann

Volume 1
Economy and Ritual
Six Studies of Postsocialist Transformations
Edited by Stephen Gudeman and Chris Hann

Thrift and Its Paradoxes

From Domestic to Political Economy

Edited by

Catherine Alexander and Daniel Sosna

berghahn
NEW YORK • OXFORD
www.berghahnbooks.com

Published in 2022 by
Berghahn Books
www.berghahnbooks.com

Library of Congress Cataloging-in-Publication Data

Names: Alexander, Catherine, editor. | Sosna, Daniel, editor.
Title: Thrift and its paradoxes : from domestic to political economy / edited by Catherine Alexander and Daniel Sosna.
Description: New York : Berghahn Books, 2022. | Series: Max Planck studies in anthropology and economy; volume 10 | Includes bibliographical references and index.
Identifiers: LCCN 2022004576 (print) | LCCN 2022004577 (ebook) | ISBN 9781800734623 (hardback) | ISBN 9781800734630 (ebook)
Subjects: LCSH: Consumption (Economics)--Social aspects. | Thriftiness. | Saving and investment.
Classification: LCC HC79.C6 T53 2022 (print) | LCC HC79.C6 (ebook) | DDC 339.4/7--dc23/eng/20220211
LC record available at https://lccn.loc.gov/2022004576
LC ebook record available at https://lccn.loc.gov/2022004577

British Library Cataloguing in Publication Data

A catalogue record for this book is available from the British Library

ISBN 978-1-80073-462-3 hardback
ISBN 978-1-80073-463-0 ebook

Contents

Illustrations

Figures

Tables

Acknowledgments

We are grateful to Chris Hann, who enthusiastically supported a reexamination of thrift building on Stephen Gudeman's classic work. Alongside Chris' continued support, this volume has benefitted from discussions about thrift with Lenka Brunclíková, Juraj Buzalka, Martin Hájek, David Henig, Don Kalb, Václav Křivanec, Ľubomír Lupták, Nicolette Makowicky, Pavel Mašek, Petr Skalník, Barbora Stehlíková, Detelina Tocheva, and Martin Tremčinský.

Daniel is grateful for discussions with Miguel Alexiades, Luděk Brož, Paul Keil, and Petr Jehlička, and, most importantly, to his coeditor, Catherine Alexander. She was the engine behind the project and the primary author of the Introduction.

The editors are delighted to thank the two anonymous, external reviewers for their excellent, thoughtful, and constructive comments, Berghahn Books for their wonderfully efficient editorial and production support, and Patty Gray for her painstaking preliminary copyediting and proofreading.

Daniel acknowledges initial support from the Wenner-Gren Foundation (Gr. Conf. 783), the Max Planck Institute for Social Anthropology in Halle, and the University of West Bohemia in Pilsen. The Czech Science Foundation (GA20-06759S) and the Institute of Ethnology, Czech Academy of Sciences supported Daniel's work on Chapter 7, the Introduction, and editorial work. The AV21 program supported the preparation of the index. Catherine is grateful to Daniel for coming up with the idea that thrift could be a productive concept to think about and to the Leverhulme Trust for a Major Research Fellowship (MRF-2018-046) that provided time to work on this. She would also like to acknowledge Samuel Williams' typically generous and creative thoughts about thrift.

Introduction

Thrift, Antithrift, Scale, and Paradox

Catherine Alexander and Daniel Sosna

One of the editors of this volume (Daniel Sosna) observed of the newly independent Czech Republic in the 1990s that carefully washing out and storing used bottles had become an outmoded activity for grandparents as younger people eagerly turned toward purchasing new consumer goods. However, a decade later, reusing plastic became cool for the younger generation, now signaling being green and European. The other editor (Catherine Alexander) learned the arts of household thrift from a mother raised in wartime Britain. She mentioned her knack for using up leftovers in 2002 to a housewife in Kazakhstan who had been extolling her own expertise in feeding her family with limited resources during the Soviet years. The reaction was dismissive: "Why? When there's no need?" Lauding a skill driven by necessity does not always translate into a habitus of value-driven actions (Alexander 2012). Clearly, thrift as virtue and rational economic action is not a given, even though economic and environmental crises seem to be ushering in a new age of thrift where such domestic concerns, more generally associated with households, have moved to the global stage and underscore national public policies.

Certain economic narratives of the twenty-first century might thus be seen as a morality tale. From this perspective, the present age, often dubbed the Anthropocene, is one where the natural world has been irreversibly damaged by human action: over-consumerism, corporate greed, inexorable capitalist expansion, resource extraction, and prodigal wastefulness that clogs the oceans and threatens the planet's survival—"overheating" in Thomas Hylland Eriksen's phrase (2016). This could be seen as an apocalyptic tale of the consequences of the forgotten values of thrift: low living and high thinking, material care and repair, temperance, saving, and wise spending. The discipline of austerity succeeds the Bacchanalia of excessive expenditure and consumerism as a morally and economically necessary corrective. Such austerity measures, after the 2008 crash, deploy an economic model arguably more suited to the thriftiness of a household or grocer's shop, one that deplores the imprudence of the feckless, indebted poor, and cuts public expenditure as a fiscally prudent measure aimed at balancing the books for the good of the nation.[1] Austerity's dour "no pain, no gain" prescription echoes the "shock therapy" applied to Latin American countries and then the former socialist bloc by international lending agencies in the 1990s. Neoliberal austerity programs cull the weak and the poor. Having been encouraged to borrow on easy credit, those least able to help themselves are now enjoined to tighten their belts and learn the value of thrift.

But such a story crashes together entirely different scales, temporalities, actions, and values. Thrift, it turns out, is at once a potent, self-evident concept, but also one that is slippery, ambiguous, and mobile as well as mobilizing. At the very least, capitalist states are ambivalent about thrift. The capital of savings is needed to fund development, but spending is also required to create profit for industry, as demonstrated by the South Korean government's change in policies from encouraging thrift to promoting spending (Nelson 1996). This volume aims to capture the pervasiveness of thrift but also how it changes shape, transforms over time, and can bear multiple meanings and connotations in different places, domains (e.g., spiritual or secular; market or household), times, and at different scales. We use "scale" here to indicate a qualitative distinction between levels that, in the context of thrift discourse, is often eclipsed to suggest the distinction is merely one of size, just another level up or down. The key intervention made by this volume is to show how contemporary practices and moralities of thrift are intertwined with austerity, debt, commerce, welfare, and patronage across various social and economic scales and are constantly renegotiated at the nexus of economic, religious, kinship, and gendered ideals and practices.

Certainly, thrift seems to be an idea whose time has come. Alongside neoliberal retractions of state investment and the insistence that people should be self-reliant, thrifty practices that minimize spending and waste through mending and making do have acquired a certain hip and middle-class chic. Recycling in the name of environmental sustainability has also become something of a moral mantra, even if its efficacy is questionable (Alexander 2022). Since 2006, there have been numerous books and special issues dedicated to the history and reemergence of thrift (e.g.

McCloskey 2006; Yates and Davison Hunter 2011; Podkalicka and Potts 2014; Yarrow 2014; Hulme 2019, 2020; Färber and Podkalicka 2019). These are rich cultural-historical accounts, largely focused on North America and Britain, which also mine literature and economics, media studies, and consumer research to trace different normative narratives. These studies make it clear that there is no simple historical evolution toward and then away from thrift as consumerism takes hold—thrift is endlessly rediscovered in different forms and at different levels from households to mutual savings groups to state-organized wartime material economies (Yates and Davison Hunter 2011).

There has been limited conversation between this body of literature and the admittedly few interventions so far from anthropology that unpack how and why thrift is performed, negotiated, and experienced in everyday lives. This volume offers a response to the under-theorization and exploration of thrift as it is practiced—and indeed practiced upon people. Perhaps it has been eclipsed as an often feminized, domestic concern, echoing the marginalization of domestic labor from mainstream economics (see, e.g., Waring 1988 and feminist economics more broadly). And yet, ripped from its domestic context, that logic has strayed across scales to legitimize state and industrial austerity programs across the world, even though states and capitalist business are qualitatively different entities: states raise taxes, corporations maximize profit. Austerity policies, in turn, have profoundly affected how most households manage to get by. How thrift actually works, therefore, demands attention. Similarly, the rhetorical and practical effects of an ideal type of thrift—cost-cutting, waste-shunning, saving—are worth scrutinizing as it travels, unmoored from its roots, and is applied to quite different contexts.

In the chapters that follow, our ethnographic explorations, both within and beyond Europe and North America, challenge and extend how thrift has been analyzed. By investigating how these ideas appear, travel, prove irrelevant, are enforced, appropriated, clash with other norms, or seem to appear in quite different cosmologies, ethnographies of thrift enrich our understandings of this familiar but most protean of concepts. Moreover, beneath the normative, often disciplinary force of crude thrifty narratives (spend less, save more, cut waste), there are ways of managing limited resources that often go unrecognized as a response to poverty. What interests us here is not so much coming up with a new one-size-fits-all definition of thrift, but tracking practices of frugality, resource care, investment, saving, and wise spending, and how such customs are understood and expressed across different geographical regions and scalar domains.

Chapters and Themes

Five themes or questions run through this book. We start by taking thrift to be the careful management of resources to ensure a person or household has enough to sustain it. It is therefore oriented toward a future, typically involving minimizing expenditure and wastefulness. But thrift is also freighted with a multitude of linked characteristics—hard work, self-discipline, sobriety, rational forethought, restraint, the desire and capacity to save and accumulate—that are often used singly as synonyms for thrift. But, to take one example, it is too easy to read thrift into sober clothes and modest comportment, which may have nothing to do with restrained saving and spending. The Dutch Golden Age may have valorized thrift as a virtue, but the monochrome portraits of prosperous merchants not only paraded rich furs and velvets but the deep black, multihued dyes that were notoriously difficult and costly to achieve (Debra Weiss pers. comm.). Another age knew how to read displays of fabulous wealth into those layered shades of night (Schama 1987). This book unpacks those companion qualities, which sometimes appear to be neither necessary nor sufficient to achieve thrifty aims, and how thrifty ideologies have played their part in disciplinary discourses typically directed toward colonized peoples and the working class.

The second element we consider is the prerequisites for thrift and whether people are able, supposing they are willing, to engage in activities that ensure a secure future. Is a surplus always possible for subsistence economies, or necessary, in conditions of abundance, or indeed wanted, where sharing has greater social value? In other words, is thrift always a choice or are there structural and material conditions or cultural logics that render it impossible, irrelevant, or repugnant? That is, how does thrift appear as an ethnographic category?

The third question follows on directly. What are the limits of thrift? When and why is it, or that array of linked qualities, repudiated? When is thrift just wrong? One immediate challenge for ethnographic comparison is that the English "thrift" is derived from Old Norse. Its subsequent encrustations of meaning in English, including its elevation to a virtue, may not seamlessly translate to other languages and places. The Portuguese term *economia* and the German *Sparsamkeit*, for example, simply emphasize spending little, saving, and living sparingly. Neither term carries much moral weight (Jason Sumich and Afia Afenah pers. comm.).[2] Nor is thrift always a virtue even in the chilly lands of North Atlantic Protestant sobriety. Without temperance it is a vice (McCloskey 2011). The figure of the miser is more consistently reviled, often in racist terms,[3] than its counterpart, the spendthrift, which in turn can attract class judgments of not knowing the value of money.

Related to the above, future-oriented temporalities are an important element in both thrifty moralities and practices, but they appear very differently according to ethnographic context. Thus, secure futures might mean intergenerational sustainability at a planetary level (World Commission on Environment and Development 1987), stewardship of resources in another lexicon, household resilience in withstanding shortage and continuing across generations (Gudeman and Rivera 1990), meeting the shorter-term demands of feeding, clothing, and educating children, or living in the present such that future salvation is assured. Calendrical and ritual rhythms also highlight the limits of thrift when a time for feasting trumps an imperative to save. Richard Wilk (this vol.) explores how discourses of both thrift and its various antitheses (e.g., laziness) are shaped by moralized temporal ontologies and orientations.

Finally, we flag up the appearance of thrift in different contexts, asking if it is always the same thing. Although, as discussed below, Maynard Keynes was not the first to identify or even name the paradox of thrift, he certainly popularized the idea that, in a recession, citizens' saving results in a sluggish economy, unemployment, and thus ultimately their inability to save (1936: 84). Nearly a century on and waist deep in another recession that apparently valorizes thriftiness, it is worth examining where and how thrift appears to migrate across scales and what paradoxes this presents—or explains.

This collection thus offers an anatomy of thrift and its paradoxes; its genealogies and reach; how it appears ethnographically in action and discourse; how it has been used, rejected, and reappropriated; and how it may serve to elide differences between, for example, individuals' comportment or economic actions, fiscal policy, and financial investment. One of the largest multinational life insurance companies is, after all, called Prudential, merging a sense of household thriftiness with financial investment. In so doing, we rethink concepts of generosity and its apparent opposite,[4] thrift, which are at once over-determined and unsystematically theorized in economic anthropology, and engage with the paradoxes that thrift often presents. This book thus contributes to a reconciliation of studies of ethics and political economy, the former often emphasizing the individual; the latter, state and supranational structures. Few though they are, thrift studies often implicitly echo feminist ethics and the ethics of care literature (e.g., Noddings 2013; Buch 2015) in their concern with relationality, connecting individuals to household, community, kin, and other expressions of mutuality. We do not propose bringing these different bodies of literature together into one plane, but suggest how and where these different analytical approaches, levels, and scales articulate or are merged, and what happens as a result.

The remainder of this introduction explores first how anthropologists have engaged with thrift as well as the curious paucity of considerations of thrift in accounts of shortage economies (e.g., war, economic depression, socialist states, and the early years of postsocialism) and the field of waste studies. The next section flips this upside down. By approaching thrift from a different angle we consider how assumptions about thrift shaped certain key anthropological debates, which in turn raised questions about the purchase of thrift as either virtue or rational economic practice beyond its familiar stamping ground of Scandinavia and the North Atlantic. What emerges recapitulates familiar anthropological moves, understanding actions within local cosmologies and value regimes as socially embedded. This in turn highlights the limits to thrift in the places where it is most familiar, when, for example, enactments of generosity and ritual observance are appropriate and thrift distasteful. Logics of thrift and antithrift are often entwined but may be either valued differently or have distinct temporal rhythms.

The final section considers what the ethnographic chapters offer in terms of understanding thrift in different regions, tracing it across scales, and exploring apparent paradoxes. Together, the following sections and chapters show that paradoxes of thrift are not only found in the incommensurate nature of household and state forms of saving. Everyday thrift may require indebtedness, be tied to generosity, or be stimulated by abundance as much as scarcity.

Max Weber and Thrift

We start with a brief discussion of Max Weber's ([1904-05] 2001) *Protestant Ethic* thesis since this is often the key reference point for thinking through thrift. Weber's proposition was that the existential terror of damnation initiated by Calvinism[5] together with the notion of vocation translated into calculative saving that produced this worldly signs of otherworldly salvation: increase of wealth through saving and profitable improvement of holdings. Such Protestant, inner-worldly asceticism (*innerweltliche Askese*) was a world away, he suggested, from the fatalistic Catholic peasant (see Rudnyckyj this vol.).

For Weber, the happy coincidence between inner-worldly asceticism and capitalist accumulation helps explain why capitalism took off in northern Europe in the sixteenth century. This mutually reinforcing duet was transformed into the consummate national characteristic of North America, alongside hard work and self-discipline, by Benjamin Franklin, Weber's favorite exemplar of capitalism (Yarrow 2014; Yates and Davison Hunter

2011). As in so many other instances, there were Soviet echoes with early twentieth-century America, both valorizing the housewifely virtue of thrift and material care, as Lewis Siegelbaum (2006: 11) describes for the Soviet regime where lack of consumer goods intensified the value placed on making do with little, if not saving.

However, Weber refers neither to thrift (Hájek et al. 2019: 65) nor the household but rather describes some of the characteristics that have come to act as metonymic shorthands for thrift: hard work, self-discipline, and saving. Weber presents a Protestant moralization of a certain kind of economic rationality that conflates practitioner with practice, person, household, and enterprise. Similarly, present frugality is intimately linked to both short-term worldly gain and eternal salvation. Thrift thus appears as both value- and goal-driven rational action, as much performative as instrumental (see Weber [1968] 2013; Kalberg 1980).

The exclusive connection between Protestantism and an ethic of hard work, frugal expenditure, and saving has long been debunked by historians noting the fourteenth-century Tuscan merchants whose account books were inscribed with "For God and profit!" as well as the emphasis placed on hard work and thrift by Cistercian orders (Andersen et al. 2016; Spalová this vol.). Extending the ethnographic range again highlights that Protestantism is far from being the only moral framework centered on thrift and/or hard work. Sinah Theres Kloß (2016: 277–79; see also Singer 1966; Darling 1934) discusses ideas of frugal spending in Asian communities, while Confucian *suzhi* discourse is concerned with what superficially appear to be Protestant (here rendered as "neoliberal") values of self-cultivation and discipline (Kipnis 2007; see also Lim and Sin Lay 2003). Confucianism emphasizes household frugality, a cultural code echoed in Japanese tradition and intensified (as elsewhere) during the second world war (Garon 2000) into a "hegemonic culture of thrift" (Uchiyama 2019) to serve national interests. But rather than join the queue of challenges to Weber, we should note his main point was that Calvin, uniquely, added predestination and eternal damnation to the religiously oriented, rational conduct of business (Weber 2001).

Although it was the first explicit, theoretical anthropological investigation of saving, Mary Douglas and Baron Isherwood's *The World of Goods* ([1979] 2002) has been oddly forgotten by subsequent studies of thrift. They open with a clear statement that seeing thrift as a positive practice and attribute is culturally dependent: "Spending only a small proportion of income may in one place and time be called thrifty, wise and provident; in another it may be held to be miserly, mean and wrong. Conversely, a high ratio of consumption may be approved as generous, magnificent and good in one culture, while in another the selfsame behaviour may be called spendthrift, feckless and bad" (2002: 12). This is then considered through their modification (2002: 24–26) of Weber's analysis through different forms of social organization, allowing the possibility of comparing accumulation practices across very different ethnographic and historical contexts. Peasants, in their formulation, are rigidly controlled by landlords, socially peripheral, and unable either to compete or band together. Bare subsistence makes saving impossible. Weber's "traditional society" is requalified as broadly egalitarian groups that typically reject individual accumulation; the group amasses wealth. Where individualism is strong, there are more incentives to accumulate but success is uncertain and risky, partly offset by insisting on the commercial virtues of honesty and hard work (2002: 25). This qualification of Weber's typology, they suggest, allows his observations about who saves when and why to be more usefully applied to a wider range of contexts.

We propose a further qualification. The peasants that Weber characterized as fatalistic and opposed to Protestant drive need to be further divided between those operating in subsistence economies,[6] where saving is unfeasible, and self-sufficient households, where thrift is valued and reserves possible. Another take is Eric Wolf's observation that most peasants did and do produce a surplus, but this could not be converted into reserves as it was immediately taken by exploitative landlords (1966: 10). Such functionally subsistence households have been analyzed through a different kind of thriftiness, such as time thriftiness: only working as much as is necessary to meet needs, dubbed the "needs: drudgery ratio", and later used by Marshall Sahlins to describe hunter-gatherer societies (1974). Again, the flexible use of unwaged family and co-operative neighborly labor (Chayanov [1923] 1966) can be seen as a form of thriftiness—or domestic exploitation.

The sense that subsistence farming is inimical to thrift is best summed up by George Foster's idea of the limited good as the driving peasant orientation: anything that is good is finite, in short supply, and cannot be augmented by any human means, including hard work and thrift (1965: 296). Moreover, he trenchantly remarks, "It is pointless to talk of thrift in a subsistence economy in which most producers are at the economic margin; there is usually nothing to be thrifty about" (1965: 307). Thrift in such a hand-to-mouth existence is neither morally nor economically valorized (see also Wolf 1966).

Stephen Gudeman and Alberto Rivera (1990) were the first anthropologists to explore thrift explicitly as an ethnographic category, juxtaposing it with classic political economy texts as conversations between local models of the economy, western folk models, and those of political economists. An updated version of that discussion by Gudeman starts this volume's ethnographic chapters. Gudeman and Rivera distinguish between the kind of saving that Weber saw as the motor of capitalism, focused on growth and profit, and the kind of saving described by rural farmers, which ensure adequate reserves are in place to enable the household to continue. The qualitative difference between these kinds of saving is played out as a distinction between household and market, replenishment as opposed to constant growth for its own sake. Such households differ from the bare subsistence described above.

The Household and Beyond: Anthropologies of Thrift

Gudeman's focus on the *oikos* or household reminds us that the virtue of frugality as minimal expense, has historically been located in the domestic, private sphere and thus sensitizes us to potential problems of extrapolating that virtue to other contexts. Such household management or economy centers on careful spending, shunning waste, and ensuring an adequate surplus to act as a reserve in case of hardship. There is also a distinction between natural increase through reproduction of people, animals, and crops, and market forms of increase based on trading, selling, and earning. The crucial point is that the household's future is one of generational continuity and security rather than the short-term, future-oriented growth that surplus indicates for capitalist enterprises. The environmental context is key: the households described by Gudeman and Rivera are relatively self-sufficient—itself a prized quality—and exist in conditions of relative uncertainty: crops may fail, animals sicken, the weather turn. Reserves are therefore a necessary investment to displace the risk of failure.

Gudeman and Hann's (2015) volume considering household economies and self-sufficiency extends the ethnographic purchase of Gudeman's long engagement with thrift (e.g., 2001: 16, 182) as also being central to practices of preservation to postsocialist, rural central Europe and Kyrgyzstan. Here, thriftiness as restricted consumption again appears as a typical house process (Gudeman and Hann 2015: 14). Their emphasis on mutuality within and beyond the household to satisfy needs (as opposed to the calculated self-interest of the market) is a useful extension of what constitutes the household as well as indicating both the labor that goes into thrift and its endpoint or goal. Nathan Light makes this explicit by shifting from self-sufficiency to what he calls "social sufficiency" (2015: 101), emphasizing that in Kyrgyz households, "thrift enables people to make better contributions to feasts and social events" (2015: 104–5). This is an important recognition that individual and household thrift are often reciprocally enmeshed with broader social relations, which are crucially, but not only, manifested at ritual moments or to fulfill the exigencies of hospitality (Candea and da

Col 2012; Rakowski this vol.). Again, Koji Mizoguchi's (2016) study of Japanese domestic groups in the Yoji period suggests that household *groups* functioned as organizational and allocative units, again shifting the emphasis from independent household units.

There are also certain rural rhythms where sharing labor is a better use of everyone's time and resources. For example, in villages in the east of Turkey, groups of women (friends, kin, and neighbors) pool their cows' milk each morning to make cheese for each household turn by turn, spending more days at the houses of those with more cows. If each woman tried to make cheese from the small amount of milk she obtained each morning, the process would be harder and more wasteful. Similarly, at harvest time, groups of men move together from one household's fields to the next (Alexander 2002). Thrift may thus draw on labor beyond the household and be aimed at increasing the common good. Mutual saving groups are another example (Mizoguchi 2016; James, Neves, and Torkelson this vol.).

A world away from such rural concerns, Daniel Miller nonetheless positions his 1998 ethnography of thrifty shopping in North London as being in dialog with two other studies of the household and house. Thus, he notes that most decisions about everyday purchases are legitimated through some kind of appeal to thrift, whether that is monetary saving (e.g., "buy one get one free," "three for the price of two," "special," or seasonal offers), buying better quality items, or cutting excess and therefore waste by buying smaller quantities (1998: 53–54). Arguably, such spending is transformed into saving (ibid.: 7). "Arguably" because the irony of shopping choices being driven by the quest for thrifty saving, which is played upon by marketing and supermarket displays, is that consumers may end up spending more, unable to resist the lure of a reduced item they had not planned on buying or cheap but rotting fruit—which subverts the ascription of utilitarian motives to thrifty actions. Assuming not only that working-class and bourgeois thrift are the same (ibid.: 135; although, see Alexander 2022) but are also as essential to North London households as to those in Gudeman and Rivera's ethnography, Miller combines this postulation with Janet Carsten and Stephen Hugh-Jones' (1995) work on the cosmological significance of the house/household to make his central point. Thrift, he suggests has moved from being a means to an end, to an end and value in itself, whether that is the experiential pleasure of finding bargains (Miller 1997: 61; see also Bardhi and Arnould 2005; Sosna this vol.) or that thrift now supplants the house as the means "by which economic activity is used to create a moral framework for the construction of value" (Miller 1998: 137). Thrift, Miller thus suggests, has a cosmological resonance, freighted with a relational significance directed toward the care of others (see also Cappellini and Parsons 2012).

Rhetorics of Thrift

Wilk raises a further point vis-à-vis thrift's antitheses, suggesting, with Miller (1998), that the apparent opposite impulses of selfish hedonism and selfless sacrifice are only rhetorically distinct: the binge is thought of as the evil twin of thrift (Wilk 2006), whereas in fact together they comprise the dialectic that drives contemporary capitalism (Wilk 2014: 322). This notion of thrift's wise spending and saving taken to pathological extremes as starvation is echoed in Sheldon Annis' (1987) account of Guatemalan peasants whose conversion to Protestantism was marked by adopting a thriftiness so austere that it amounted to economic anorexia (1987: 142) as a means of exerting control over an otherwise chaotic and terrifying social environment.

Thrift thus accumulates normative meanings and signs that play out in virtue-judgmental complexes, neatly indicated by Wilk's (2014 and this vol.) summary of the Caribbean distinction between the "grasshopper" young men, who are living for the day, as opposed to the "ant" grown-ups, who are responsible, saving and investing for the future (2014: 322). Such distinctions, as explored in some of the chapters here (James, Neves, and Torkelson; Diz; Wilk), are endlessly replayed as mechanisms of disapproval directed toward a subordinate group variously characterized as juvenile, undisciplined, lazy, or spendthrift—even if, as James, Neves, and Torkelson show, the people being castigated are in fact phenomenally adept at budgeting, using debt rather than money, despite the rapacity of many lenders. Thrift also has a long history of being a disciplinary mechanism of colonizing states, as Nancy Hunt described in her study of the Belgian Congo, where women were given "lessons in gardening, domestic economy and thrift" (1990: 458, see also Grant 2005: 53 and 106; and Kloß 2016: 277–79). Syed Hussein Alatas' *The Myth of the Lazy Native* (1977) was a hugely influential study of how colonized Southeast Asian people were consistently denigrated from the sixteenth to nineteenth centuries. The one group escaping the baseless accusations were subject, as he says, to another racial stereotype: "the patient, plodding, thrifty, industrious Chinaman" (1977: 75). Enjoining the virtues of hard work, thrift, and sobriety upon the laboring classes has long been a device to manufacture "respectability" and tractability. Austerity discourse once again displaces the structural logics of capitalism to individual responsibility (Gibson-Graham 2014).

Although the North Atlantic region and, to a lesser extent, colonized regions have their own traditions of thrift being either cultivated or enforced, the many regions of the world under state socialism in the twentieth century were often defined by chronic shortages (Kornai 1979), which necessitated mending and making do long after other places had left behind wartime rationing. Yet little has been written on the effects of such a lack of goods alongside a state-promoted ethic of thrift—and indeed comradely care for objects—on household provisioning (pace Fehér, Heller, and Márkus 1983; Siegelbaum 1998; Schlecker 2005; Alexander 2012). It is worth remembering that shortage might range from nothing to erratic supplies to unfinished or unusable items, the former requiring alternative modes of provisioning (e.g., dacha gardens or shadow economies), the latter a range of creative skills (Alexander 2012; Gerasimova and Chuikina 2009).

In an atypical inversion of how colonizers caricatured the colonized, or indeed how the authorities judge subordinate groups (Wilk this vol.; Alexander 2022), in both Soviet and post-Soviet periods, thrift and restraint (Rausing 2004: 146) were used as national virtues that defined Estonians against Russians who were said to be "happy-go-lucky and hospitable, lacking industry, application, and predictability, drinking and letting themselves go" (ibid.: 21) and who had no sense of thrift as a virtue (ibid.: 22). Zsuzsa Gille's (2007) evocation of the "cult of waste" in postwar, socialist Hungary describes how habits of collecting recyclables for the nation were inculcated in the population, although inappropriate storage often rendered such collections unthrifty and dangerous as chemicals leaked through rusting barrels. Gille emphasizes a political economy of material thriftiness rather than its effects on domestic economies. Meanwhile, in Vietnam, the experience of state rationing and the promotion of thrift continues to shape citizens' conception of the promised society (Schlecker 2005). There are generational differences in attitudes toward thrift but also what appears to be a paradox: younger people see thrift as outmoded in the new market economy but also judge as wasteful the etiquette of regularly providing more food that can be consumed. This is explained as the mingling of two thrifty traditions. Presocialist rural Vietnam was marked (like many rural areas) with long periods of austerity occasionally punctuated by ritual feasting. Under socialism, festivities were marked only by a thrifty cup of tea and sweets, which utterly failed to embody the care, affection, and communal obligations that lavish feasting should signal.

Thrift in Waste and Discard Studies

To these interventions we add the renewed attention that thrift, or related material practices, has received from scholars of waste and discard studies (e.g., Strasser 2000; Gille 2007; Alexander and Reno 2012; Eriksen and Schober 2017; Hawkins 2006; Sosna, Brunclikova, and Galeta 2019; see also Gudeman 2001) who unpack micropractices, within as well as beyond households, revealing productive consumption within and between households as recovery, reuse, recycling, repair—and varieties of secondhand exchange (Holmes 2019). These acts appear as necessity and/or positive affect via the requisite creative skills and imagination (Martínez and Laviolette 2019; Alexander 2012), often robustly challenging the moralizing discourse of the "throwaway society" (Gregson, Metcalfe, and Crewe 2007). Susan Strasser's (2000) work is a particularly fine study of the move in the United States from household practices of conserving scraps, which were driven by necessity, to such expertise becoming valued and turned to demonstrations of skill divorced from their conservation roots. Quilt making thus moved from a means to use leftover material to a craft for which makers buy "ready-made scraps."

William Rathje's "garbology" (household waste analysis) upended assumptions that poor households shop for the cheapest goods on offer by showing that they typically purchase smaller, and therefore pro rata more expensive packages of goods than wealthier households (Rathje and Murphy 2001: 65–66). This highlights the structural constraints on thrifty expenditure, as Robert Tressell ([1914] 2012) vividly demonstrated in his novel *The Ragged-Trousered Philanthropists*, where, for example, the rich bought good quality shoes that proved cheaper in the long run than the endless pairs of poorly made shoes that were all the workmen could afford.

Weirdly, there are almost no studies of how domestic actions to minimize wastefulness fit within a broader framework of thrifty household provisioning, or if reuse and recycling are seen as ethical or simply necessary (pace Alexander 2022; Holmes 2019; Sosna, Brunclikova, and Galeta 2019). In other words, studies of household provisioning or shopping are rarely brought into the same frame as material strategies for delaying or reducing consumption by stretching the utility of items or indeed foraging either for wild food or scraps and discarded objects to be repurposed. What the studies above reveal, however, are the multiple and mutable everyday ethics and affects that shape acts of material care, plus the importance of material qualities and indeed storage in thinking through capacity for thrift (see also Balbo 2015; Alexander and Reno 2012; Alexander et al. 2009). They further show that thrifty actions of recovery and repair can also carry an affect of pleasure (Sosna this vol.; Alexander, Smaje, Timlett, and Williams 2009; Alexander 2012; Reno 2015), recalling the fun of the bargain hunt, irrespective of whether it may work out as a saving (Miller 1997; Bardhi and Arnould 2005). Nonetheless, the relationship between thrift and repair has not been systematically analyzed. A recent anthology on repair mentions thrift only once and that is simply a case of saving money by cheating (Khalvashi 2019: 106).

What we may take from such studies is that thrifty practices of saving money and materials through bargain hunting, sharing labor, and repair are widespread but rarely studied and even less in the round to reflect the numerous strategies to provide the household with security. These studies also suggest that repair, sharing, and saving money often serve as insurance against economic uncertainty. Although most of the studies above are centered on the household as a physically fixed entity as well as the kin it shelters, there is a sense that households, however self-sufficient, may often be embedded in broader communities. Moreover, even where thrift is valued, there are times when it is offensive, which adds a calendrical rhythm to Douglas and Isherwood's point that in other places and times thrift may be mean and wrong. The next section homes in on such ideas of antithrift.

Antithrift?

This section thinks through how thrift operates, or doesn't, beyond the North Atlantic regions where thrift is particularly freighted with moral valences. Such ethnographies may not explicitly reference thrift, but by understanding how a concern for thriving plays out through other environmental conditions (e.g., abundance) and different sociocultural logics, the material and cultural prerequisites for different forms of thrift are revealed, as well as their limitations. By moving to ethnographic contexts where thrift has less overt economic, social, and moral purchase, we gain a better understanding of the kind of thrift that actually exists in the places that most fervently embrace the rhetoric of its promise.

Agustin Diz notes (pers. comm.) that Marshall Sahlins' (1996) tracing out of a "western cosmology" of consumption and scarcity from the initial fall from grace (and abundance) onward not only provides a genealogy in which austerity is just the latest expression of this concern with scarcity, need, abundance, and ethics, but also implies that antithrift often seems to be "just around the corner." Thus David Hume (2006: 16) pointed out that if we did not live in a world of scarcity, we would not need a justice system. Keynes (1963: 369–70) imagined a future abundance that would require a reimagination of morality. Even Walt Rostow (1959) wrote that the final stage of capitalism would be an era "Beyond Consumption;" a time when "the problem and human agenda imposed by the fact of scarcity" would come to an end (1959: 14). Thus, although thrift/antithrift and scarcity/abundance are often distinguished as separate "states," perhaps it is more productive to think of them as two sides of the same coin (see Diz 2017 and this vol. for thrift and antithrift entanglements).

Arguably, rejecting the universal purchase of thriftiness as frugal saving toward future prosperity was foundational to social anthropology. Chris Hann and Keith Hart suggest that nineteenth-century economic anthropology aimed to test whether the principles underpinning contemporary western society were appropriate for a global system (2011: 1) or indeed were universal. Thus, Bronisław Malinowski revealed nonutilitarian logics and values impelling social action: the Trobriand Islands most emphatically did not conform to the ideals of bourgeois Central Europe. Writing about gift exchange, Malinowski noted that "there is no trace of gain from a utilitarian or economic perspective" (1978: 175). The complex gift exchanges he described appeared to turn commonplaces on their head. Status and social standing derived from giving away rather than possessing material wealth, the goal of utility maximization achieved through diligent thrift. While barter and utilitarian trade coexisted with prestations, the former lacked the prestige of the latter.

But Malinowski's discussion of abundance[7] and accumulation throws further shade on familiar contexts of resource scarcity, where hard work and careful accumulation counter uncertainty. In contexts where self-sufficiency is prized, such stocks act as a buffer against hard times, enabling resilience—the means to an end. But where increase and profit are valued, accumulation itself is the goal (Gudeman and Rivera 1990). All this presupposes an initial condition of shortage, or at least the likelihood of lean periods, suggesting that where this is not the case, exertion and amassing are irrelevant. But Malinowski documents that even though "all the necessities of life are within easy reach . . . abundance is valued for its own sake . . . beyond any possible utility . . . [the] love of accumulation for its own sake. Food is allowed to rot" (1978: 173). And considerable labor goes into creating such super abundance, not merely surplus but excess. Public waste, you might say, displaces private gain. The observation inspired Georges Bataille's ([1949] 1988) insistence that all human economies are driven to work, produce, and store surplus in the service of wasteful luxury. Douglas and Isherwood's ([1979] 2002) brief typology of which groups are more likely to save and why might have tempered such a claim.

Such magnificent giving and wasting is the very antithesis of thriftiness with its "waste not want not" logic. Clearly this accumulation is not to secure future material security. Rather, the piles of rotting food demonstrate the gardeners' skill, much as the prized artistry of craftsmen creating unusable but beautiful objects is juxtaposed with the mundane products of the despised inlanders Malinowski calls "the industrials" (1978: 189). Hard work aimed at accumulation thus appears despite plentiful resources, suggesting that building stocks against scarcity is not the sole driver of such actions. Potlatch rituals are the apogee of such a value regime.

Later studies of gift exchange investigated the division between the spectacular moment of exchange and the eclipsed women's work of, for example, cultivating pigs for gifting (M. Strathern 1988; Josephides 1985) and the complex negotiations required to amass enough to give (A. Strathern 1971). Perhaps, to stretch the term, we might see such careful work of growing, husbanding, and saving as thrifty but in the service of a different value system, privileging social relationships and creativity and the event of giving it all away. This interplay between privileged and discarded or eclipsed moments reappears, from a different angle, in Laura Rival's (2002) discussion of a Huaorani antiproductive trope that dismisses their own subsistence labor in favor of marveling at the forest's "natural abundance," not recognizing the labor of past generations that created such profusion. At the very least, this shows the limits of thriftiness and work aimed at individual maximization, but also reminds us that thriftiness and generosity are almost as entangled in Vietnam and Kyrgyzstan as in Melanesia and the Amazon, although in the latter regions the effort of producing such magnificence can be "disappeared" as Rival describes (2002) or eclipsed (M. Strathern 1988).

The debates around hunter-gatherers in the 1980s and 1990s were partly shaped by the assumed characteristics of thrift and rational behavior described above. Thus, the prevailing model until the 1990s was that these groups typically did nothing but hunt or gather, while James Woodburn further suggested a division into immediate-return and delayed-return systems (1980) where the former constituted instant consumption, the latter postponed consumption by using storage, with a suggestion that this carried greater social investment (Bird-David 1992a: 25).

There are several reasons for the immediate-return system. Food preservation in certain climates can be hard, while the constant mobility that is critical for hunter-gatherers makes physical storage impractical. Added to this, the year-round abundance of easily available food reduces the necessity of accumulation. Even when environmental conditions allow for storage, as Sahlins says, "Food storage . . . may be technically feasible, yet economically undesirable, and socially unachievable" (1974: 32). There is also, following Sahlins, a different sense and temporality to affluence, which again shifts how we consider the purpose of thrift. If careful accumulation is unnecessary to see people through future lean periods, then wealth or affluence may change to present-focused satisfaction of wants (see Wilk this vol.).

Nurit Bird-David changed the plane of discussion, suggesting a culturally distinct "cosmic economy of sharing" (1992b: 28) linking groups together. She demonstrated that while most hunter-gatherer groups have been engaged in other economic activities for centuries, these are less prized than hunting skills and are also brought within the norm of immediate sharing. Gifts or portions may move from interhousehold unit exchanges within a group to those that link groups to each other. Arguably, this is also a different mechanism for offsetting potential future risk, subsuming individual units into broader sharing communities.

The question these debates provoke is whether we should understand thrift broadly as a rational mechanism for ensuring security, which plays out in some circumstances as household or individual accumulation for reserves and in others as a sharing economy[8] or gift exchange system that maintains social relations. All three instances valorize one mode, whether self-sufficiency, gift obligations, or sharing, while engaging in many kinds of economic interactions. The second approach considers thrift as careful resource management that allows reserves, gifts, or sharing, or indeed all three at different points, but acknowledges that functional explanations of security are inadequate to encompass fully the cultural logics of gift exchange and sharing economies. The narrowest definition would be to take thrift as a category of economic action that pertains in circumstances of resource insecurity in sociocultural settings that value self-sufficiency, and is marked by both its means (frugal spending and accumulating reserves), and end (resilience, longevity, and sustainability). While the last is the easiest to work with, and the commonest, it can also lead to the moral censure of those whose careful planning is aimed at different goals or different ways of ensuring resilience.

Storage, which often seems a prerequisite for thrift (qua saving), has therefore less salience in most hunter-gatherer moral-economic universes but is crucial in very different circumstances. Although rarely mentioned, the socialist economy of shortage made storage a vital element in smoothing over erratic food supplies. Balconies and dachas were crucial for enabling periodic gluts to be stored, such as a sack of potatoes or bottled fruit and vegetables for the winter months, as well as the tools and equipment needed for such thriftiness (Alexander 2012). One manifestation of abrupt economic change in Kazakhstan in the early 2000s was the sheer quantity of glass jars and tools for gardening and building being sold by roadsides. This was explained as the need to earn money, but was also related to the new lack of *time* (with increased work hours) for cultivating dacha gardens and preserving produce, as well as higher fuel costs to travel to dachas. Without accessible storage and time, the resources necessary for thrift were severely curtailed. A growing interest in the affordances of storage again draws attention to the narrow bandwidth of thrift as a virtue: excess is as much a vice as too little. Thus, an inability to control stored accumulation risks being seen as pathological hoarding (Newell 2018).

All of which brings us to the limits of thrift.

The Limits of Thrift

The previous sections highlight two kinds of limitations to how we think about thrift. First, the various elements associated with thrift (minimizing outgoings, locating bargains or scraps to be repurposed, utilizing creative skills in making and remaking, working hard, developing self-discipline, planning carefully, saving, and storing) may exist and be given meaning and moral weight in quite different cultural logics. But when all or some of these elements are aimed at spectacular wasting, complex gift exchange, ritual observance, or sharing, we might wonder what the careful future-oriented thrift of the household aimed at replenishment has to do with any of this; and perhaps it doesn't at all—other than to note that its mechanisms are similar in form if not always meaning in other places.

But this also serves to remind us that thrift as frugality, its most common synonym, has its limits everywhere. There are times when it is wrong, even more so for those of high status and/or wealth. It is rare to find a place where largesse and generosity are not required at some point for ritual, celebration, or hospitality in some form (Bakhtin 1984; Schlecker 2005). The Roman virtues located *frugalitas* or simplicity in the domestic domain, *liberalitas* or generosity in the public sphere—needless to say, these were gendered spaces of virtue. Thus, whether a "bread and circuses" sop to appease the masses, the appropriate behavior of a political leader, a Melanesian Big Man, or the "ruinous feasts" that Clarendon described seventeenth-century English aristocrats being obliged to host (quoted in Trevor-Roper 1951; see also Alexander, Gregson, and Gille 2013), giving is typically linked to high status and the public sphere (see also Dietler and Hayden 2001). Hamlet's first quip is to decry the "thrift" that led to his father's funeral feast being turned into his mother's wedding banquet (Act 1, Sc 2, l,179–80). Arnold Bennett's stingy Ephraim Tellwright is roundly mocked for behaving inappropriately for his wealth and status (1902).[9] However, this is not only an Anglophone theme. Al-Jāḥiẓ's six-hundred-page *Kitāb al-Bukhalā'*, or *Book of Misers* (1978), dates back to 800 CE; and there are countless other examples. The common theme of these stories is that misers mistake means for the end, failing to spend wisely to maintain a material life and human relations. Thus, the moral necessity to turn enough profit (but no more) to glorify God, provide for pilgrims, and charitable giving is one of the monasteries' concerns in Barbora Spalová's chapter (this vol.).

On a more mundane level, failure to spend *tout court* can be unthrifty: refusing the regular care and cost of keeping a roof watertight may end up as a cataclysmic expense; the false bargain, however thrilling the hunt, is costly. Thriftiness therefore carries a sense of prudence and balance (see Spalová and Wilk this vol.), of navigating between hoarding, miserliness, and prodigality. As the frequently recycled aphorism has it: moderation in all things—especially moderation.

A final refutation of thrifty logic appears in Sophie Day, Evthymios Papataxiarchis, and Michael Stewart's *Lilies of the Field* (1998), which focuses on marginalized people who, it is suggested, refuse future-oriented thriftiness qua saving as an act of resistance (but see Wilk this vol.). Acting in the present also suggests a more flexible, improvisatory approach to an uncertain world where savings may vanish in currency devaluations or soaring inflation. Questions of capacity may also limit thrift.[10] Hand-to-mouth existence does not allow for material investment whether in extensive or intensive social relations. Accessible storage can be crucial for a household to prosper or get by during lean periods. Finally, the arts of thrift are vital whether darning, turning worn sheets sides-to-the middle, patching a roof, or countless other tasks—but they require time and sometimes tools.

Our opening understanding of thrift was that it comprised actions primarily aimed at household self-sufficiency, as a countermeasure to conditions of scarcity or uncertain supply. This sense of thrift can now be qualified. The household is not necessarily the unit of thriftiness or its endpoint; rather, a more expansive sense of communal or spiritual well-being might be sought (see Rakowski and Spalová this vol.). As such, we need to consider when and why thriftiness is actively devalued and when culturally mediated ideas of human thriving may require the antithesis of thrift.

What remains under-theorized, and what the last section discusses, is how, where, and why ideas and practices of thrift often rooted in the household have traversed different scales and to what effect.

Scale and Paradox

Bernard Mandeville (1714) first noted an apparent paradox of thrift: "As this prudent economy, which some people call Saving, is in private families the most certain method to increase an estate, so some imagine that, whether a country be barren or fruitful, the same method if generally pursued (which they think practicable) will have the same effect upon a whole nation, and that, for example, the English might be much richer than they are, if they would be as frugal as some of their neighbours. This, I think, is an error." Popularized by Keynes (1936: 85; see also Samuelson [1948] 1998), the "paradox of thrift" suggests that an increase in individuals' saving serves to reduce overall demand, output, and hence, eventually, the wealth of the national economy, a paradox updated in 2009 as the "paradox of deleveraging" (Eggertson and Krugman 2012). Debates continue over whether there are scalar differences between individuals and the national economy in how thrift is practiced, what they might be, and indeed if "the global" is now another scalar concern. Thus, for example, another angle onto the scalar paradoxes of thrift could be that thrift is crucial to the engine of capitalist innovation and productivity at national and supra-state levels but leads to widespread environmental degradation and indeed to savage divides between metropolis and provinces, city and rural areas (Collier 2018). Friedrich Hayek (1929) and later other neoclassical economists rejected the paradox of thrift arguing variously (and controversially) that increased individual savings in turn stimulate production, or that export is a way of maintaining demand and production (i.e., the paradox of thrift incorrectly assumes a closed system). The insight that thrift as virtuous economic practice might have scalar limits is productive, echoing other limiting factors above.

This final section draws out how our ethnographic chapters extend the understandings of thrift examined above partly by considering how thrift moves across, or is affected by, different scales and domains, and the paradoxes this explains or presents. The first four chapters (Gudeman; James, Neves, and Torkelson; Diz; and Rakowski) are explicitly concerned with household thrift in, respectively, Panama, South Africa, Argentina, and Mongolia. The next three chapters, while nominally in the very different ethnographic settings of Czech monasteries (Spalová), Indonesian industry (Rudnyckyj) and a Czech landfill (Sosna), also show how practices and normative ideas of household thrift underpin rhetoric, belief, and action in these very different domains. The final chapter (Wilk) echoes Gudeman's dialogic approach to excavating thrift narratives, bringing history into conversation with Belizean folk models that use thrift and laziness as modes of approbation and censure.

Each chapter offers further angles onto thrift based on its ethnographic specificity with subthemes highlighting other connections between chapters: thrift as a normative or disciplinary mode (James, Neves, and Torkelson; Diz; and Wilk); the many meanings and affects attributable to thrifty actions, or laziness (Sosna and Wilk); the role of worldly and spiritual asceticism (Spalová and Rudnyckyj); how thrift is a virtue of moderation (Spalová and Wilk) and can manifest in conditions of abundance (Diz and Sosna). As this introduction indicates, each chapter presents a different kind of engagement with thrift's futures.

However, all chapters can be seen as being in conversation, whether directly or indirectly, with the kind of household thrift described by Gudeman. The contributors take this core idea and explore, for example, how regional, national, and global economies; local mutual saving schemes; loans; recovered objects for gifts or sale; and state welfare all variously shape how everyday economies are managed. To understand household thrift, it is crucial to take account of these multiple, imbricated scales. Conversely, as Rudnyckyj draws out, locating state or industrial austerity as an extension of household thrift gives it a spurious legitimacy.

We start with an updated version of Gudeman and Rivera's classic engagement with rural household thrift (1990), which opens noting how thriftiness has become a pleasurable practice: "a means to ends activity became an end itself." The paradox here is highlighted by Keynes: the kind of thrift that enables a household to continue has a perverse effect on a market economy, which is grounded on a qualitatively different kind of thrift. Saving is enabled through minimizing expenditure and avoiding waste where possible. Although there is occasional recourse to local markets, the ideal here is the self-sufficient *oikos*. While future-oriented, it is not aimed at short-term constant growth, which is the radically different aim of accumulation in a market context. The next three chapters examine how such long-term thrift operates in very different contexts and where people are often at the mercy of state policies and market vagaries.

James, Neves, and Torkelson's chapter starts with the paradox of poor households in rural and peri-urban South Africa becoming embroiled in multiple forms of debt in order to provide education and care for family members. While this appears as a paradox to some observers, it is a necessity where state welfare payments are inadequate, or simply unpaid. Moreover, far from being "financially illiterate," the women who head the households in this study are extraordinarily canny in how they weave together different income sources to manage their budgets. Such sources range from a variety of loans, from viciously predatory loan sharks to local rotating savings and credit associations (*stokvels*). These women's struggles to provide exemplify the harsh ethical and economic choices of practicing thrift *in extremis*, the centrality of debt rather than money to such book balancing, and the ease with which such alternative means of thrifty management may be overlooked.

In some senses, Agustin Diz's chapter flips the South African example on its head, but it also shows that household thrift can only be understood through the interplay of the state and broader economies. Again, state welfare payments are a vital resource for indigenous Guaraní households, but here such grants are lavish. Such wealth has been enabled by a global boom in soybean production and filtered through various national and regional brokers. Despite such local prosperity, welfare is still focused on women as responsible for household thrift. Indeed, the various forms that houses take (from mud huts to robust constructions) is read locally as an indication of wise thriftiness versus lack of foresight, prefiguring Wilk's discussion.

Tomasz Rakowski's chapter, focusing on a largely postpastoral community of Torghuts in rural and urban Mongolia, opens with the paradox of thrift, or wise stewardship of resources, as simultaneously keeping together while giving away. This makes sense as an extension of pastoral logics where a group's survival relies on cooperation and generosity, echoing the discussion of sharing economies above. A further paradox emerges from how the principle of giving and maintaining operates across scales and domains as diverse as the local township and region, the urban business community of Torghut migrants, national politics, and rituals to preserve cosmological harmony. Far from finding distinct forms of thrift and different logics separating household from economy, profane from sacred spheres, Rakowski shows a common logic of preserving the life force at each scale, which therefore appear as recursively related—at once different and the same.

Spalová considers two Czech monasteries following the Rule of Benedict, which advocates frugality qua living sparingly for the monks' spiritual salvation. Simultaneously, they have a duty to glorify God through beautiful buildings that endure and to provide charity. Such obligations present a dilemma as to how much they should profit from their resources to fulfill these commitments. Spalová suggests there are distinct forms of thrift: individual asceticism (frugality) and calculative management for the monasteries' holdings (thrift). Both are subject to moderation. Excessive asceticism is as frowned upon as luxurious living. Profit seeking is tempered to provide just enough to meet the monasteries' responsibilities. Ensuring monasteries have the wherewithal to continue, fulfilling their spiritual and earthly purposes, mirrors the logic of household thrift. Their business dealings echo social enterprises where profit is channeled back into the communities to which they are connected. This nuances the kind of thrift typically associated with market enterprise as well as highlighting how household thrift may appear in quite different domains, as the next chapter also shows.

In critical dialogue with Weber's emphasis on worldly asceticism shaping western capitalism, Rudnyckyj explores the changing purchase of such ideas where economies have long been shaped by quite different religious, social, and economic forms: Islam, moral economies of patronage, and soft budget regimes where deficit and over-spending have little effect. The chapter focuses on the introduction of cost-cutting measures associated with market capitalism elsewhere that aim to minimize costs and wastefulness and maximize growth. To galvanize its workforce, the management of a steel company relies on reinterpretations of Islamic texts to instill worldly ascetic values, including thrift and hard work, in workers. The implication is that by drawing on a household model of thrift at the scale of state or industry, households are reimplicated in the effects of cost-cutting as workers keep or lose their jobs in ensuing austerity regimes.

Returning to the Czech Republic, but remaining in the world of work, Sosna's chapter considers the apparent paradox of landfill workers who appear to be at once thriftily retrieving usable items while wasting other resources such as fuel and utilities at the site. The paradox is resolved by switching from a lens of ecological thriftiness or resource management to understanding many of these actions as part of the household thrift and reciprocity encountered in previous chapters. Items salvaged from the landfill may be sold, used at home to avoid spending, or given as gifts. Money received from fiddling fuel usage similarly replenishes household coffers. Intertwined with these reasons are the joy of hunting for recoverable items and wasting utilities as acts of resistance against an unpopular employer.

We end with Wilk's chapter that reminds us that thrift and cognate attributes, such as laziness, are ethical economic behaviors and thus forms of judgment and boundary markers. Further, they are essentially twined with temporal ontologies. In Wilk's neat phrase, thrift is time travel, displacing present labor to future security, enacting foresight and prudence. Unthrifty prodigality and laziness are present-oriented and often linked to other tropes of being infantile and primitive. The paradox is that these figures of speech are not only familiar from colonial discourse about subordinate groups, but also are used by Belizeans to describe a common individual and national pathology. Such images are also customary at the scale of global political economy as states are judged on whether they are "responsible" (thrifty) and thus worthy of becoming indebted to international lending agencies. Wilk ends our ethnographies of thrift with the pointed observation that there is much to be said for a slower, more present-oriented way of life. In another lexicon, this might be considered mindfulness.

Together, these ethnographies at once expand and contract how we think about thrift. The drive for households and kin groups to secure their longevity and well-being is profound and widespread. Those households, however, are frequently enmeshed with wider kin groups, neighbors, and communities that share labor, exchange gifts, receive charity, or lend, demand, and jointly save money. Such communities may orchestrate ritual giving alongside, and as part of, enabling the survival of individual households. The household, sometimes stretching across village and city, proves elastic in its organization of resources.

But most strikingly, it is apparent that household thrift is also profoundly shaped by global commodity prices, state welfare regimes, and the competence or otherwise of officials and regional and local economies, including complex credit mechanisms and the affordances of waged work. Without taking into account how households are affected by but also navigate these multiscalar circuits, we cannot begin to understand how people craft a good life in an uncertain world. The fact that the concept of thrift crosses so many boundaries within and between disciplines makes thrift into a fruitful connection between theory and action, or philosophical and practical approaches. As this book shows, ideas of thrift carry us beyond individual ethnographic studies, to the kind of ethnological comparison that was once central to anthropology.

Acknowledgments

Hannah Brown, Agustin Diz, Chris Hann, Deborah James, Jason Sumich, Darren Theil, Rick Wilk, and Samuel Williams have been anything but thrifty with their generous ideas and suggestions. The anonymous reviewers have likewise been both liberal and thoughtful in their excellent comments. We are grateful to them all.

Catherine Alexander is Professor of Anthropology at Durham University. Drawing on fieldwork in Turkey, Kazakhstan, and Britain, she has written widely on economic anthropology and material culture, including households, recycling, and waste. Recent publications in this area are *Economies of Recycling* (coedited with Joshua Reno, 2012), *Moral Economies of Housing* (coedited with Maja Hojer Bruun and Insa Koch, 2018), *Indeterminacy: Waste, Value and the Imagination* (coedited with Andrew Sanchez, 2019), and *Technologies of Unknowing Waste* (coedited with Patrick O'Hare, 2020).

Daniel Sosna is a senior researcher in the Department of Ecological Anthropology, Institute of Ethnology, Czech Academy of Sciences. He received his PhD in anthropology from Florida State University, and his research resulted in the book *Social Differentiation in the Late Copper Age and the Early Bronze Age in South Moravia (Czech Republic)* (Archaeopress, 2009). Daniel is a specialist on ethnographic and archaeological research of waste regimes with a regional focus on Central Europe. He coedited the book *Archaeologies of Waste: Encounters with the Unwanted* (Oxbow Books, 2017).

Notes

1. See Catherine Alexander (2022) for a detailed historical ethnography of how moralized ideas of household thrift have been used in Britain (and elsewhere) to justify savage cuts to public expenditure that directly prevent low-income households from enacting the very thrift they are enjoined to practice.
2. Other German speakers suggest a range of moral overtones to *Sparsamkeit*.

3. Shylock, who confuses his daughter with his ducats, is described in animal metaphors.
4. "Apparent" because, as this Introduction and the following chapters make clear, this is a false dichotomy. Rather, thrift typically appears as a means to enable the equally morally necessary act of generosity.
5. Despite being called *The Protestant Ethic*, Weber is clear that the particular ethic to which he refers was driven by ascetic Protestantism starting with Calvin.
6. Understood as those where surplus is minimal or nonexistent.
7. Malinowski describes islands' agricultural fertility (1921: 2) such that the islanders' hard work is richly rewarded.
8. Contemporary discourse about a new sharing economy is divided between celebrating its potential for thriftiness and sociality and seeing such claims as a mask for exploitative, predatory economic relations (Frenken and Schor 2017).
9. Thanks to Deborah James for this reference.
10. Another instance where expansion is rejected is where pastoral communities may limit herd size to one that is manageable or convert surplus animals into a different kind of reserve, such as land (Barth 1961: 106).

References

Alatas, Syed Hussein. 1977. *The Myth of the Lazy native: A Study of the Malays, Filipinos and Javanese from the 16th to the 20th Century and its Function in the Ideology of Colonial Capitalism*. London: Frank Cass & Co.

Alexander, Catherine. 2012. "Remont: Work in Progress." In *Economies of Recycling: The Global Transformation of Materials, Values and Social Relations*, edited by Catherine Alexander and Joshua O. Reno, 255–75. London: Zed Books.

———. 2022. "The Simple, Bare Necessities: Scales and Paradoxes of Thrift on a London Public Housing Estate." *Comparative Studies in Society and History*. Preprint published online by Cambridge University Press, February, 2022. DOI 10.1017/S0010417522000159.

———. 2002. *Personal States: Making Connections between People and Bureaucracy in Turkey*. Oxford: Oxford University Press.

Alexander, Catherine, Nicky Gregson, and Zsuzsa Gille. 2013. "Food Waste." In *The Handbook of Food Research*, edited by Anne Murcott, Warren Belasco, and Peter Jackson, 471–85. London: Bloomsbury.

Alexander, Catherine, and Joshua O. Reno, eds. 2012. *Economies of Recycling: The Global Transformation of Materials, Values and Social Relations*. London: Zed Books.

Alexander, Catherine, Chris Smaje, Rose Timlett, and Ian Williams. 2009. "Improving Social Technologies for Recycling: Interfaces, Estates, Multi-Family Dwellings and Infrastructural Deprivation." *Proc of Inst of Chartered Engineers. Waste and Resources Management* 162(1): 15–28.

Al-Jāḥiẓ. 1978. *Kitāb al-Bukhalā'*. Beirut: al-Maktaba Attakafiya.

Andersen, Thomas Barnebeck, Jeanet Bentzen, Carl-Johan Dalgaard, and Paul Sharp. 2016. "Pre-reformation Roots of the Protestant Ethic." *The Economic Journal* 127(604): 1,756–93.

Annis, Sheldon. 1987. *God and Production in a Guatamalan Town*. Austin: University of Texas Press.
Bakhtin, Mikhail. 1984. *Problems of Dostoevsky's Poetics*. Translated by Caryl Emerson. Minnesota: University of Minnesota Press.
Balbo, Andrea, ed. 2015. "Storage." *The Journal of Human Palaeoecology* 20(4): 305–436.
Bardhi, Fleura, and Eric Arnould. 2005. "Thrift Shopping: Combining Utilitarian Thrift and Hedonic Treat Benefits." *Journal of Consumer Behaviour* 4(4): 223–33.
Barth, Frederik. 1961. *Nomads of South-Persia: The Basseri tribe of the Khamseh Confederacy*. Oslo: Humanities Press.
Bataille, Georges. (1949) 1988. *The Accursed Share: An Essay on General Economy. Vol. 1 Consumption*. New York: Zone Books.
Bennett, Arnold. 1902. *Anna of the Five Towns*. London: Chatto and Windus.
Bird-David, Nurit. 1992a. "Beyond 'The Hunting and Gathering Mode of Subsistence': Culture-Sensitive Observations on the Nayaka and Other Modern Hunter-Gatherers." *Man* 27(1): 19–44.
———. 1992b. "Beyond 'The Original Affluent Society': A Culturalist Reformulation." *Current Anthropology* 33(1): 25–47.
Buch, Elana. 2015. "Anthropology of Aging and Care." *Annual Review of Anthropology* 44(1): 277–93.
Candea, Matei, and Giovanni da Col, eds. 2012. "The Return to Hospitality: Strangers, Guests and Ambiguous Encounters." *JRAI* 18(S1): Siii–S217.
Cappellini, Benedetta, and Elizabeth Parsons. 2012. "Practising Thrift at Dinnertime: Mealtime Leftovers, Sacrifice and Family Membership." *The Sociological Review* 60(S2): 121–34.
Carsten, Janet, and Stephen Hugh-Jones, eds. 1995. *About the House: Lévi-Strauss and Beyond*. Cambridge: Cambridge University Press.
Chayanov, Alexander. (1923) 1966. *The Theory of Peasant Economy*, edited by Daniel Thorner, Basile Kerbly, and R. E. F. Smith. Manchester: Manchester University Press.
Collier, Paul. 2018. *The Future of Capitalism: Facing the New Anxieties*. London: Allen Lane.
Darling, Malcolm. 1934. *Wisdom and Waste in the Punjab Village*. Oxford: Oxford University Press.
Day, Sophie, Evthymios Papataxiarchis, and Michael Stewart, eds. 1998. *Lilies of the Field: Marginal People Who Live for the Moment*. Comparative Essays on Marginality and Autonomy (Studies in the Ethnographic Imagination). London: Routledge.
Dietler, Michael, and Brian Hayden. 2001. *Feasts: Archaeological and Ethnographic Perspectives on Food, Politics, and Power*. Washington, DC: Smithsonian Institution Press.
Diz, Agustin. 2017. *The Afterlife of Abundance: Wageless Life, Politics, and Illusion among the Guaraní of the Argentine Chaco*. PhD diss., London School of Economics and Political Science.
Douglas, Mary, and Baron Isherwood. (1979) 2002. *The World of Goods: Towards an Anthropology of Consumption*. London: Routledge.
Eggertson, Gauti, and Paul Krugman. 2012. "Debt, Deleveraging, and the Liquidity Trap: A Fisher-Minsky-Koo Approach." *The Quarterly Journal of Economics* 127(3): 1,469–513.

Eriksen, Thomas Hylland. 2016. *Overheating: An Anthropology of Accelerated Change.* London: Pluto Press.
Eriksen, Thomas Hylland, and Elizabeth Schober, eds. 2017. "Waste and the Superfluous." Special Issue. *Social Anthropology/Anthropologie Sociale* 25(3): 282–352.
Färber, Alexa, and Aneta Podkalicka, eds. 2019. "Thrift, Dwelling and TV." *Journal of Current Cultural Research* 11(3–4): 421–550.
Fehér, Ferenc, Agnes Heller and György Márkus. 1983. *Dictatorship Over Needs.* Oxford: Blackwell.
Foster, George. 1965. "Peasant Society and the Image of Limited Good." *American Anthropologist* 67(2): 293–315.
Frenken, Koen, and Juliet Schor. 2017. "Putting the Sharing Economy into Perspective." *Environmental Innovation and Societal Transitions* 23: 3–10.
Garon, Sheldon. 2000. "Luxury Is the Enemy: Mobilizing Savings and Popularizing Thrift in Wartime Japan." *The Journal of Japanese Studies* 26(1): 41–78.
Gerasimova, Ekaterina, and Sof'ia Chuikina. 2009. "The Repair Society." *Russian Studies in History* 48(1): 58–74.
Gibson-Graham, J. K. 2014. "Rethinking the Economy with Thick Description and Weak Theory." *Current Anthropology* 55(S9): S147–53.
Gille, Zsuzsa. 2007. *From the Cult of Waste to the Trash Heap of History: The Politics of Waste in Socialist and Postsocialist Hungary.* Bloomington: Indiana University Press.
Gille, Zsuzsa, and Martin Hájek. 2017. "Introduction to the Special Section: Discourses of Economic Behaviour in Times of Instability." *Sociologický Časopis* 53(6): 799–803.
Grant, Robert. 2005. *Representations of British Emigration, Colonisation and Settlement.* New York: Springer.
Gregson, Nicky, Alan Metcalfe, and Louise Crewe. 2007. "Identity, Mobility, and the Throwaway Society." *Environment and Planning D: Society and Space* 25(4): 682–700.
Gudeman, Stephen. 2001. *Anthropology and Economy.* Cambridge, UK: Cambridge University Press.
Gudeman, Stephen, and Chris Hann, eds. 2015. *Oikos and Market: Explorations in Self-Sufficiency After Socialism.* Oxford: Berghahn Books.
Gudeman, Stephen, and Alberto Rivera. 1990. *Conversations in Columbia: The Domestic Economy in Life and Text.* Cambridge, UK: Cambridge University Press.
Hájek, Martin, Petr Kaderka, Jiří Nekvapil, and Tomáš Samec. 2019. *Kdo šetří, má za tři? Diskurz šetrnosti v proměnách české společnosti.* Praha: SLON.
Hann, Chris, and Keith Hart. 2011. *Economic Anthropology: History, Ethnography, Critique.* Cambridge: Polity Press.
Hawkins, Gay. 2006. *The Ethics of Waste: How We Relate to Rubbish.* Washington, DC: Rowman and Littlefield.
Hayek, Friedrich. 1929. "The Paradox of Savings." In *Profits, Interest and Investment: and Other Essays on The Theory on Industrial Fluctuations.* London: Routledge & Kegan Paul.
Holmes, Helen. 2019. "Unpicking Contemporary Thrift: Getting on and Getting by in Everyday Life." *The Sociological Review* 67(1): 126–42.

Hulme, Alison. 2019. "Austerity and Everyday Life: Perspectives on Practices of Consumption and Thrift." *Journal of Consumer Culture* 19(4): 441–47.
———. 2020. *A History of Thrift*. Manchester: Manchester University Press.
Hume, David. 2006. *An Inquiry Concerning the Principles of Morals*. New York: Cosimo Classics.
Hunt, Nancy Rose. 1990. "Domesticity and Colonialism in Belgian Africa: Usumbura's Foyer Social, 1946–1960." *Signs: Journal of Women and Culture in Society* 15(3): 447–74.
Josephides, Lisette. 1985. *The Production of Inequality: Gender and Exchange Among the Kewa*. London: Tavistock.
Kalberg, Stephen. 1980. "Max Weber's Types of Rationality: Cornerstones for the Analysis of Rationalization Processes in History." *The American Journal of Sociology* 85(5): 1,145–79.
Keynes, John Maynard. 1936. *The General Theory of Employment, Interest and Money*. London: Palgrave Macmillan.
———. 1963. *Economic Possibilities for Our Grandchildren. In Essays in Persuasion*. New York: W.W. Norton & Co.
Khalvashi, Tamta. 2019. A Ride on the Elevator: Infrastructures of Brokenness and Repair in Georgia. In *Repair, Brokenness, Breakthrough: Ethnographic Responses*, edited by Francisco Martínez and Patrick Laviolette. Oxford: Berghahn Books.
Kipnis, Andrew. 2007. "Neoliberalism Reified: Suzhi Discourse and Tropes of Neoliberalism in the People's Republic of China." *The Journal of the Royal Anthropological Institute* 13(2): 383–400.
Kloß, Sinah Theres. 2016. *Fabrics of Indianness: The Exchange and Consumption of Clothing in Transnational Guyanese Hindu Communities*. New York: Springer.
Kornai, János. 1979. *Economics of Shortage*. Amsterdam: New-Holland Publishing.
Light, Nathan. 2015. "Self-Sufficiency Is Not Enough: Ritual Intensification and Household Economies in a Kyrgyz Village." In *Oikos and Market: Explorations in Self-Sufficiency After Socialism*, edited by Stephen Gudeman and Chris Hann. Oxford: Berghahn Books.
Lim, Cheryl, and Chua Sin Lay. 2003. "Confucianism and the Protestant Work Ethic." *Asia Europe Journal* 1(3): 321–22.
Lucas, Gavin. 2002. "Disposability and Dispossession in the Twentieth Century." *Journal of Material Culture* 7(1): 5–22.
Malinowski, Bronisław. 1921. "The Primitive Economics of the Trobriand Islanders." *The Economic Journal* 31(121): 1–16.
———. (1922) 1978. *Argonauts of the Western Pacific*. London: Routledge and Kegan Paul.
Mandeville, Bernard. 1714. *The Fable of the Bees or Private Vices, Publick Benefits*. London: J. Roberts.
Martínez, Francisco, and Patrick Laviolette, eds. 2019. *Repair, Brokenness, Breakthrough: Ethnographic Responses*. Oxford: Berghahn Books.
Marx, Karl. (1851) 2003. *The Eighteenth Brumaire of Louis Bonaparte*. New York: International Publishers.
McCloskey, Deirdre. 2006. *The Bourgeois Virtues: Ethics for an Age of Commerce*. Chicago: University of Chicago Press.

———. 2011. "The Prehistory of American Thrift." In *Thrift and Thriving in America: Capitalism and Moral Order from the Puritans to the Present,* edited by Joshua Yates and James Davison Hunter, 61–87. Oxford: Oxford University Press.
Miller, Daniel. 1998. *A Theory of Shopping.* Cambridge: Polity Press.
Mizoguchi, Koji. 2016. "The Household as a Node of Communal Collaboration between Settlements and Tension within Settlements: A Case Study from the Yayoi Period in Northern Kyushu (Japan)." *Journal of Anthropological Research* 72(2): 158–77.
Nelson, Laura. 1996. *Measured Excess: Status, Gender, and Consumer Nationalism in South Korea.* New York: Columbia University Press.
Newell, Sasha. 2018. "Uncontained Accumulation: Hidden Heterotopias of Storage and Spillage." *History and Anthropology* 29(1): 37–41.
Noddings, Nel. 2013. *Caring: A Relational Approach to Ethics and Moral Education.* Berkeley: University of California Press.
Podkalicka, Aneta, and Jason Potts. 2014. "Towards a General Theory of Thrift." *International Journal of Cultural Studies* 17(3): 227–41.
Rathje, William, and Cullen Murphy. 2001. *Rubbish! The Archaeology of Garbage.* Tucson: The University of Arizona Press.
Rausing, Sigrid. 2004. *History, Memory, and Identity in Post-Soviet Estonia: The End of a Collective Farm.* Oxford: Oxford University Press.
Reno, Joshua. 2015. *Waste Away: Working and Living on a North American Landfill.* Berkeley: University of California Press.
Rival, Laura. 2002. *Trekking Through History: The Huaorani of Amazonian Ecuador.* New York: Columbia University Press.
Rostow, Walt Whitman. 1959. "The Stages of Economic Growth." *The Economic History Review* 12(1): 1–16.
Sahlins, Marshall. 1974. *Stone Age Economics.* New York: Aldine de Gruyter.
———. 1996. "The Sadness of Sweetness: The Native Anthropology of Western Cosmology." *Current Anthropology* 37(3): 396–415.
Samuelson, Paul. (1948) 1998. *Economics.* New York: McGraw-Hill Education.
Schama, Simon. 1987. *The Embarrassment of Riches: An Interpretation of Dutch Culture in the Golden Age.* New York: Random House.
Schlecker, Markus. 2005. "Going Back a Long Way: 'Home Place,' Thrift and Temporal Orientations in Northern Vietnam." *JRAI* 11: 509–26.
Siegelbaum, Lewis. 1998. "'Dear Comrade, You Ask What We Need': Socialist Paternalism and Soviet Rural 'Notables' in the Mid-1930s." *Slavic Review* 57: 107–32.
———, ed. 2006. *Borders of Socialism: Private Spheres of Soviet Russia.* London: Palgrave Macmillan.
Singer, Milton. 1966. "Religion and Social Change in India: The Max Weber Thesis, Phase Three." *Economic Development and Cultural Change* 14(4): 497–505.
Sosna, Daniel, Lenka Brunckilova, and Patrik Galeta. 2019. "Rescuing Things: Food Waste in the Rural Environment in the Czech Republic." *Journal of Cleaner Production* 214: 319–30.
Strasser, Susan. 2000. *Waste and Want: A Social History of Trash.* New York: Owl Books.
Strathern, Andrew. 1971. *The Rope of Moka: Big-men and Ceremonial Exchange in Mount Hagen New Guinea.* Cambridge, UK: Cambridge University Press.
Strathern, Marilyn. 1988. *The Gender of the Gift.* Berkeley: University of California Press.

Tressell, Robert. (1914) 2012. *The Ragged-Trousered Philanthropists*. Ware, UK: Wordsworth Classics.

Trevor-Roper, Hugh. 1951. "The Elizabethan Aristocracy: An Anatomy Anatomised." *The Economic History Review* 3(3): 279–98.

Uchiyama, Benjamin. 2019. *Japan's Carnival War: Mass Culture on the Home Front, 1937–1945*. Cambridge, UK: Cambridge University Press.

Waring, Marilyn. 1988. *If Women Counted*. New York: Harper & Row.

Weber, Max. (1904-05) 2001. *The Protestant Ethic and the Spirit of Capitalism*. Chicago: Fitzroy Dearborn Publishers.

———. (1968) 2013. *Economy and Society*. Berkeley: University of California Press.

Wilk, Richard. 2006. "Consumer Culture and Extractive Industry on the Margins of the World System." In *Consuming Cultures, Global Perspectives: Historical trajectories, Transnational Exchanges*, edited by John Brewer and Frank Trentmann, 123–44. Oxford: Berg.

———. 2014. "Consumer Cultures Past, Present and Future." In *Sustainable Consumption: Multi-disciplinary Perspectives in Honour of Professor Sir Partha Dasgupta*, edited by Alistair Ulph and Dale Southerton, 315–36. Oxford: Oxford University Press.

Wolf, Eric. 1966. *Peasants*. Englewood Cliffs: Prentice Hall.

Woodburn, James. 1980. "Hunters and Gatherers Today and Reconstruction of the Past." In *Soviet and Western Anthropology*, edited by Ernest Gellner, 95–118. London: Duckworth.

———. 1982. "Egalitarian Societies." *Man* (N.S.) 17: 431–51.

World Commission on Environment and Development. 1987. *Our Common Future*. Oxford: Oxford University Press.

Yarrow, Andrew. 2014. *Thrift: The History of an American Cultural Movement*. Amherst: University of Massachusetts Press.

Yates, Joshua, and James Davison Hunter, eds. 2011. *Thrift and Thriving in America: Capitalism and Moral Order from the Puritans to the Present*. Oxford: Oxford University Press.

1

Making Savings

STEPHEN GUDEMAN

When I was young, my family often put together meals from leftovers. I wore hand-me-downs from my brother and watched my father steam unfranked stamps off envelopes, which is a practice I adopted until I learned it is illegal. Years later when I saw Panamanian peasants patch their clothes, save their uneaten rice for the next day, and reuse the metal nails they had, I recognized their practices, but only during fieldwork in Colombia did I see these disparate practices as illustrations of thrift and understand its place in economy. Later, when I undertook studies in Guatemala, Cuba, and parts of Eastern Europe, I saw other patterns of frugality. In the meanwhile, being thrifty became a satisfying practice for me.

I carried out the research in Colombia in the late 1980s with Alberto Rivera. We worked throughout the mountainous region that stretches from the Caribbean Coast to Ecuador. In these rural areas that are loosely connected to markets, the predominant economic institution is the house. Crops and animals are raised principally for home consumption but may be marketed for cash to purchase other things for the house.

On the first day of our fieldwork a man spoke at length about making savings (*hacer economias*) and economizing (*economizar*). The need to make savings and ways of doing so entered our field conversations many times after. Making savings, I slowly learned, applies to diverse and inventive practices whose connection is not immediately apparent.

After that initial talk, I realized that making savings belongs to two worlds, the house and the market, and has a double sense—being thrifty and hoarding. In the house economy at the margin of a market, being thrifty and holding the savings sustains the group. Thrift also helps corporate entities to achieve profits; but holding these savings may negate the functioning of the larger markets in which they participate. To sort out this contradictory position of thrift, I followed several textual trails, but when I saw that the distinction between being thrifty and keeping the savings had been used to advantage by John Maynard Keynes ([1936] 1964), the historical discussions and disagreements became much clearer. The textual conversation about thrift and saving was sometimes convoluted, but an examination of our ethnography and the changing theories has much to suggest about the relationship between practices and textual production, and between the margins and centers of market economies.

I use "making savings" to translate *hacer economias*, but terms such as being "thrifty," "parsimonious," "frugal," "abstinent," or "economical" can be employed. Economizing is common to both the house and market economies. In rural Colombia, being thrifty means controlling expenditures to have leftovers, which increase the base or holdings of the house. In the market sphere, economizing controls disbursements to have a profit. Leftovers in the rural house and the unspent income of the corporation are savings, but they are used differently. House remainders, whether food that does not spoil or partly used materials, are held as a precaution against the future or hedge against uncertainty; and when they are traded, the purpose is to replace the holdings. In the market sphere, savings are exchanged with the purpose of increasing capital, but corporations and individuals also keep a portion of their savings as a precautionary measure. John Maynard Keynes ([1936] 1964) termed this tendency to hold wealth in a market economy "liquidity preference," and observed that it is due to the "precautionary motive."

Until Keynes wrote about the propensity to hoard and explained its effect on the functioning of markets, the long-dominant house practice of keeping the savings was passed over in the central market texts, even though the making of savings or thrift was not. His recognition of the desire to keep or hold back, it might be suggested, allowed him to construct a new macroeconomics or larger model of the market economy that included practices of the house in addition to those of the corporation.

Ways of Being Thrifty

In the Colombian house economy, making savings is part of the larger task of managing a house well (*mandar bien*). Managing well means ensuring the smooth working of all house relationships. The man and woman must assist one another; the children must be trained to respect authority and to work. When there is shared labor and shared care for the work, the house is well run.

Managing well also means making savings. A house gathers agricultural produce from the land in a venture that it does not fully control. Once gathered, the harvest constitutes a stock for living that the house does control. Being thrifty presumes the resources of a house are tight and applies to the way they are used.

Economizing also means allocating and expending goods so that there are leftovers for other uses, that nothing is wasted, and that a reserve is built for the future. Making savings stands in opposition to waste, prodigality, and luxury. Being thrifty runs through all house practices from agricultural production to housekeeping to preserving, conserving, and storing.

Managing well also means taking care or being thrifty in the use of money. Just as making leftovers and making something of them are ways of being frugal, so avoiding the expenditure of cash by substituting material uses for money costs is a way of being thrifty. As one man explained, "One uses up the base [holdings of the house] but in order to avoid buying. Don't sell anything; keep it for eating, and less will need to be bought." If the base is sufficient and carefully used, or if something is replaced "inside" the house, he continued, money does not have to be secured and expended: "When it does not go out the doors, that is making savings." To make savings one must have materials in the house and produce the means for living to avoid the need to buy and the trader's gain or profiting.

When people purchase in stores, they try to spend as little as possible, for then "money remains." Buying less, owning fewer clothes, and buying inexpensive goods are ways to be thrifty, which has an impact on the way small stores stock and sell their inventory. Packaged foods reach the countryside in very small sizes because the people ration their money when purchasing. Stores make money in the same way. The inventory of rural stores itself is limited, and the goal is to have rapid turnover so that less financial investment is needed. For both houses and stores, these practices save money, although they require the expenditure of labor time. For those with some financial wealth, buying in bulk is thrifty because it is less expensive per item; but this form of purchase is difficult to accomplish, given the marketing structure in the countryside and small inventories, the lesser size of packages produced for consumers, the way suppliers make money through many small-lot sales, and the peasants' shortage of cash.

Parsimony in the use of house materials is of a piece with the way cash is expended. Economizing in the home is a shifting set of experiments. A domestic crop provides food for the house, which means food does not have to be bought—this is thrift. People try to provide their own seed, obviating the need for its purchase. Some crops serve several purposes, such as providing food for humans and fodder for animals, and this is a way of making savings because there is less loss of the harvest. Certain crops, such as maize, require less labor or materials to raise, which releases money or work time for other household activities. As one agriculturalist said, "The worker uses less food, so more remains to exchange."

Using house labor is the thriftiest way to raise crops, as is trading labor with other houses. If laborers must be hired, paying them in kind rather than cash saves money, and remunerating them partly with meals is a way to be thrifty. For those with ample land, deploying sharecroppers who receive part of the harvest instead of money is a form of frugality. Even in the smallest house, a garden with herbs and tomato plants or a patio with a few fruit trees makes savings: "Everything serves."

The domestic production of commodities is done parsimoniously. A potter tries to secure clay from land he owns or to which he has free access. If stubble from the fields can be used instead of purchased wood or charcoal to fuel his kiln, more economies are made. The working of the clay is done at the house, which serves as the processing shelter.

Comparable strategies are employed in consumption. The people are careful not to cook too much food, for it may be wasted and the need to buy will arrive sooner. There are limits to belt-tightening, however. To go below what the house needs to support its own work means the base will not be restored. The fire in the kiln must be hot enough to bake the pottery, so if scrub from the field is not sufficient to provide the heat, wood must be purchased.

Making do and savings

Tools have a patchwork and patched-up quality. Machetes are domestically repaired. Most of the small iron sugarcane mills, which a few people have, came from the United States and were made in the early twentieth century. Over time gears, casings, and pistons break. If the equipment were held commercially, it would be discarded, but grinders and other instruments are used far beyond their anticipated service time at the cost of frequent repairs by house labor.

Making do, an important way of being thrifty, is practiced with invention. Materials are fully used, reused, and put to new uses—a process also applied to the leftovers and waste of the larger economy. Castoff plastic containers for holding petroleum products, gathered in towns, are used for carrying and storing liquids or catching rainwater. With their tops sliced off, they serve as measuring vessels for seed. Old tires are cut into pieces that are remade into sandals, and small oil tins become kerosene lamps. Objects held in the countryside are given many tasks. One afternoon I watched a family baking bread, pastry, and cookies for a holiday. As the food emerged from the outdoor oven, the family used metal pot lids and roofing materials as trays, and the dough was rolled on a bed.

Making do is possible only because the people have many and broad skills and learn new ones. Most stick and thatch houses are lashed together with vines without the use of a nail, and if constructing this type of building is the skill of only a few, most people can make a bed of local cane and wood. For sending tomatoes to the market, the people fashion crates from wood scraps and used nails. Women, in addition to their domestic duties, tend animals and harvest cash crops; although to use a woman's skills most fully, the people sometimes spend money and buy a sewing machine. The act of forming a household itself is considered parsimonious. To support field laborers the woman prepares a brew and the man provides the materials for it, with neither paying for the work of the other.

Making savings means engaging in ceaseless activity. Working long days means that one is not wasting time, which implies the house is not wasting food. The people's definition of being rich is to have a sufficient base so that work is unnecessary while their idea of luxury, as in the waste of owning and feeding pigeons, shows that savings are not being made.

Owning land is thrifty. By raising a variety of crops, trading use of the land for labor via sharecropping, combining agriculture with pastoralism, and relying on products of the latter to fertilize the former, which is a way of internalizing exchange, the market can be avoided and money saved.

Keeping animals is thrifty in another way. Holding the agricultural leftover in animals keeps the base for future use. Cows and goats yield milk, a no-cost food, while hens provide eggs and sheep provide wool. Most of the animals require little expenditure of labor, their maintenance costs are low, and their growth augments the base.

A Long Conversation: Thrift

Practicing thrift is common to the house as well as market participants, but it has a different position in each. Corporate participants use thrift to manage their flows and build reserves that may be invested in profit making activities, while the rural house saves to preserve and build its base for contingencies. What is the connection of the two modes of parsimony? Is material thrift in the house evidence of the market's influence or is economizing with cash a domestic carryover to the market?

In my view, the practice of being thrifty began in the domestic economy in earlier times and subsequently was deployed in commerce; but the textual history of thrift is complex, for it shows a shift from a focus on material things to an emphasis on handling money.

The written model of the domestic economy begins in Greek times, and the main Greek texts emphasize the importance of managing well both house relationships and goods. Subsequent Roman texts give attention to thrifty agricultural techniques and practices but also hint at the importance of care in the expenditure of money. Later, as the market sphere grew, the house more and more had to handle money, and by the fourteenth century running a household well had much to do with the thrifty use of cash.

Leon Battista Alberti's ([1433–41] 1971) *Della famiglia*, as I shall explain, is a benchmark in this transition from handling things to handling money with its contrasting voices concerning the house and its management of money. After Alberti, the route of inscription takes several paths, two of which I shall follow. According to Max Weber ([1920] 1958), being thrifty is a central component of the Protestant ethic, culturally and ideologically crucial for modern capitalism. Sombart ([1913] 1915), Braudel (1986), and others partly disagree, holding that capitalist relationships began far earlier, but they concur that the practice of making savings is important in the development of capitalism. Part of this argument hinges on the origin of parsimony, although the disagreement may be incorrectly focused.

The second textual path leads into modern economics, for starting with the Mercantilists and early French writers and continuing through Smith and Mill, the concepts of thrift and abstinence become linchpins in the textual understanding of the way capital funds are created and augmented. This line of argument ends in a contradiction with Mill's claim that abstinence from current consumption creates capital yet does not influence spending patterns in the consumer market.

There were counter voices. Malthus disagreed with this smooth vision of the house practice in the market; however, his voice remained unheard until Keynes. To recount every step in this long history is not my project and beyond my capacities. I shall suggest some of the ways the house practice of thrift developed, was appropriated, and transformed in the market, and then gave rise to contradictions in models of its center, all the while remaining a practice of the house and the periphery.

Early Texts

Thrift does not appear in Aristotle's seminal text *Politics*. He focuses on the management of the household and its internal relationships, such as the relation of master to slave, husband to wife, and parents to children: "the business of household management is concerned more with human beings than it is with inanimate property" (1946: 33). Household economy is not directed to acquisition but to securing necessities, and household life is not a means to an end but a complete action (praxis). Aristotle is aware that monetary gains can be made, and he recounts some of the ways in which fortunes are amassed through monopoly control of resources (1946: 30–31), but household possessions are for use. They are not instruments for the accomplishment of something else nor is the house directed to ceaseless acquisition, which falls within the unnatural realm of exchange. Because the use of currency pertains mostly to "retail trade," which is not a household function, the house management of money is not Aristotle's concern.

Like Aristotle's *Politics*, Xenophon's fourth-century BCE text on household management (1923) had a formative impact on those to follow. It was translated from the Greek by Cicero and became known among Roman writers on agriculture, who through their texts influenced practices of succeeding centuries. Xenophon speaks of increasing "the estate by showing a balance" (1923: 363), but the recognition of gain is subsidiary to that of running the estate through careful management (1923: 517).

Xenophon assumes that only the earth yields the things by which people live and then moves swiftly to household administration (1923: 401). The text is one of the earliest written on management practices. In Xenophon's estimation, it is not the knowledge of farming itself or the intelligence of the farmer that makes for success but the care, hard work, and trouble of the manager (1923: 521).

Xenophon uses metaphors to explain and construct the roles of female and male in the household. The tropes are taken from the animal world, such as the beehive with workers and a queen, from the military with armies and commanders, from ships with captains and crews, from the polity, and from music. House relationships are partly modeled after other domains. Like these busy worlds, the successful house is characterized by thrift and ceaseless work. Slack and slothfulness are to be avoided (Xenophon 1923: 517).

The principal Latin texts on the household, estate, or villa are by Cato, Columella, Varro, and Palladius (Amerlinck de Bontempo 1987). The emphasis now shifts from social relationships within the house to farming practices, and the villa as a user of money. For example, Cato recognizes the estate as a locus of currency circulation and emphasizes the importance of care in expenditure so that there may be remainders (Cato 1933: 5–8). "Remember that a farm is like a man however great the income, if there is extravagance but little is left" (Cato 1933: 5). His text mingles money accounts with product calculations and extols parsimony in both. He recommends, for example, that after reviewing the tasks accomplished, the owner should: "Give orders that whatever may be lacking for the current year be supplied; that what is superfluous be sold. . . . Sell worn-out oxen, blemished cattle, blemished sheep, wool, hides, an old wagon, old tools, an old slave, a sickly slave, and whatever else is superfluous. The master should have the selling habit, not the buying habit" (1933: 9). His text is not about profit making in exchange but about carefully managing a house by setting aside sufficient amounts from returns to cover subsequent expenditures, by keeping superfluities within the villa, and by reproducing the villa through replacing its holdings.

Precepts on farming and animal husbandry have a prominent place in the texts of Varro (1934), Palladius (1976), and Columella (1941) as well. Their concern with the techniques of estate functioning is a new voice, but it fits the domestic model. Attention is given to controlling house losses, with little emphasis paid to market activity or profit making. The notion of being thrifty with money is voiced only as part of good housekeeping.

Towards Modern Texts

The Roman and Greek texts on the domestic economy proved to be influential models right through the Middle Ages, and they were intensively reworked in the Scholastic thought of Aquinas and others (Roll 1973), but it is most interesting to reengage this long conversation on thrift and the domestic economy at a later period, when markets were more fully developed.

In his masterful study of the development of the market economy, Fernand Braudel, with some reluctance, turns to the question of when capitalism began. Max Weber had argued that the crucial moment was the sixteenth century, when the Protestant ethic called for a new form of worldly action, but Werner Sombart thought that capitalism had arisen earlier, and Braudel agrees. "Fourteenth-century Florence," he says, "was a capitalist city" (1986: 578). Regardless of who stands in the right, some of the textual evidence cited is of capital interest. Sombart drew ammunition for his argument from Alberti's *Della famiglia* ([1433–41] 1971) in which Braudel claimed to find a new set of themes: forethought, the considered use of money and time, and "thrift exercised willingly" (Sombart [1913] 1915: 106). Braudel calls these "good bourgeois principles" (1986: 579). He admits that Alberti's work is one in a long line of "housekeeping manuals" filled with homely advice and of little "relevance to the world of trade" (1986: 580), but he argues that it bespeaks the existence of a capitalist spirit in Florence at the time.

Thrift, along with hard work, has often been identified as the "bourgeois virtue" (Fox-Genovese and Genovese 1983). Parsimony is said to be the practice of the rising and prosperous middle class, being a willingness to forgo present pleasures and amusements in service of the future. When linked to rational action, it implies controlling and disciplining current wants in the service of greater ends. Sombart called this combination *The Quintessence of Capitalism* ([1913] 1915), and on this point he and Weber agreed. Weber ([1920] 1958) had proposed that parsimony, as opposed to prodigality, was a key feature of the Protestant ethic. Faith was to be proved by objective monetary results, achieved consistently over a lifetime. In certain forms of Protestantism there was not only a "this-world" turning but also a "calling" to ceaseless work in order to show signs of being one of the elect through worldly success. The pure pursuit of money and gain was condemned, for they were not to be enjoyed, nor was individual industry to cease with success. Ostentation and self-indulgence were detestable to the asceticism that was inherent in this religious form. On Weber's account, religiously impelled asceticism, directed to the material realm, led to thrift and the accumulation of capital, which should be put to work. The religious model of Luther and Calvin produced both industry and frugality, and ultimately riches.

I must demur, because thrift is pervasively practiced in rural Colombia among Roman Catholics and within a cosmological framework in which labor is an effort, and success is a result of God's power expressed through nature. Weber might have countered that this discovery does not belie his argument because the particulate features of the Protestant ethic are not unique to it and once articulated the ethic shifts in a secular direction. This response admitted, the historical roots of Colombian rural culture, it must be said, predate the presumed rise and spread of the Protestant ethic. Thrift, savings, ceaseless work, and avoiding the unnecessary use of resources are found precisely where—on Weber's argument—they ought not to be.

This ethnographic observation seems to align me with Sombart (and Braudel) as opposed to Weber, for if being thrifty predates the rise of ascetic Protestantism and is separate from it, Weber must be wrong. Thriftiness with money, however, is initially the voice of the domestic economy as it encounters the growing sphere of market exchange. It is the domestic formulation of monetary and exchange relationships. One must disagree with Sombart not only for fixing on economizing or making savings as the original capitalist essence but also for locating this activity within the market as opposed to the house, which was exactly Weber's ([1920] 1958: 194–98) critique of Sombart in a learned footnote that placed the work of Alberti in the stream of Greek and Roman texts on the house economy. The point at issue involves not only the practice of making savings but also the way the resulting accumulations are used.

How, then, shall we read Alberti's *Della famiglia*? The scholarly argument has centered on one section of the work that consists of four parts, all with a domestic focus. The first concerns relations between the generations, the second love and marriage, and the fourth friendship, while attention has been drawn to the third, which concerns "good management." This third section is about the well-run house, not the profit-making individual, and the conversation, cast in a form recalling Xenophon's dialogue, ranges widely over many domestic themes of the period. Alberti's discussion of material practices would be especially well understood in contemporary Colombia where household need or necessity is persistently voiced, and luxury is viewed as a waste: "Those who use no more than is sufficient for whatever is needed and save the rest . . . I call good managers. . . . Men labor to earn money so that they will have it in case of need. While in good health, they provide for illness, just as an ant in the summer provides for the winter ahead. Possessions, therefore, are to be used to satisfy needs; when there is no necessity, they are to be saved" (Alberti [1433–41] 1971: 169–71).

Alberti presents a house text about thrift and holding a reserve written within the context of the long conversation that began in Greek and Roman times, although it gives more attention to money use. Sombart gives it a capitalist interpretation, however. He particularly draws attention to one phrase: *sancta cosa la masserizia*. Sombart first terms this the principle of "Holy Economy," then says that what Alberti meant by *masserizia* is not clear, and finally treats the Italian *masserizia* as meaning "economy" in the modern sense ([1913] 1915: 105). The English text, however, reads: "Thrift is a sacred thing; how many evil desires and dishonest appetites it curbs!" (Alberti [1433–41] 1971: 168). Weber, too, was worried by Sombart's understanding of "sacred thrift," and he interpreted it as "a principle of maintenance . . . not of acquisition" ([1920] 1958: 195). Sombart dissimulates here, for *masserizia* has several usages that make good sense in the context of Alberti's discussion, are instances of the domestic voice, and can be seen as applications of the house model as it encounters the market. According to one authoritative dictionary (*Sansoni Dictionary of the Italian and English Languages* 1972), *masserizia* can be used for:

1. Furniture and fittings or household goods
2. Fittings and stock, such as equipment, tools, and implements
3. Stewardship
4. Saving and economy

The meaning could not be clearer: *masserizia* is the good management or stewardship of the domestic holdings, which includes, but is not limited to, being frugal with money. In addition, *far masserizia* means, "to economize or save," "to do or make," which is comparable to the Spanish *hacer economias*. Sombart, in the service of his argument, interprets Alberti's domestic use of "economy" as if he intended it to apply only to exchange and the market, but Alberti was expressing not so much a "bourgeois mentality" as the domestic economy's response to exchange. Sombart's argument, while ostensibly calling on history, lacks historicity, because it displaces Alberti's voice from its position in a long and changing conversation to make it a reflection of Sombart's own.

Alberti's text is particularly interesting because it is one of the first written expressions of the way the house was managing itself in the market by trying to save on the expenditure of money and hold it. Being thrifty with money developed out of good housekeeping, which has always meant care in the use of materials. As the market grew and domestic units became greater participants in it, careful house management came to be applied to the use of money. The aim was to create reserves. Eventually, the house practice was used in conversations about market transactions, which leads us to the texts of economists.

Several stages may be distinguished in the written, market conversation about thrift. In the view of Tribe (1978), the period from 1600 to 1800 CE saw the final development and then the demise of the "agricultural treatise." During the early years of this period, writers were still listening to, and sometimes plagiarizing, Xenophon and the Latin authors. Emphasis was placed on the relation of the house to land and on its internal "good ordering" (Tribe 1978: 55). The husbandman was visualized as a solitary figure, not even linked to the local economy.

In most of the texts the larger system also was seen as a form of house holding. The Mercantilists, for example, were broadly united in the view that goods were to be provided for national needs just as the house provided for its needs. Remainders could be sold internationally with the balance received in goods and currency, which increased national wealth. Mercantilism displayed a greater interest in trade than the prior texts on the house, but this interest was linked to ensuring national self-sufficiency, and it echoed the house problem of achieving a just price and fair exchange. As one Mercantilist argued, there is "a great similitude between the affairs of a private person, and of a nation, the former being but a little family, and the latter a great family" (quoted in Haney 1949: 143).

By the 1750s a new model was emerging according to which the house farm is enmeshed in a system of exchange and its produce is circulated within the larger society. Calculation, landlord–tenant relations, and record keeping all became subjects for textual conversation, and the house was no longer seen as "the economy" (Tribe 1978: 78). This period did not mark the complete disappearance of the house model, for it was now projected on the more inclusive state. Political economy was viewed as the wise regulation of a royal household in which the monarch helped guide the circulation of the national product. This use of the house model for the nation culminated in James Steuart's *An Inquiry into the Principles of Political Oeconomy*, which began with a consideration of thrift:

> Oeconomy, in general, is the art of providing for all the wants of a family, with prudence and frugality. If any thing necessary or useful be found wanting . . . we immediately perceive a want of oeconomy. The object of it, in a private family, is therefore to provide for the nourishment, the other wants, and the employment of every individual. . . .
>
> What oeconomy is in a family, political oeconomy is in a state: with these essential differences, however, that in a state there are no servants, all are children: that a family may be formed when and how a man pleases, and he may there establish what plan of oeconomy he thinks fit; but states are found formed, and the oeconomy of these depends upon a thousand circumstances. . . .
>
> The principal object of this science is to secure a certain fund of subsistence for all the inhabitants . . . to make their several interests lead them to supply one another with their reciprocal wants. . . .
>
> It is the business of a statesman to judge of the expediency of different schemes of oeconomy, and by degrees to model the minds of his subjects. ([1767] 1966: 15–17)

Steuart's text, like a statesman's function, was an act of modeling and persuading. He projected the known house model on the political ordering of the larger economy. Notably, although he assumed thrift to be an important part of household and state management, he did not apply it to market practices.

Anne Robert Jacques Turgot's *Reflections on the Formation and the Distribution of Riches* ([1770] 1898), which followed Steuart, was both a Physiocratic text and a precursor of later interpretations. As the work unfolds, it evinces a shift from the house to the market, and it mixes the two by using thrift as the linked practice. Turgot claimed that the land provides all wealth. By economizing on what the earth yields, capital accumulates (Turgot [1770] 1898: 97). This is the house model. He also states that capital exists as money, that it is used throughout the economy, and that money is the "subject of saving" ([1770] 1898: 98). This is the emerging market model, and it implies that capital is not accumulated solely through making savings from the land's produce. The French term used here is *l'épargne*, which has the ambiguous triple meaning of thrift, economy, and saving. Turgot's work captured a shift in which the domestic lexicon was appropriated, taken apart, and then partly reprojected on exchange as if the two applications—for materials in the house and for money in market transactions—were the same.

Adam Smith made greater use of the idea of thrift and did so in the context of the market. His *An Inquiry into the Nature and Causes of the Wealth of Nations* was published only nine years after Steuart's *Principles*. The latter may have brought to a close the period in which the domestic model was maximally projected outside its home domain, and Smith may have established a new model for the market, but his text retained parts of the earlier conversation. He argued, for example, that savings from current consumption, as in the house, are made through frugality and constitute capital: "Capitals are increased by parsimony, and diminished by prodigality and misconduct. Whatever a person saves from his revenue he adds to his capital. . . . Parsimony, and not industry, is the immediate cause of the increase of capital. Industry, indeed, provides the subject which parsimony accumulates. But whatever industry might acquire, if parsimony did not save and store up, the capital would never be the greater" ([1776] 1976: 358–59).

Smith's text was different from Turgot's, with its emphasis on land as the first source of wealth, and he more fully projected the practice of thrift on the market participant. But because the market enterprise was not completely established in the text, most of Smith's examples had an individualistic and house resonance, which helped bridge the two spheres of house and business.

Smith saw frugality as involving the interplay of expenditures and leftovers, of controlling one to have the other but elevated this house practice to the status of a human "principle": "The principle which prompts to expence, is the passion for present enjoyment; which, though sometimes violent and very difficult to be restrained, is in general only momentary and occasional. But the principle which prompts to save, is the desire of bettering our condition, a desire which, though generally calm . . . never leaves us . . . the principle of frugality seems not only to predominate, but to predominate very greatly" ([1776] 1976: 362–63).

Smith placed great trust in self-interest, but he did not attend, from within the economic realm, to the determinants of parsimony and prodigality. They were counterpoised "passions" whose balance was perhaps determined, as Weber later argued, by something like the Protestant ethic. Still, along with his contemporary David Hume, Smith produced a ringing defense of frugality: "Every prodigal appears to be a public enemy, and every frugal man a public benefactor" ([1776] 1976: 362). This textual appropriation of the house practice for the market ultimately led Smith along a new path. He argued not only that parsimony increases capital, but also that the latter is used to produce more: he welded together being thrifty and investing the savings, while teasing apart being thrifty and holding the savings:

> What is annually saved is as regularly consumed as what is annually spent, and nearly in the same time too; but it is consumed by a different set of people. That portion of his revenue which a rich man annually spends, is in most cases consumed by idle guests, and menial servants, who leave nothing behind them in return for their consumption. That portion which he annually saves, as for the sake of the profit it is immediately employed as a capital, is consumed in the same manner, and nearly in the same time too, but by a different set of people, by laborers, manufacturers,

> and artificers, who reproduce with a profit the value of their annual consumption. ([1776] 1976: 359)

Smith's main theme was that all money accumulated by thrift is spent rather than hoarded. Some expenditures pay for food and services in the home, while other spending is used as capital for the manufacture of goods. One is unproductive expenditure; the other is productive. Either way, all money is spent, and cash has no store-of-value function: "The sole use of money is to circulate consumable goods" (Smith [1776] 1976: 361). This was a crucial reevaluation of the house practice of thrift, and it gave making savings a new rationale. We might summarize this developing model by saying thrift yields savings, savings provide capital, and capital is spent on goods and labor, which are employed productively to provide more goods. There are no pauses; there is no keeping of wealth. For Smith, the crucial distinction was between spending on the manufacture of goods and spending for domestic services. One leads to the growth of capital, and the other does not. The house rationale for being thrifty and accumulating savings to have a reserve for future use was deleted from his contribution.

In France, Jean-Baptiste Say interpreted and elaborated the work of Smith. In his *Treatise on Political Economy* ([1803] 1964) he argued that only saving augments productive capital and that savings are made from current consumption by frugality. He agreed with Turgot and Smith that thrifty practices had increased in modern times but considered this due to "the advances of industry," because more efficient processes of production had tempted owners of capital to use it for making profits. For J. B. Say, capital could be endlessly accumulated through frugality and industry, and these heightened practices of his time undermined the older one of hoarding wealth ([1803] 1964: 116–18).

Say's rereading of frugality as prompted by profit seeking was of a piece with his larger model of the economy. A savings, he contended, was always expended or consumed, and he attacked the counter voices of Sismondi and Malthus by arguing that "the accumulations of the miser are now either vested in reproduction . . . or . . . production" ([1803] 1964: 111). All this fits Say's Law, which in many ways was the logical conclusion of the argument that thrift delivers savings, which provide capital for consumption: "When the producer has put the finishing hand to his product, he is most anxious to sell it immediately, lest its value should diminish in his hand. Nor is he less anxious to dispose of the money he may get for it; for the value of money is also perishable. But the only way of getting rid of money is in the purchase of some product or other. Thus the mere circumstance of the creation of one product immediately opens a vent for other products" ([1803] 1964: 135).

According to Say's Law, there is no overproduction of goods or shortfall of demand, for the sale of a product yields—through the return it gives on land, labor, and capital—the purchasing power to buy, and this power is exercised. For the economy as a whole, returns from production make up exactly sufficient demand to purchase what is produced. The act of "saving" only influences the distribution of spending between present consumption and investment for the future. Monetary savings are always offset by their expenditure.

John Stuart Mill finally and fully articulated this classical model of the economy. He held that capital is the result of saving, even when there are increases in productivity that yield capital: "To consume less than is produced, is saving; and that is the process by which capital is increased" (Mill [1848] 1929: 70). Mill, like Smith, was an observer of the world and admired peasant smallholders. To some degree he used them to model middle-class savers. Both, he said, are frugal; they economize and exercise self-control. In contrast, day laborers are "usually improvident" and "spend carelessly" ([1848] 1929: 286–87). Savings are the result of abstinence from consumption. Saving enriches while spending impoverishes, so the prodigality of some, such as day laborers, forces others to economize ([1848] 1929: 163, 72–73). Mill saw thrift as being common to both the house and corporate actors but not the laborer.

Mill further argued that profit is the return for prior abstinence ([1848] 1929: 462). To persuade a holder of capital to forgo current consumption, a return must be paid, and profit is that reward ([1848] 1929: 36). Mill observed that cultures differ in their propensity to accumulate, and this motive varies with the profit or income it can be expected to realize ([1848] 1929: 164–65, 173, 72–79). He clinched the profit-as-reward-for-abstinence argument by drawing an analogy between the house and business: "The cause of profit is, that labour produces more than is required for its support. The reason why agricultural capital yields a profit is because human beings can grow more food than is necessary to feed them while it is being grown . . . from which it is a consequence, that if a capitalist undertakes to feed the labourers on condition of receiving the produce, he has some of it remaining for himself after replacing his advances" ([1848] 1929: 416–17). Mill's claim "from which it is a consequence" was intended to persuade the reader of an identity between house expenditures with its returns in agriculture and monetary costs and returns in manufacturing. Making savings has the same function in both, which is to create capital. But Mill, an ethnographer of his time, knew that savings were not always accumulated for investment and that he had not taken full enough account of the link between being thrifty and building reserves in the house: "The tendency of peasant proprietors . . . is to take even too much thought for the morrow. . . . They deny themselves reasonable indulgences, and live wretchedly in order to economize. In Switzerland almost everybody saves . . . among the French . . . the spirit of thrift is diffused through the rural population . . . there are numbers who have hoards in leathern bags, consisting of sums in five-franc pieces" ([1848] 1929: 286–87).

Mill's recognition of contrary practices at the European periphery posed a problem for the developing model of the center. Mill argued that profit arose from the investment of savings accumulated by thrift; profit was the reward for this abstinence, and it motivated different degrees of thriftiness. Yet Mill knew that peasants practiced thrift simply to have savings for the future and never received a reward for their abstinence. If both peasants and capitalists had the same frugal practices, how could their difference be explained?

Mill rid himself of this problem by the device of redefinition or perhaps omission. Pure savings, he said, are not capital. "If merely laid by for future use, it is said to be hoarded; and while hoarded, is not consumed at all. But if employed as capital, it is all consumed" (Mill [1848] 1929: 70). To preserve the profit-as-reward-for-abstinence argument, Mill—with J. B. Say—had to omit the possibility of hoarding in the market circuit. With this shift, the textual conversation came full circle: capital was made by abstinence or hoarding, yet capital was not a hoard! Mill had drawn a similarity between capitalists and peasant householders on the basis of their common practice of economizing, giving thought to the morrow, and having the spirit of thrift. This similarity provided a model for the way capital was built, and it was used to justify the taking of profit. But among householders, thrift is practiced to have a reserve, so to keep the profit argument intact Mill deleted this implication of the older, appropriated model.

Hoarding and Keynes

After Mill, the consideration of hoarding fell aside until Keynes ([1936] 1964) reinstituted it, neatly turning everything about by claiming that interest paid on money is the reward for not hoarding. He thus distinguished making savings from keeping them. In Keynes's model, interest is not a reward for abstinence, thrift, or waiting but a return for giving up the security of keeping a liquid hoard. Keynes did not write about the domestic economy, but his transformed model allowed him to draw an implicit distinction between the house and market economies: "In the absence of an organized market, liquidity-preference due to the precautionary-motive would be greatly increased; whereas the existence of an organized market gives an opportunity for wide fluctuations in liquidity-preference due to the speculative-motive" ([1936] 1964: 170–71).

With Keynes, hoarding and temporal hitches reentered the market model, and the phenomena of business cycles and political action in the economy again became textual concerns. By his implicit recognition of domestic frugality and saving, Keynes was able to construct a new macroeconomics; but in a sense, he was only restating the Colombian folk voice that being thrifty or making economies is not the same as seeking a profit or making money.

Thus, what had begun as the house modeling of thrift, which still persists in Colombia, was appropriated and slowly reevaluated in the texts of economists to model the accumulation of capital. In this intellectual appropriation and transformation of a people's practice, the act of thrift—with all that it potentially implies about liquidity preference and hoarding, money used as a store of value, and under consumption—was for a long while veiled, perhaps to distance the new model from those from whom it had been taken. Thrift and saving had been shifted from one conversation to another and reapplied. Only after some time was the original voice and practice rediscovered.

Keynes himself once justified his profession in a grand set of phrases: "The ideas of economists and political philosophers, both when they are right and when they are wrong, are more powerful than is commonly understood. Indeed the world is ruled by little else. Practical men, who believe themselves to be quite exempt from any intellectual influences, are usually the slaves of some defunct economist. Madmen in authority, who hear voices in the air, are distilling their frenzy from some academic scribbler of a few years back" ([1936] 1964: 383).

The anthropologist wonders whether the economist has it back to front, for to judge by the Colombian ethnography it would appear that many of those "voices in the air" come first from the practices and articulations of living folk and are then frantically distilled and transformed by academic economists into textual forms that—as the writings of Aristotle, Xenophon, Cato, Aquinas, Smith, Mill, and Keynes suggest—have their persuasive force on one another and on the long conversation in which we all participate.

Acknowledgments

I provide here a revised portion of Chapter 9 in our book, *Conversations in Colombia: The Domestic Economy in Life and Text*, by Stephen Gudeman and Alberto Rivera. Cambridge, UK: Cambridge University Press, 1990. Reprinted with permission.

Stephen Gudeman received his professional training at Cambridge and has carried out fieldwork in Panama, Colombia, Guatemala, and Cuba, as well as overseen a field project in Eastern Europe. He is emeritus professor at the University of Minnesota and the author or editor of twelve books and 150 publications.

References

Alberti, Leon Battista. (1433–41) 1971. *Della famiglia.* Translated by Guido A. Guatino. Lewisburg: Bucknell University Press.

Amerlinck de Bontempo, Marijose. 1987. "'Praedium,' 'fundum,' 'villa' y hacienda: La perspectiva de los agrónomos latinos." In *La hererodoxia recuperata,* edited by Susana Glanrz, 375–95. México: Fondo de Cultura Económica.

Aristotle. 1946. *The Politics.* Translated by Ernest Barker. London: Oxford University Press.

Braudel, Fernand. 1986. *The Wheels of Commerce.* Translated by Siân Reynolds. New York: Harper and Row.

Cato. 1933. *On Farming.* Translated by Ernest Brehaut. New York: Columbia University Press.

Columella. 1941. *On Agriculture.* Translated by Harrison Boyd. London: Heinemann.

Fox-Genovese, Elizabeth, and Eugene D. Genovese. 1983. *Fruits of Merchant Capital.* New York: Oxford University Press.

Haney, Lewis H. 1949. *History of Economic Thought,* 4th edn. New York: Macmillan.

Keynes, John Maynard. (1936) 1964. *The General Theory of Employment, Interest, and Money.* New York: Harcourt, Brace and World.

Mill, John Stuart. 1929 (1948). *Principles of Political Economy,* ed. W.J.Ashley. London: Longmans, Green.

Palladius. 1976. *Traité d'agriculture.* Translated by René Martin. Paris: Société D'Edition "Les Belles Lettres."

Roll, Eric. 1973. *A History of Economic Thought.* 4th ed. London: Faber and Faber.

Say, John-Baptiste. 1964 (1803). *A Treatise on Political Economy.* New York: Sentry Press.

Smith, Adam. (1776) 1976. *An Inquiry into the Nature and Causes of the Wealth of Nations,* edited by Edwin Cannan. Chicago: University of Chicago Press.

Sombart, Werner. (1913) 1915. *The Quintessence of Capitalism.* New York: Dutton.

Steuart, James. (1767) 1966. *An Inquiry into the Principles of Political Oeconomy,* edited by Andrew S. Skinner. Chicago: University of Chicago Press.

Tribe, Keith. 1978. *Land, Labour and Economic Discourse.* London: Routledge and Kegan Paul.

Turgot, Anne Robert Jacques. (1770) 1898. *Reflections on the Formation and the Distribution of Riches.* New York: Macmillan.

Varro. 1934. *On Agriculture.* Translated by William Davis Hooper. London: Heinemann.

Weber, Max. (1920) 1958. *The Protestant Ethic and the Spirit of Capitalism.* Translated by Talcott Parsons. New York: Scribner.

Xenophon. 1923. *Oeconomicus.* Volume 4. Translated by E. C. Marchant. Cambridge, MA: Harvard University Press.

2

Saving, Investment, Thrift?

Welfare Beneficiary Households and Borrowing in South Africa

Deborah James, David Neves, and Erin Torkelson

For at least a century, getting and spending money have been topics of moral and social contestation in the lives of Black South Africans.[1] With recent changes, disputes, for decades taking place along the fault line of gender, have become fiercer, but have also seen new protagonists enter the fray. In a setting where proletarianization was rapid, extensive, and often brutal (Cooper 2002), its decline has been experienced with even more disruption. Since the end of apartheid and the advent of democracy in the 1990s, the ANC (African National Congress) government, in partnership with entrenched White capital (Fine 2019), pursued economic liberalization and financialization. These economic policies led to growth in the economy without an accompanying growth in waged work (Marais 2011), unleashing a virtual epidemic of borrowing and lending (James 2015). Against this backdrop, women in rural and peri-urban areas have pursued practices of householding and husbandry, attempting to get by on state welfare payments while also saving (eking out household money to cover costs over a longer period) and investing (contributing to solidaristic social relationships). As the introduction to this volume demonstrates, such thrifty practices have ambiguous consequences. They are caught up with complex patterns of indebtedness that might seem the very opposite of thriftiness but are interwoven with it, variously enabling and stalling careful household management.

One key mechanism through which Black South Africans—villagers and township residents alike—save money and practice thrift is through membership in the financial mutuals known as *stokvels*.[2] Such clubs, a feature of rapidly urbanizing societies worldwide, from China and Indonesia (Geertz

1962) to sub-Saharan Africa (Ardener 1964, 2010; Bähre 2007; Krige 2014; Rodima-Taylor 2014), typically take the form of rotating savings and credit associations (ROSCAs). Members contribute standard amounts at regular intervals throughout a cycle (usually a year). They then take it in turns at successive meetings, or when urgent needs arise, to receive the accumulated amount in cash, using this for expenditures normally beyond their reach. Although they are often seen as "traditional," they are not in fact rooted in ancient custom (Shipton 2007); they emerged in Black South African communities in tandem with oscillating labor migration and urbanization (Bähre 2007; Kuper and Kaplan 1944), often—as burial societies—responding to the need to repatriate the bodies of deceased migrants (Delius 1996; see also Thomson and Posel 2002).

Women's clubs, which had come into being in tandem with the somewhat later development of female migration, provided support and solidarity, as well as a means to save earnings (James 1999, 2015; Mager and Mulaudzi 2012). They are nowadays often seen as quintessentially female,[3] being associated with care for the household (*go hlôkômêla lapa*), whereas "men just want to eat." A central intention of (women's) savings clubs, observed clothes peddler Sophie Mahlaba, is to stop men from wastefully squandering money ("eating" money—*go ja tšhêlêtê*).

> Since men are in any case said to be incapable of cooking and unaware of what household goods and provisions might be required, there would be little point in their joining clubs aimed at replenishing such stocks. Women also point to the cyclical character of the clubs' savings activities and the way this feature helps mothers who are obliged to meet very particular expenses at year-end: providing food and drink for Christmas festivities; stocking pantries with dry goods and cleaning products to last well into the new year; and—when the school year begins—buying new school uniforms, shoes, books, and stationery for their children, as well as paying school fees. (James 2015: 129)

This is a partisan view in a long-standing dispute; the opposite has also been argued to be true. Men in migrant laborer households, showed Ferguson, were committed to long-term investment in cattle while their wives strove tirelessly to convert those cattle for cash in order to cover immediate expenses (Ferguson 1985). But much has changed over the ensuing thirty years. Women now increasingly hold sway over householding because of shrinking wage-labor and the corresponding importance of the state pension and other forms of welfare (known as "social grants"). In addition, the severe toll HIV/AIDS has taken on households has left widows or younger unmarried mothers to look after not only their own but also relatives' children. The narrative of a wife's responsibility for the domestic domain thus retains great force and has even intensified (James 2015: 127); and, as the principal recipients of welfare (on behalf of their children, via the Child Support Grant), it is they—with their *stokvel* membership—who play a pivotal role. Adding to the complexity of how financing is moralized, *stokvels* have enjoyed a contradictory relationship with formal finance and investment. Viewed by some as a means of adjusting—even a step on the road—to financial formality (e.g., Geertz 1962; Krige 2012), and often making use of special bank accounts to store and save members' contributions temporarily, they have also been used in South Africa by those seeking to escape the disadvantages of banking (often seen as skewed against the needs of Black people and as unduly bureaucratic with high transaction costs) and especially to evade the steep costs of credit entailed in purchasing goods on installment by buying them for cash instead (James 2015: 143).

But seeking such escape, on the face of it, seems increasingly futile. At the same time as these changes were taking place, momentous developments were occurring in the world of high finance. With state aid (through a process of public procurement), large financial companies have turned poor welfare recipients into clients, a process that has also been noted in Brazil and Chile, where it has been dubbed the "collateralization of social policy under financialized capitalism" (Lavinas 2018: 502). Listed multinational Net1 UEPS (Universal Electronic Payment Systems) Technologies (hereafter Net1), through its Cash Paymaster Services (CPS) business, won a government contract to deliver social grants in South Africa, using its proprietary smart-card technology. It extended loans to grantees and used social grants to recoup repayments for the debts incurred. In South Africa, as in Chile and Brazil, welfare dependents' incorporation into the market has thus been ensured by a regular benefit that the state pays, which lenders then use to secure their repayment automatically; "we are witnessing the collateralization of social policy: credit and debt, along with new financial devices, are becoming the cornerstones of what used to be social protection systems, so as to respond to the needs of finance-dominated capitalism (Lavinas 2018: ibid.). In the South African case, following public outcries, Net1's contract was withdrawn, and its role taken over by the Post Office (SAPO). This move was viewed as a triumph for welfarist policy against capitalist extraction, yet it raised further problems. Some commentators and critics of the extractive lending practices adopted by the company (outlined below) endorse an idea of "thrift" in which existing resources ought to be made to stretch to cover monthly expenses (see James 2015: 44–45, 163). While this has proved persuasive for various parts of the concerned citizenry and might be a model of prudence ideal for bourgeois householders (Gudeman this volume), in a context of low employment such literacy implies less the working out of a reasoned budget and apportioning of income than simple belt-tightening. But the social grant-recipient women portrayed in this chapter do make plans about future finance and allocate money to different purposes, engaging in the management of household resources to keep things going. Although they "don't have savings," much like the Buenos Aires shack-dwellers documented by Ariel Wilkis (2017), they "do have debt." Alongside the social investment represented by *stokvel* membership, they count on being able to borrow—not as an aberration, but as an essential element in the household budget.

This chapter shows how the increasing predominance of women in managing and budgeting for the household, in part through *stokvel* membership, has intersected with their advancing "financial inclusion." While social grants have enabled welfare recipients to access credit through more formal means, such credit has not simply replaced communal rotating savings and credit schemes but rather has articulated with them. This in turn has prompted social reformers and activists to impose rights-based ideas about sound financial practice. Taking place against a backdrop of clashing value systems, irreconcilable viewpoints, and incompatible ideas about the uses to which money ought to be put and how it should be stored, the chapter documents the new and not-so-new practices of saving, investment, and borrowing through which "thrift" is constituted. Local models of household economy are centered on husbanding resources rather than spending them heedlessly, but this requires the borrowing of money from various sources: something that itself constitutes an investment or form of thrift. Depicting householders' practices in terms of dichotomous opposites—such as frugality vs profligacy—is misleading; thrift has ambiguities that can make it both a vice and a virtue.

Ethnographic Context and Research Methods

The research on which this chapter draws was done in collaboration with, and its agenda was shaped by, human rights organization Black Sash (James, Neves, and Torkelson 2020).[4] The aim was to explore the effects of the latest developments in "reckless lending" in South Africa. These came in the wake of the explosion of indebtedness during the 1990s, when the twin forces of liberalization and financialization enabled Black people formally excluded by "credit apartheid" to borrow extensively (see James 2015; Neves 2018; Torkelson 2020). Our sample, covering a wide range of spatial contexts—urban and rural, centrally situated and remote—revealed the prevalence of a widening range of lenders offering loans to social grant beneficiaries, and showed how the apartheid history of each of these areas, as well as their proximity to or distance from urban centers (see Table 2.1 and Figure 2.1), has shaped local lending practices. Thus, for example, the industrial hub of Uitenhage (see Figure 2.1) had an extensive range of types

Figure 2.1. Map of fieldsites. © Elsabe Gelderblom/Black Sash.

of borrowers, including most of those identified below (see Table 2.1 for the typology) but with a predominance of EFT (electronic funds transfer)/debit order and cash/debit order lenders. In the remoter sites—Hammanskraal, Khutsong, and especially Taaiboschgroet—cash lenders and "loan sharks" predominate. We worked collaboratively with the local partners of Black Sash, mostly small NGOs, who identified five to ten indebted welfare beneficiaries in each site. Our methodology consisted of a case-study approach focused on in-depth interviews coupled with a semistructured survey instrument designed, trialed, and refined over two years in partnership with Black Sash, combined with the documentary analysis (of research participants' bank statements, contracts, etc.). We interviewed welfare recipients, seeking to understand their responsibilities and obligations to their household, strategies for budgeting throughout the month and year, and how they made decisions about spending, saving, and borrowing. In addition, we drew on local knowledge to survey communities and identify different types of lenders.

Table 2.1. A typology of lenders and lending in South Africa.

Lending Context	**Lenders**					
Transfer/ Repayment	**EFT/ Debit Order**	**Cash/Debit Order**		**Cash/Cash**		
Examples of Lenders (to social grant recipients)	National/ Corporate EPE/Money-line (facilitated by CPS/Net1), Finbond	Regional ABC, Top-up, Mashabalala	Regional/Local Payday/Chinese lenders (e.g., Wen, Zhang)	*Mashonisa* (small)	*Mashonisa* (medium)	*Mashonisa* (large)
Social Connection	None	Little to none	None	Kin, neighbors	*Stokvels*, slightly larger, more distant from borrower	Largest, most socially distant
Terms of the Loan	3–6-month loans, about 5% interest per month (excluding fees)	3–6-month loans; about 30–60% interest per month	1-month loans, given in cash; about 30–60% interest	30% interest monthly, does not retain borrower card, negotiable terms and time frame	30–50% interest, may retain card but not PIN, less negotiable terms and time frame	50–100% interest, retains card and PIN, little negotiation
Characteristics of Lending System	High-tech, biometric-verification, formal printed contracts	Hybrid system. Combines formal banking or payment system with cash disbursement of the loan, written or verbal contracts		Personalized and relational. Relies on ATM banking/ cards to claim repayment, but uses informal handwritten or verbal contracts or ATM statements		

To make sense of the complex lending landscape, we mapped the variety of lenders and types of lending we discovered. Table 2.1, although subdivided into separate categories based on the practices by which money is transferred by lenders to their grant-recipient clients and then repaid by borrowers to these lenders, ought rather to be read as a continuum. It follows a series of gradations from what are often called "formal" practices, on the left-hand side, to increasingly "informal" ones on the right. However, the forms of borrowing and lending it portrays defy a simple categorization along formal/informal lines (Hart 2015), since many face-to-face cash transactions rely on, or are facilitated by, hi-tech debit orders and banking infrastructure. Interest rates vary widely, as do the ways in which these are communicated to borrowers. The registered lenders on the left-hand side of the table publish their rates on preprinted forms (and carbon copies are given to borrowers) and appear largely to comply with the stipulations of the National Credit Act (NCA), although high interest rates are often obscured by calling these "initiation" or "service fees" (Gregory 2012). The *mashonisas*[5] (loan sharks) on the right-hand side of the typology, in contrast, mostly charge higher rates of interest, comply with no legal stipulations, and often fail to record repayments or inform borrowers of their remaining debts, or do so by using ATM "mini statement" printouts or exercise books.

Those lenders normally thought of as "formal," who rely on sophisticated financial systems such as the EFT/debit order system and the functionality of Net1's EasyPay Everywhere or EPE ("green") card, include Moneyline and Finbond in the first column of Table 2.1. Moneyline is a registered Financial Services Provider and a subsidiary of Net1; Finbond is a Mutual Bank partially owned by Net1. Both are large firms with multiple branches nationwide. Because banking the unbanked had initially been made possible through the contract awarded to Net1 that afforded it a kind of "lock-in" (Breckenridge 2019), this enabled debit-order based lending—from it and other lenders—for social grant recipients, even following the termination of its contract. The South African state had effectively subsidized the creation of a monopoly and gave Net1 preferential access to 17 million social grant beneficiaries through its control of the payment system and its flows (Torkelson 2020). Net1 restructured the low-income lending market by creating the EPE bank account that allowed for early and automatic debit order deductions from these grant beneficiaries, enabling other microlenders with debit order facilities—and even those without—to later benefit from Net1's innovations.

The second column of Table 2.1 contains types of lenders that grant loans in cash but collect repayments using debit orders on borrowers' bank accounts. They include businesses known as cash loans, microlenders, and payday loan enterprises, which may have several branches but are regionally based and much smaller than the large financial services companies or mutual banks. Their loans are typically repaid over three to six months, with repayment collected through debit order on a bank account. Among these are the "one time" lenders (who collect the total repayment in one go), many run by Chinese nationals. All rely on the financial system established by EFT/debit orders both to check the creditworthiness of borrowers and to collect repayments.

The lenders in the far-right column both lend to borrowers and collect loan repayments in cash. Lumped together as *mashonisas* (sometimes termed "loan sharks"), they vary widely depending on the size of their businesses and the nature of their relationship with borrowers. Rates of interest charged increase as one moves toward the far right of the column. These lenders range from friends, family, or neighbors who help out with a loan but still charge interest, through local "neighborhood" or "village" *mashonisas*, to those more "distant" in both spatial and relationship terms. The latter typically do not have close connections to those who borrow from them, are more affluent than their clients, and charge the highest interest (50–100 percent).

It is against the backdrop of this wider borrowing landscape that activities in the cash/cash column—and especially borrowing and lending by members of financial mutuals or *stokvels*—take place. Such savings coexist with the banking system, albeit in ambivalent ways. Policy makers after apartheid initially disparaged them but have more recently come to embrace and advocate them as a catch-all solution to financial problems. Participation in these clubs, far from diminishing since the advent of democracy when people gained greater access to formal financial services, has intensified. Banks, in an attempt "to try and capture some of the pools of money which continue to circulate outside the formal banking system" (Krige 2014: 66), established special *stokvel* accounts where clubs temporarily deposit their money, but many householders have used *stokvels* instead to keep their savings beyond the reach of the finance industry. Overall, the borrowing and lending that *stokvels* enable is entangled with, and inseparable from, the hi-tech financial arrangements that EFT/debit order lenders facilitate.

Investment, thrift, and indebtedness are thus interconnected in unexpected ways. Poor people, in circumstances of widespread poverty and unemployment, caring for many dependents, continue to need money beyond what they receive from the state or earn from precarious wage labor. Borrowing has continued apace. While this debt explosion has much in common with its counterparts across the globe, especially in countries of the Global South (Servet and Saiag 2013), what distinguishes the South

African case is the very swift and extensive "financial deepening" indicated in Table 2.1. Women's borrowing using the electronic transfer/debit order systems is intertwined with their cash borrowing from *mashonisas*.

Thrift here embodies a contradiction. If thrift is one important principle of a local model of household economy that centers on careful husbandry rather than profligacy, it also necessitates the taking out of loans from various sources—something which can, itself, be seen as a kind of investment or form of saving and thus as reconcilable with "traditional" conceptions of thrift (Gudeman this vol.). People borrow from their neighbors or fellow villagers, on the one hand, in transactions that are often mediated via *stokvels*, and they offer loans to them, on the other—borrowing and lending cannot be neatly separated. The membership of such associations enables people to anticipate and budget for expenditure as documented below, but also requires them to borrow from *other* sources to keep up their subscriptions, often driving them into difficulties. The exact calculus of which debt is more pressing (to the *stokvel* or to the outside lender—who might herself be a member of another *stokvel*) is made more complex by group pressure not to interrupt the payment cycle. Indeed, some of the neighborhood people who loan money to others—as *mashonisas* (loan sharks)—are doing so because they belong to the type of *stokvel* that requires its members to lend out money at interest, known as ASCRAs (accumulated savings and credit associations) (Ardener 2010; Bähre 2007). *Stokvels* that, in one register, are serving as savings enabling thrift or investment mechanisms are, in another, acting as sources of indebtedness. Added to these contradictions are the activists and lawyers, policy makers, and even those in the business community who question what is a fair interest rate, how much can and should be charged to those taking out "unsecured loans," and how regulation might curb or cap these charges. Such questions are difficult to answer given the convoluted relationships in play.

Saving and Investment, or Borrowing?

The cases of welfare recipient/borrowers documented below illustrate some of the ways in which these apparently discrete types of loans connect to each other in low-income households, and the ambiguities entailed in keeping a thrifty household in this low-resource setting. Most hail from the rural areas in or near the former Bantustans that were migrant labor reserves during the height of the mining and industrial economy in the apartheid era—Port St. Johns (Eastern Cape), Limehill (KwaZulu Natal), and Taaiboschgroet (Limpopo) (see Figure 2.1). Only one of the sites mentioned below—Khutsong (Gauteng)—is a township in which mine workers and their families were able to put down roots and reside in the longer term. In all these sites, rural and peri-urban alike, unemployment is now highly prevalent.

The Overdetermination of Borrowing in Port St. Johns

Athandwa is a fortysomething woman who lives in the village of Nonxeni, approximately 30 km outside Port St. Johns (Figure 2.1) in what was once the Transkei Bantustan. Educated to grade nine (two years of secondary schooling), she is currently unemployed, but has intermittently worked as a domestic cleaner for Black middle-class households. From late 2013 to 2014 she spent four months working on a public employment scheme, involved in road construction, for which she was paid R90 daily.[6] Even then she was compelled to take out a loan, because the scheme's workers were not paid on time by the project contractor and needed money for transport. Since then she has regularly borrowed money, although sometimes leaving intervals between the loans, repaying the sum and owing nothing for a month or two, before borrowing again. At the time of research, she was in a recurrent cycle of debt.

Even by impoverished village standards, single mother Athandwa's household is poor and vulnerable. This is evident from the two single-roomed mud "flats" (rectilinear huts) where they live. As the only survivor of five sisters, she explained that "everybody depends on her." Her household consists of herself and her three children—her son had until recently been studying at a regional university while the other two are in school—as well as a nephew and niece who live with her after the death of their mothers, Athandwa's sisters. She receives welfare payments for the four minor children, but bureaucratic failures mean these payments amount to less than they should. For her niece, whose mother died in 2009, Athandwa receives a Foster Care Grant. But for her nephew (as for her own two children) she collects Child Support Grants, although she ought to be entitled to the fourfold greater Foster Care Grant in the case of her nephew. The social workers responsible for arranging these insisted, obstructively and unlawfully, that it was the duty of the boy's absent father and paternal grandparents to support him.

In terms of expenditure, in an average month, Athandwa reportedly spends R800 on groceries that are "never enough" for the household members, R700 on school transport, and R100 on electricity that routinely runs out before month end. Beyond this, her regular outgoings are contributions to *stokvels* and insurance schemes. These, listed in a rather matter-of-fact manner as normal budgetary items, included R85 funeral insurance to Zidlekaya in Port St. Johns, R150 toward one *umcalelo/stokvel* that yielded a lump sum to buy December groceries, and R500 toward another *umcalelo/stokvel* with three members.

Athandwa has taken loans from a broad range of lenders (see Table 2.1). To cover some of her expenses, she borrows from a *mashonisa*. This *mashonisa* is neither small-scale nor based in the village, but an affluent member of the local elite. She maintains an office in Port St. Johns, with other business interests including local retail. She is a prominent, middle-aged businesswoman, characterized as "rich" as well as being unsympathetic and confrontational. She drives new cars, and her children reportedly attend "good schools" in Mthatha. Athandwa and the local fieldworker decline to name her. Efforts to visit her office failed; a suspicious administrator indicated that she was perpetually unavailable.

Athandwa is locked in a recurrent cycle of debt with this *mashonisa*. She first took out a loan from her in 2017 to pay for the children's school uniforms and transport as well as to meet her son's university costs. Athandwa repaid the loan, and then, securing domestic work for three months, managed to survive without further borrowing. Thereafter she borrowed again to buy a school uniform and pay for school transport. She estimates that school related expenses routinely run to R500 a child per year (she enumerated R200 shoes, R150 a jersey [cardigan], etc.). Typically, she borrows a sum of R1,000 that incurs R400 interest monthly (i.e., 40 percent). The lender retains Athandwa's bank card and PIN code. The transactions are entirely informal, unregistered, and illegal, with no documents or paperwork issued.

Athandwa's shifting arrangements were affected by the changeover from Net1 to SAPO discussed earlier. Before her employment on the public employment scheme, she had held a Standard Bank account, but then—partly in order to facilitate borrowing—she applied for a "green card" (EPE) and the Standard Bank account lapsed, unused. She reopened it (see Figure 2.2) in mid-2018 when, as a result of an advice campaign against EPE, she abandoned this EPE account. Prior to 2017, she had regularly borrowed from Net1's Moneyline. She most recently took out a loan from them of R1,650 in March 2018, and repaid R250 monthly over six months. She judged Moneyline preferable to the *mashonisa*, because it did not retain the bank card or deduct more than announced, and it charged lower interest. However, her loan overlapped with the one she had taken out from the *mashonisa*: Moneyline—unlike the *mashonisa*—is compliant with legal requirements not to lend larger sums. Despite this account of Moneyline's preferability as a moneylender, Athandwa thus continued to borrow from the higher-interest *mashonisa* to tide her over. As with the case of Mpho, who is discussed later in this chapter, the cycles of repayment to formal (and lower-interest) lenders like Moneyline did not always respect the urgent temporalities imposed by household needs.

Athandwa is reportedly very stressed by the debt; she feels that *umboi bumile* (life has stopped). Despite these sentiments, she does not know how to survive without recurrent borrowing. Her case illustrates some of the overlapping reasons for, and forms of, indebtedness found in the research. In her case, as in many, these ranged from illness and death (twinned with the increased number of dependents that resulted) through precarious, uncertain, and intermittent employment. Having once worked—but always on a casual basis—as a domestic cleaner, she later found (as did others in this study) that government employment on a public works scheme provided no long-term security. Other reasons for indebtedness, in her case, included the failure of systems of state welfare. The second Foster Care Grant to which she was entitled was not forthcoming; instead, she was subjected by government social workers to paternalistic and moralizing lectures on how relatives—clearly disengaged—"ought to help." The state bursary to which her son was certainly entitled was, likewise, never delivered. Finally—seemingly less pressing, but nonetheless crucial—Athandwa's case echoed those outlined below in that she was likely using her EFT/debit order borrowings to pay for her *stokvel* contributions. Although she did not spell out the role these played in her household management, they were crucial to whatever arrangements of thrift she was able to negotiate and enabled her to negotiate the cyclical inconsistencies of repayment she became involved in as different needs arose.

Building from this case but focusing on the theme of savings clubs, the following story illustrates the ambivalent part they play in householders' arrangements.

Borrowing to Invest, in Limehill

Hannah lives with her mother, her two children, her late sister's two children, and the orphaned child of an extended family member. Their home is in Limehill, KwaZulu Natal, a so-called "resettlement camp" that became infamous in the late 1960s when it was set up to receive the inhabitants of a mission station that had been designated a "black spot" and became the object of forced removal by the apartheid government (Desmond 1971). It is remote from urban areas such as Ladysmith, and opportunities for work—scarce across South Africa—are even more sparse in this settlement. The primary income in the household is Hannah's mother's pension and four Child Support Grants, paid in respect of Hannah's own and her sister's children. A further child, daughter of an extended family member, is an orphan. Hannah aims to apply for a Foster Care Grant to enable her care, but she requires a government social worker to drive the legal process—help that has been unforthcoming. The household also gets some income from

Hannah's informal selling of vegetables in Ladysmith and (formerly) her yearlong employment—that ended in June 2019—on a government public employment project.

Hannah belongs to three *stokvels* whose arrangements illustrate varying types of forward planning centered on community and household. One requires a relatively low-level cash commitment, at R30 per month, and is used to pay for food and drinks and other items required for community get togethers or when neighbors are in need. A second involves a payment of R120 per month and is for Christmas clothes and groceries. The contribution for the third is R150, paid not regularly but whenever someone is holding a ceremony (typically a funeral) in the settlement: there have been as many as five in one month. After five years, if a member has never drawn on this fund, she receives R4,000 as a one-time payout. Hannah was fortunate enough to receive this payout once; on this occasion she experienced her *stokvel* membership as very advantageous. At other times she feels more ambivalent; being a member has put pressure on her to take out loans from EasyPay/Moneyline on several occasions in order to pay her contributions. One of her *stokvels* has monthly meetings with a roll call. When your name is called, she says, you must go up to the front to make your payment. If you fail to do so, you experience shame. In addition, because every payment (and nonpayment) is carefully recorded in a ledger book, you will have to pay double the following month. After a series of missed payments, you will likely be asked to leave the group.

Overdue *stokvel* payments led Hannah to take out an EPE card so that she could borrow from Moneyline to cover the shortfall. If Moneyline did not exist, she says, she would have to cancel her *stokvel* membership. But she is sure that the *stokvels* have helped her, even if paying off a loan means cutting down on food, a large and expensive part of her budget in a household of seven. Taking the loans for the *stokvels* enables her to "pay for things for her children . . . Christmas clothes" that she would not be able to do otherwise. Although she explains that the grant is "a gift from the government" to support her children and she does not want to use it to borrow money, it is the only resource that can serve as collateral. The loans are thus a necessary burden. However, she had finished paying her most recent Moneyline loan over three months prior to our interview, and she was trying to switch her "green" EPE for a "gold" SASSA card issued by SAPO (see Figure 2.2). She had phoned EPE, but failed to get help or advice about canceling the card. After three months, she was still receiving her grant money through EPE, which makes borrowing easier, and she is wary of this.

Hannah's *stokvel* membership illustrates the unexpected ways in which investment and indebtedness are connected. Belonging to a *stokvel* is viewed by many—including policy makers, activists, and welfare beneficia-

Figure 2.2. Pensioner with EPE's "green card." © Erna Curry/Black Sash

ries—as a valuable way of planning and saving for future expenditure that typically occurs at Christmas or on the occasion of a death. It thus features as a form of "saving." But it also requires grant holders/members to borrow from other sources in order to keep up payments. It thus increases the pressure on budgets that are already stretched and can drive people further into debt. *Stokvels,* as in Hannah's case, do not operate as an alternative to formal loans, but may be a facilitator of them. This is so not only when, as above, members come under pressure to keep up their payments, but also when, as below, members of other *stokvels* are obliged to lend out or "invest" the lump sums they receive for the benefit of the group overall and its members. The two systems of social obligation can combine to make for a perfect storm of borrowing.

Negotiating with the Mashonisa in Khutsong

As can be seen from the following case, the need for loans to cover household expenses can converge with a local *mashonisa*'s imperative to lend money in order to invest her *stokvel* payout and "make the money grow." Patricia, a sixty-three-year-old woman, lives in the township of Khutsong, Gauteng, near the mining town of Carletonville. Once relatively prosperous, the town and its surrounding mines have seen job opportunities slashed with the decline of deep level gold mining. Patricia's household consists of herself and her two granddaughters, both of whom are at school. They are the daughters of her son, who was unemployed when he died some years ago; their mother died soon thereafter. Patricia was previously employed as a domestic worker in Carletonville, but the household currently has no waged members, and its survival depends on social grants. She has a monthly pension of R1,800 and, until the oldest grandchild turned twenty-one, received two monthly Foster Care Grants of R1,000 each.

In need of cash, Patricia was advised by her friends to approach a woman from a nearby neighborhood, known to offer loans, who belongs to a *stokvel*. Patricia herself had previously been a member of a *stokvel*, but it had recently disbanded. Financial mutuals often dissolve when the weight of nonpayment by defaulting members becomes too great, or when the treasurer—sometimes in cahoots with a bank cashier—absconds with the funds. In this case, borrowing cash from a community (and *stokvel*) member appeared to be the best option. In contrast to Hannah, Patricia did not consider borrowing from the EFT/debit order lender Finbond, although it had offices nearby and another of Patricia's neighbors had used one of its loan products. It was because of Patricia's lack of mobility, the cost of transport, and general neighborhood mores and customs, that she took a loan from a *mashonisa*. As outlined above, *mashonisas*, often tarred with the same brush as "loan sharks," vary widely as to the terms and conditions they offer. In this case, Patricia managed to negotiate a loan—like that available in the EFT/debit order sector—with repayments stretched over several months, at roughly similar rates, and founded on trust and neighborly relationships.

The issue that emerged as being at least as important as these flexible repayment rates, for Patricia, was her wish not to give over her ATM and ID cards to the *mashonisa*. Confiscating these cards and keeping them to ensure repayments on payday is a widespread practice among South Africa's loan sharks, as in other countries of the Global South (see Parry 2012). "I didn't want to leave my ID with her, or even my card. I told her, 'I don't want my things to stay with other people.' So she gave it back," says Patricia. This lender also proved flexible in offering to make a house call. In January Patricia asked to borrow R3,000: "I called her to come to my house; it was too far for me to walk." The normal practice would have been to have her repay R3,900 the following month (30 percent interest). Instead, she negotiated, asking whether she could stretch the payment over three months—R1,300 each month—but without extra interest. "I told her that I don't want to suffer." They agreed verbally on these terms. Instead of keeping Patricia's card, this lender fetches it at month end: "she trusts me; she knows where I live." The *mashonisa* withdraws what is owed to her from the ATM, then gives Patricia a mini statement printout so Patricia can see what has been taken. "She is very good; she doesn't cheat you." It is interesting to note how, in this resource-poor neighborhood where borrowers and lenders cannot easily be distinguished, the lender had her own cashflow problems: of the total R3,000, she had enough cash to give Patricia only R1,200 in the first instance, adding the rest at a later stage. Thus, both loan and repayment were stretched out over a period of time.

Here, the degree of trust established was of particular importance. Knowing a borrower, and knowing where that borrower lives, made it unnecessary for the *mashonisa* to retain the card. The local *mashonisa* belonged to the type of *stokvel* (known as an accumulating savings and credit association—ASCRA—in the literature) that requires its members to lend out money and collect interest. In such a *stokvel*, each member is obliged to get the money back—she "shoulders all the risk"—but this translates into pressure put on neighbors who borrow and threaten to default. Because the organization thus comprises a group of intermediaries who take private responsibility for the use of group funds, collateral is built into the structure of the club itself (Bähre 2007; Elizabeth Hull, pers. comm.; James 2015: 144). All in all, *stokvels* that serve as savings (even investment) mechanisms in one way, act as sources of indebtedness in another.

Patricia's account showed her to be a woman for whom conventional notions of household thrift—backed up by ideas about the advantages of "financial literacy"—were particularly apposite. She was well aware of the negative consequences of borrowing at high rates of interest, even under the "favorable" conditions she had managed to negotiate with her *mashonisa*. She was keenly aware of her (almost adult) grandchildren's insistence that the grants were intended "for them" rather than "for her"; an irony considering that she had no use for these welfare grants other than the quintessentially gendered activity of sustaining the household. And she stated her intention to stay out of the hands of loan sharks, however benevolent, in future.

Higher Earnings and Conflicting Debts in Taaiboschgroet

The case study that follows is about a household with relatively higher levels of income and a greater number of interlocking repayment obligations. This borrower, like Athandwa and Hannah, had been taking out EFT/debit order–based loans from EPE/Moneyline to cover *stokvel* repayments, among other things. In her case, however, there were a greater number of *stokvel* and funeral club memberships, alongside other repayment obligations. These payments had entangled her in crosscutting obligations to both EFT/debit order and cash/cash lenders, many of which she seemed unable to compute.

Mpho, a thirty-seven-year-old woman, lives in the village of Taaiboschgroet (Ga-mamadi), a settlement in Limpopo Province. Remote from sites of commerce, it too has a history mapped by the spatial separations of apartheid; situated on a former White farm added to what was then a Bantustan, it was populated by former labor tenants evicted from White farms in the 1970s (at the time, farmers wanted only full-time workers to live on their farms and, in a practice that continues today, they hired extra labor seasonally.) Trucks arrive to collect workers (mostly women) who stay on the farms until the end of the season for casual work at the minimum wage. In Bochum (70 kms away) are branches of various banks, but few grant beneficiaries use formal financial facilities (apart from Net1, which sends a mobile facility to distribute grants monthly and simultaneously offers Moneyline loans). This opens a gap that is exploited by mobile agents of other loan companies, insurance salesmen, and *mashonisas.*

Mpho, unmarried, lives with her partner, who is twenty years older than she is and has never been employed, and their three children, all of whom are schooling. The household's income consists of three Child Support Grants (totaling R1,260pm [per month]) plus the earnings from her work in an NGO that offers homebased care to sick people and that yields R3,500pm. She disputes, however, that this is "a proper job." As with many NGOs in South Africa, its reliance on a "mixed economy" of funding sources, patchworking together state grants and charitable donations, gives it a precarious existence. Women working in such organizations find their fortunes waxing and waning, often being pushed back into the status of volunteer when the money dries up and called back into waged work when it is again forthcoming (see James 2015: 42–43).

Mpho estimates her monthly expenses as follows: electricity (R200pm), food (R800pm), airtime (R120pm), satellite TV or "dish" (R130pm), and transport of her child to and from primary school (R100pm). She has also bought a bed on "hire purchase" (installment) for which she pays R450pm. Beyond this, she belongs to numerous savings schemes. One is a *stokvel*/society with thirty-two members, to which she contributes R200pm. At the end of the year each member gets groceries to the value of R2,400 that, she says, last her for several months. In addition, the household makes many funeral contributions, all paid in cash. Such schemes, like *stokvels,* often necessitate borrowing. They range from more "formal" (but often borderline illegal) policies (to which mainly younger people pay monthly contributions, in cash, to agents parked at the pay point on the day when grants are paid) to various neighborhood-based associations (to which older grant holder/pensioners more frequently belong). Mpho subscribes to both. Each month she pays a R70 subscription to a provider in the former category, whose representative arrives in a car on grant payday to collect the cash. The rest are incurred at neighborhood level. There is R50 for "cattle" (money collected to buy a beast for slaughter in the case of a death in the neighborhood), R70 for those in the same neighborhood as her, and R150 contribution to a kitty to meet other funeral expenses. In addition, there are two amounts of R100 each that are incurred not monthly but only on the event of a death in a specific family.

Her outgoings include repayment on three loans: one to EPE/Moneyline and two to *mashonisas*. In order to avail herself of the former, she took out an EPE "green card" in 2014 (see Figure 2.2). Since then, she has become accustomed to taking out an EPE/Moneyline loan every six months, commencing as soon as the last payment ends. She borrows R1,000, and repays R220pm over a six-month period. She has done this about six times. She took out the first loan, in January, to buy school uniforms for her children. The next one, in July, she took out to buy winter clothing for her children. Both have now become recurrent.

The *mashonisas* from whom she borrowed, in contrast, are local lenders—from *mo gae* (here at home). The first loan was for R1,500; with the interest, the repayment is supposed to be R2,250 (slightly less than the "going rate" of 50 percent). Asked if the repayment was over several months, she said sometimes she manages to repay the interest only, but other times she pays nothing because she has no money. She said she was unable to calculate her total outgoings: "if you could remember that amount of money, you would get a heart attack."

On the EPE/Moneyline loan, the way to see if you have finished paying, she says, is when you go to collect your grants and receive the full amount. The *mashonisas*, in contrast, handwrite the repayments in a book. The *mashonisa* she first approached for a loan keeps her EPE card. When grant payday comes, the *mashonisa* withdraws the full amount in cash from the ATM and gives her what is left over. She is more circumspect about how much she then pays to the second *mashonisa*, or how she pays it. Asked whether people in this village think they are being cheated or robbed—a claim often heard—by *mashonisas*, she says "I cannot say that. They are helping us in the middle of the month when we have no money." She does not object to having her card kept because "we are looking for money." She sometimes goes to the *mashonisa* to check her balance, and they agree on the outstanding amount. Asked why she went to the second *mashonisa*, she explains she would not want to go to the first one for a further loan midmonth—better to approach a different one. One reason she borrows from *mashonisas* is to cover the cost of the funeral societies and *stokvel* membership. Asked whether she prefers EPE to the *mashonisa*, she says "all of them are good." Her welfare income is available only on grant payday at the beginning of the month; a further EPE loan is available only at the end of the six-month repayment period, but the *mashonisa* will "lend you money any time." Asked about whether her entire income might have been divided/budgeted to better effect, she answers simply, "It's not enough." She could do with advice to manage her affairs, she says, but ultimately the family's income is "too small." According to the information we gathered, the family's income amounts to R4,760, with an estimated expenditure of R2,300, in addition to which she has R220 deducted by EPE and pays about R660–750 to the first *mashonisa* and an undisclosed amount to the second one: totaling R3,270 monthly. Other unforeseen expenses occur sporadically, such as those incurred when taking a child to the doctor (R500, plus R70 for transport to get to town).

The case study of Mpho throws up some interesting contrasts to that of Patricia. Unlike Patricia, who has a considerably lower income and proportionately fewer debts and repayment obligations, and who calculates her incomings and outgoings with great care, Mpho has a larger income but also pays out more to lenders across the spectrum illustrated in our table. Her obligations in respect to diverse *stokvel* and funeral club memberships are on a par with those of Hannah, from our second case study above. There is a certain temporal regularity, and a corresponding rationale, to Mpho's package of loans. The EFT/debit order–based loans she takes out every six months are calculated as necessary to buy clothes for her children as the seasons change. The second *mashonisa* loan, taken out in midmonth (as was true in many other cases), is logically pinned to a different—but equally pressing—temporal rhythm.

Nevertheless, her debts in general—including for *stokvel* payments—are more difficult to compute, as she herself acknowledges. This inability to get an overview of debts is linked to the confusing array of repayment systems at play and the mixture of technologies used across the lending spectrum. These create a jumbled hybrid of owings and obligations, something that is particularly evident if one tracks the whereabouts of the key piece of infrastructure that makes this all possible: the "green card." As noted earlier, these cards were made available by Net1, the company that held the original contract to deliver social grants. Although concerns about reckless lending contributed to the contract's being withdrawn from the company and ultimately awarded instead to the post office (SAPO), many people opted to retain their EPE "green cards" (see Figure 2.2). They did so because, given that SAPO does not yet have the capacity to deliver payouts nationally, Net1/EPE has by default been able to retain many "customers" in some sites. In addition, in Taaiboschgroet where Mpho lives, EPE's "grant payday" is at the beginning rather than the middle of the month. Demonstrating the importance of temporal rhythms to payment in this low wage environment, it was this early payment date—alongside its facilitating of the habituated borrowing from EPE/Moneyline to which she had become accustomed—that predisposed Mpho to keep the "green card" rather than switching to a SAPO ("gold card") account.

Although Mpho is nominally the holder of the bank account to which the green card is linked, she is the owner and keeper of the card itself in name only. It is in fact physically held—as in numerous other cases—by the *mashonisa* who gave her the first loan. This withholding of cards makes it difficult for a grant recipient/borrower to calculate what she owes to whom, because she is unable to get a mini statement from the ATM. Recall how the only time Mpho becomes aware whether her EPE loans have been paid off is when she receives her grant at month end. To enable her to collect the grant, the *mashonisa* "lends" her the card. Mpho's friend Julia tried changing from the "green" to the new "gold" card issued by SAPO in an attempt to escape the *mashonisa* from whom she had borrowed. But the *mashonisa* accosted her in the queue when she came to collect her grant and took the card from her "by force." The *mashonisa*'s retention of the card also makes it difficult to keep various kinds of borrowings—as was previously a widespread practice (James 2015: 33, 109, 133)—in separate savings segments parceled off from each other. While paying money to a *stokvel* or to numerous funeral clubs certainly enables the putting aside of money for future use and makes it possible to ringfence savings for groceries or to cover the costs of good neighborliness, getting into debt to make this possible creates a crosscutting jumble of incompatible obligations. Hi-tech biometric data and electronic banking systems, seemingly a world away from the crudeness of relatively small cash-based transactions, here converge to form a proliferation of clashing scales.

Conclusion

Discussions of grants and credit in South Africa are often polarizing, centering on whether grants should be used only for necessities or also for things often considered luxuries. But sometimes activists hold seemingly contradictory views at once. They might defend the right of poor people to borrow for luxuries like a child's birthday party with cake, while also thinking that borrowers who fail to budget appropriately ought to be subject to "disciplinary discourses" (see the Introduction) or taught "financial literacy,"[7] and that lenders ought to be regulated "from above" by the state and its institutions such as the National Credit Regulator (James 2015: 76–77). Such injunctions highlight the paradoxes of thrift. Were the possibilities afforded by EFT/debit order loans (seemingly more "reasonable" despite padding out interest rates with initiation fees and the like) to be eliminated overnight, this would certainly go some way to solving what is generally acknowledged as problem debt. But it would also restrict the possibilities of borrowing at what have become, and now present themselves as, the most reasonable (or least exploitative) rates. Those who, despite their best intentions, are unable to make do with the limited possibilities afforded by welfare payments would thus be severely affected.

As the introduction to this volume points out, thrift is thus an ambiguous modality: it can be both a vice and a virtue. These ambiguities extend beyond Keynes' "paradox of thrift," whereby "an increase in individual saving serves to reduce overall demand, output and hence, eventually, the wealth of the national economy." Household thrift, as the introduction makes clear, is shaped by state welfare regimes, commodity prices, the competence or otherwise of officials, and complex credit mechanisms. Depicting householders' practices in terms of dichotomous opposites—such as parsimony vs extravagance, or austerity vs debt—is thus misleading.

The case studies presented here speak to the themes of this volume by demonstrating how ideas and practices of thriftiness vary across different geographical settings—each with a long-term history of marginality and disadvantage stretching back into the apartheid era—within a single country. These territorial inequalities intersect, albeit unevenly, with the mortality of the HIV/AIDS pandemic that has left so many women caring for orphaned grandchildren, nephews, and nieces. Those in the remotest areas, who have ended up there because of histories of displacement and dispossession, have fewer alternatives than those in less peripheral sites. They are beset by levels of unemployment that are only temporarily alleviated by state run employment schemes. They are also disadvantaged by their distance from services, economic opportunities, and medical facilities. In these ways they continued to experience the ongoing legacies of "credit apartheid" long after the apparent abolition of apartheid at the level of state law (Department of Trade and Industry 2002, 2004; James 2015). The newest manifestation of that apartheid, paradoxically, is the swift financial deepening that has brought every grant beneficiary within the ambit of the hi-tech financial services sector.

These cases illustrate how, despite these displacements, disturbances, and disadvantages, women with access to social grants (and to the loans for which the latter have served as collateral) have devised novel ways of practicing household thrift. Ever mindful of the imperative to "invest" rather than "eat" money, women have taken advantage of diverse options to negotiate across the terrain of diverse lenders and the differentiated temporalities of the credit cycle. Rhythms of shortage, now set by banks and *mashonisas* rather than the seasonal agricultural cycles that structured temporalities for their grandparents, must be offset by longer-term plans.

The experience of lack that is typically experienced in the middle of the welfare payment cycle (i.e., in midmonth), or in the middle of the six-month repayment period offered by EFT/debit order lenders like Moneyline, predispose grant recipients to extra borrowing, often—because they have few alternatives—from the most extractive of lenders. But they often use the loans to pay into social savings schemes that have longer-term phases: the yearlong sequence of the *stokvel* and the sequence of the funeral society that is potentially, but not always, more protracted because it is pinned to the life cycle itself. Despite what sound like overdetermining structural features, the women make their own plans. They have an attitude reminiscent of Chayanov's Russian peasants—oriented toward careful budgeting and investment where possible—that echoes earlier emphases on "caring for the household" and on preventing the undue squander entailed in "eating" one's money.

Acknowledgments

Thanks to the LSE's KEI fund for supporting this research; to Lynette Maart, Hoodah Abrahams-Fayker, and Theresa Edlmann of Black Sash who coordinated the project (and Mandy Moussouris who helped bring it into existence); to Black Sash partner organizations and their personnel (Alexa Lane, Abigail Peters, Evashnee Naidu, Jerome Bele, Bridget Magasela, Zoleka Ntuli Nobuzwe Banda Funeka Xolo, Motsi Khokhoma, Janaap Odendaal, Phineas Kopa, Speelman Nkoana, Rose Mosedame, Moyabo Manakane, Mpho Tsutse, Paseka Mthini) and all our interlocutors in the field for their assistance; and to participants in the LSE's "brown bag lunch" seminar for helpful suggestions.

Deborah James is Professor of Anthropology at the London School of Economics. Her book *Money from Nothing: Indebtedness and Aspiration in South Africa* (Stanford University Press 2015) explores the lived experience of debt for those many millions who attempt to improve their positions (or merely sustain existing livelihoods) in emerging economies. She has also done research on advice (especially debt advice) encounters in the context of the UK government's austerity program.

David Neves works as an independent researcher, and is a research associate at the Institute for Poverty, Land and Agrarian Studies (PLAAS), University of the Western Cape. His research straddles the areas of poverty, vulnerable livelihoods, and social policy.

Erin Torkelson is a lecturer in Geography at Durham University and a Mellon Postdoctoral Scholar in Geography at the University of the Western Cape. Her current research explores the collision between normative assumptions about cash transfers as public goods and the lived experiences of cash transfers as private debts.

Notes

1. Even while White borrowing and debt has vastly outstripped Black borrowing and debt (Posel 2010), worries about sustainability and poverty keep the policy focus on Black people.
2. This kind of club is known as *umcalelo* in isiXhosa, *lehodisana* in Sesotho (from the verb *go hoda*, to pay, in its causative reciprocal form: to cause to pay back to each other). But the term *stokvel*, based on the English "stock fair" or simply the English word "society," is now more commonly used.
3. Men-only *stokvels* have also been noted (and now seem to be on the rise). Most, whether male or female, are single-gendered groups that exist to fulfil needs thought of as gender-specific.
4. The Black Sash is a human rights organization focused on issues of social justice and aiding those excluded on both racial and economic grounds.
5. The Zulu word *mashonisa* relates to the verb stems *-shona* (to sink, become poor, die) and *-shonisa* (to impoverish, cause to become poor) (Dent and Nyembezi 1969: 481). It may be translated as "one who impoverishes" or who "takes and continues to take indefinitely" (Krige 2011: 144). In popular parlance the plural is *mashonisas* (Siyongwana 2004: 851; Krige 2011: 151).
6. At the time of research, R1 was equal to £0.05 (R100 was equal to £5).
7. Angelique Arde, "SA's First Financial Literacy Survey," IOL, 11 November 2012, https://www.iol.co.za/personal-finance/sas-first-financial-literacy-survey-1420710.

References

Ardener, Shirley. 1964. "The Comparative Study of Rotating Credit Associations." *Journal of the Royal Anthropological Institute* 94(2): 201–29.

———. 2010. "Microcredit, Money Transfers, Women, and the Cameroon Diaspora." *Afrika Focus* 23(2): 11–24.

Bähre, Erik. 2007. *Money and Violence: Financial Self-Help Groups in a South African Township*. Leiden: Brill.

Breckenridge, Keith. 2019. "The Global Ambitions of the Biometric Anti-Bank: Net1, Lockin and the Technologies of African Financialization." *International Review of Applied Economics* 33(1): 93–118.

Cooper, Frederick. 2002. *Africa Since 1940: The Past of the Present*. Cambridge, UK: Cambridge University Press.

Datta, Kavita. 2012. *Migrants and Their Money: Surviving Financial Exclusion*. Bristol: Policy Press.

Delius, Peter. 1996. *A Lion Amongst the Cattle*. Johannesburg: Ravan Press.

Dent, G. R., and C. L. S. Nyembezi. 1969. *Scholars' Zulu Dictionary*. Cape Town: Shuter and Shooter.

Department of Trade and Industry, with Reality Research Africa. 2002. *Credit Contract Disclosure and Associated Factors*. Pretoria: Department of Trade and Industry.

Department of Trade and Industry. 2004. *Consumer Credit Law Reform: Policy Framework for Consumer Credit*. Pretoria: Department of Trade and Industry.

Desmond, Cosmas. 1971. *The Discarded People: An account of African resettlement in South Africa*. Harmondsworth: Penguin.

Ferguson, James. 1985. "The Bovine Mystique: Power, Property and Livestock in Rural Lesotho." *Man* (NS) 20(4): 647–74.

Fine, Ben. 2019. "'Post-apartheid South Africa: It's Neoliberalism, Stupid!'" In *Race, Class and the Post-Apartheid Democratic State*, edited by John Reynolds, Ben Fine, and Robert van Niekerk. Pietermaritzburg: University of KwaZulu-Natal Press.

Geertz, Clifford. 1962. "The Rotating Credit Association: A 'Middle Rung' in Development." *Economic Development and Cultural Change* 10(3): 241–63.

Gregory, Chris A. 2012. "On Money Debt and Morality: Some Reflections on the Contribution of Economic Anthropology." *Social Anthropology* 20(4): 380–96.

Hart, Keith. 2015. "How the Informal Economy Took over the World." In *Informal Market Worlds Reader: The Architecture of Economic Pressure*, edited by P. Moertenboeck, H. Mooshammer, T. Cruz, and F. Forman, 33–44. Amsterdam: NAI010 Publishers.

James, Deborah. 1999. *Songs of the women migrants: performance and identity in South Africa*. Edinburgh: International African Institute/Edinburgh University Press.

James, Deborah. 2015. *Money from Nothing: Indebtedness and Aspiration in South Africa*. Palo Alto: Stanford University Press.

James, Deborah, David Neves, and Erin Torkelson. 2020. *Social Grants: Challenging Reckless Lending in South Africa*. Cape Town: Black Sash.

Kar, Sohini. 2020. "Accumulation by Saturation: Infrastructures of Financial Inclusion, Cash Transfers, and Financial Flows in India." In *Financialization: Relational Approaches*, edited by Chris Hann and Don Kalb, 64–85. New York: Berghahn Books.

Krige, Detlev. 2011. Power, identity and agency at work in the popular economies of Soweto and Black Johannesburg. D.Phil. diss., University of the Witwatersrand, Johannesburg. http://wiredspace.wits.ac.za/handle/10539/10143.

Krige, Detlev. 2014. "Letting Money Work for Us: Self-Organization and Financialization from below in an All-Male Savings Club in Soweto." In *People, Money and Power in the Economic Crisis*, edited by Keith Hart and John Sharp, 61–81. New York: Berghahn Books.

Kuper, Hilda, and Selma Kaplan. 1944. "Voluntary Associations in an Urban Township." *African Studies* 3(4): 178–86.

Lavinas, Lena. 2018. "The Collateralization of Social Policy under Financialized Capitalism." *Development and Change* 49(2): 502–17.

Mager, Anne Kelk, and Maanda Mulaudzi. 2012. "Popular Responses to Apartheid: 1948–c. 1975." In *The Cambridge History of South Africa*, edited by Robert Ross,

Anne Kelk Mager, and Bill Nasson, 369–408. Cambridge, UK: Cambridge University Press.
Marais, Hein. 2011. *South Africa Pushed to the Limit: The Political Economy of Change*. London: Zed Press.
Neves, David. 2018. "The Financialisation of the Poor and the Reproduction of Inequality." In *New South Africa Review 6: The Crisis of Inequality*, edited by Gilbert M. Khadiagala, Sarah Mosoetsa, Devan Pillay, and Roger Southall, 84–100. Johannesburg: Wits University Press.
Parry, Jonathan. 2012. "Suicide in a Central Indian Steel Town." *Contributions to Indian Sociology* 46(1&2): 145–80.
Posel, Deborah. 2010. "Races to Consume: Revisiting South Africa's History of Race, Consumption and the Struggle for Freedom." *Ethnic and Racial Studies* 33: 157–75.
Rodima-Taylor, Daivi. 2014. "Passageways of Cooperation: Mutuality in Post-Socialist Tanzania." *Africa: Journal of the International African Institute* 84(4): 553–75.
Servet, Jean-Michel, and Hadrien Saiag. 2013. "Household Over-Indebtedness in Contemporary Societies: a Macro-Perspective." In *Microfinance, Debt and Over-Indebtedness: Juggling with Money*, edited by Isabelle Guérin, Solène Morvant-Roux, and Magdalena Villarreal, 45–66. London: Routledge.
Shipton, Parker. 2007. *The Nature of Entrustment: Intimacy, Exchange and the Sacred in Africa*. New Haven: Yale University Press.
Siyongwana, Paqama Q. 2004. "Informal Moneylenders in the Limpopo, Gauteng and Eastern Cape Provinces of South Africa." *Development Southern Africa* 21(5): 861–66.
Thomson, Robert J., and Deborah Posel. 2002. "The Management of Risk by Burial Societies in South Africa." *South African Actuarial Journal* 2(1): 83–127.
Torkelson, Erin. 2017a. "Deductions from Social Grants: How It All Works." GroundUp, 3 March. https://www.groundup.org.za/article/deductions-social-grants-how-it-works/.
———. 2017b. "Sophia's Choice: Farm Worker Has to Decide Which of Her Children to Feed." GroundUp, 15 March. https://www.groundup.org.za/article/sophias-choice-farm-worker-has-decide-which-her-children-feed/.
———. 2020. "Collateral Damages: Cash Transfer and Debt Transfer in South Africa." *World Development* 126.
Wilkis, Ariel. 2017. *The moral power of money. Morality and economy in the life of the poor*. Palo Alto: Stanford University Press.
———. "The Moral Performativity of Credit and Debt in the Slums of Buenos Aires." *Cultural Studies* 29(5–6): 760–80.

3

Wages, Patronage, and Welfare

Thrift and Its Limits in Argentina's Gran Chaco

AGUSTIN DIZ

This chapter explores the ways in which Indigenous Guaraní communities in Argentina's Gran Chaco region engage with and manage wages, patronage, and welfare. It argues that the temporal and spatial scales at which welfare policies, extractive cycles, and even democratic politics operate drive the experiences of Guaraní households, imbuing economic resources with gendered social potency. The chapter shows how resource flows come together in ambiguous ways that weave together households and political communities. Contrary to arguments that posit thrift as a universal and pervasive strategy, the Guaraní case demonstrates how different resources are managed differently depending on the sets of social relations within which they circulate. Specifically, we will see that "antithrift" (see the Introduction)—a logic more attuned to generosity, sharing, and even excess in the short-term—is key to Guaraní livelihoods. Thrift and antithrift thus become central to the way in which Guaraní populations are integrated into broader political and economic structures. As they play out in the context of everyday life, the macroscales of extractive industries, national welfare, and even global financial markets articulate with local ideas of gender, household, and community.

Similar to the forms of thrift discussed in the introduction to this volume, thrifty practices among the Guaraní tend to reflect an ethical stance of restraint, typically in opposition to forms of consumption and expenditure that are deemed irresponsible and wasteful. In this sense, thrift is understood as a future-oriented strategy for the management of scarce resources; one that is most closely associated with the household economy. However, we will see that settlement-level politics rejects thrift and that antithrift emerges as a desirable political practice that prioritizes the circulation of resources in the present over their accumulation for the future. While thrift characterizes the intrahousehold management of resources and the family, antithrift is central to the conduct of interhousehold relationships and closely related to notions of provision and redistribution. At first glance, the distinctions between the separate realms of intra- and interhousehold life seem to hold. However, these contrasts dissolve over the courses of everyday life, and such neat separations become increasingly difficult to tease out when we look at arrangements within individual households. In as much as thrift and antithrift emerge as interlocked aspects of Guaraní life, they are not so much opposite and opposing logics as they are entangled strategies for managing distinct resource flows (see Introduction).

After contextualizing the analysis within Guaraní history, I describe three distinct resource flows that are central to contemporary subsistence: wages, patronage, and welfare. Each flow generates unique logics of thrift and antithrift and mobilizes and valorizes different sets of social relations. I then take the case of a particular family to show how these three flows play out within an individual household. Over the course of this chapter, I argue that acquiring, managing, and spending different types of resources requires distinct circuits of labor and cooperation, which has the effect of inscribing the different resource flows within separate yet overlapping spheres of mutuality. In a sense, the chapter tracks the economic spheres of "house, community, commerce, finance and meta-finance" as set out by Stephen Gudeman (2016: 14). In doing so it shows how these spheres combine locally to generate tensions and articulations between mutuality and market logics (Gudeman 2008).

The Guaraní and the "Post-neoliberal" Moment

The Guaraní populations who are the focus of this chapter descend from labor migrants who traveled from Bolivia to Argentina and from war refugees who fled Bolivia in the 1930s (Hirsch 2004). The settlements I worked with between 2012 and 2017 lie in the northwestern province of Salta, near the Bolivian border. Settlement populations ranged from roughly two hundred to two thousand individuals. While more than twenty thousand people self-identify as Guaraní in Argentina (INDEC 2004), they remain an underrepresented minority when compared to the larger nonindigenous populations that inhabit nearby towns like Tartagal and Aguaray (Diz 2017).

Historically, the Gran Chaco has been one of Argentina's most important commodity frontiers. The successive booms and busts of sugar cane plantations, sawmills, haciendas, and hydrocarbons have played an important part in both regional and national economies, and they have been of central importance to the livelihoods of Guaraní settlements and households. At various points in the Chaco's history, Guaraní workers found employment on sugar cane plantations, sawmills, haciendas, and oil and gas fields. However, these extractive industries are currently in decline and demand for Guaraní labor has waned. Most recently, the Chaco has seen the rapid expansion of soybean production, an industry that capitalized on a recent global commodities boom (2000–2014) and provided the basis for a marked increase in redistributive welfare under a post-neoliberal government (2003 and 2015). During the time of my fieldwork a lack of infrastructure and market access made autonomous agriculture risky and unprofitable. Instead, people's livelihoods were most often secured through an assortment of unstable jobs, patronage, and welfare payments (Diz 2018).

I conducted fieldwork among the Guaraní at the height of Argentina's post-neoliberal era. After the political and economic meltdown that engulfed Argentina in 2001, a neo-Peronist coalition, under the guidance of Néstor Kirchner and Cristina Fernández, governed the country between 2003 and 2015. This new center-left political force, known as the Kirchneristas in reference to their first leader, was part of the so-called "post-neoliberal turn" in South America (Grugel and Riggirozzi 2012). Capitalizing on the global commodities boom, post-neoliberal governments favored neo-extractive development, in which states, rather than private corporations, took on a greater role in natural resource extraction and used revenues to expand social spending and distribution (Savino 2016). This redistributive tendency earned the Kirchneristas the label of "export-oriented populists" (Richardson 2009) for their ability to forge broad-based electoral coalitions and gain popular support, while furthering extraction and deepening dependency on global markets (Svampa 2015).

While the Chaco's traditional industries are in decline, the region has seen a boom in soybean production (Lapegna 2016). This boom, which was replicated in various parts of the country, was central to state revenue during the post-neoliberal era, and it enabled the creation of new redistributive welfare policies. As we will see, these policies had a crucial impact on Guaraní settlements, which had never had such regular access to government benefits. As with similar forms of welfare throughout the Americas (Peck and Theodore 2010; Lavinas 2013), the relatively small payments Guaraní people received were designed to be investments in human capital that would enable poor citizens to join and contribute to the market. At the national scale, the logic exemplifies an attempt to combat Maynard Keynes' "paradox of thrift" in the sense that it sought to incentivize expenditure and financial inclusion among the poorer segments of the population who might otherwise be inclined to accumulate and save (see Introduction to this vol.). At the local level, though, programs worked to curb profligacy by locating their expenditure within a model that assumed thrifty household management. Here we find an important scalar tension in how thrift plays out within policy and lived experience.

Guaraní people's increased incorporation into waged labor markets, their receipt of welfare benefits, and, most recently, their increased access to credit have transformed the material conditions of their lives. As a result, people often told me that their grandparents and great-grandparents, "the ancients" as they were often called, lived a life of poverty and dependence on forest resources. In contrast to the ancients, people felt that they were now better off and experienced access to money, store-bought food, cell phones, motorcycles, or sound systems as clear indicators of progress. The following sections examine the different ways in which sources of wealth are managed and experienced in Guaraní settlements. Starting at the level of the household, I will expand outward toward the political community and national politics, showing how the different levels articulate with each other on the ground.

Houses, Wages, and Thrift

Perhaps the most visible indicator of the shift between the ancients' poverty and today's relative affluence can be found in the change Guaraní houses have undergone over the last two decades. In this section, I will provide two portraits of individual families and the houses in which they live. We will see thrifty strategies of saving, accumulating, and investing that have enabled people to upgrade their houses, but we will also see that these strategies of thrift are closely entwined with nonmarket obligations of mutuality.

The first portrait is that of Indalecio's family. Indalecio is a Guaraní man who was in his late sixties at the time of our interview. His life history reflects the boom and bust cycles of the Chaco's economy. In his youth he worked as a logger in the nearby forests, but his fortune changed when he found a job with an oil and gas subcontracting company in the late 1990s. Over a fortunate run of four years, he was able to string together several jobs with this company. But when the hydrocarbon industry hit hard times, he was laid off. By the time I met him, he no longer had an income and dedicated most of his time to a small agricultural field that yielded some crops but was not enough to sustain his large family.

Indalecio's house was home to five of his unmarried sons and daughters and was composed of three different kinds of buildings. The first had a thatched roof, supported by wooden beams, and closed off on one side by a wall of irregular wooden slats. Adjacent to this was a bare-bricked, rectangular house with a corrugated iron roof and shuttered windows. Finally, there was another rectangular house with white-plastered walls, a similar corrugated roof, and glass windows. The houses were surrounded by a carefully maintained, swept dust patio and shaded in parts by a number of mango trees. To one side of the three buildings stood a pile of bricks, wire coils, and rebar mesh. Indalecio had accumulated these materials because he hoped to continue to expand his house. Walking past the house and toward the edge of the patio stood Indalecio's son's house, a small hut with mud brick walls and a thatched roof.

The second portrait is of Angela's family. She is a single woman who was in her late twenties when we spoke. When I lived in her settlement, she worked as a teacher in the settlement's primary school and lived with her elderly parents and three younger siblings. She also helped her married sisters who lived in houses near the parental household and took care of their children. Like Indalecio, Angela's father tended to a small agricultural field that did not provide for the family's subsistence. Her two brothers were unemployed, as were her brothers-in-law. The family depended heavily on her income. Every month Angela handed most of her wages to her parents for the family's subsistence; but like Indalecio, she also spent part of the money to pay for small amounts of bricks, cement, iron sheets, and steel bars that would go toward building a new house for her family.

While Angela paid for the materials because she had a job, her unemployed father, brothers, and brothers-in-law were in charge of building the new house. The whole process of house building was slow and gradual, since Angela could only buy the materials in piecemeal fashion and her male relatives only worked on the house sporadically. In fact, while work had begun before I arrived in the settlement in 2012, the house remained incomplete in 2017 when I last visited. In the meantime, Angela, her parents, sisters, and some of her nieces and nephews still lived in the old wooden shack they had built in the 1980s. Angela's judicious management of her wages and her careful purchase of construction materials exemplify the kind of thrifty house economy in which "slow accumulation" enables savings to be "put into the house," and illustrates an overarching ethos of "making-do" (Gudeman 2016: 16–17).

In comparing these two examples, we can begin to tease out situated and historically inflected understandings of thrift among the Guaraní. Until recently, most families lived in mud brick huts like Indalecio's son's or wooden shacks like the one Angela lived in. However, over the last couple of decades, sporadic access to temporary employment and wages has enabled families to upgrade to brick-walled houses like Indalecio's or the one Angela was slowly having built. People refer to these houses as *casas de material* (material houses). While mud huts and casas de material are both functioning houses, they are not equivalent to each other in as much as they index different degrees of access to income. Mud houses were generally associated with poverty and backwardness, a vivid reminder of how the ancients used to live, and most people I spoke to aspired to live in *casas de material*. The most striking of these brick houses had been built in the early 2000s following a minor surge in employment opportunities in the oil and gas industry. They had smooth cement floors and some even had glass windows and insulated roofs. A few included small annexes with iron-barred windows that could double as a small shop for everyday goods. While the oil jobs facilitated house construction for many, other families took a more piecemeal approach, portioning off a fraction of their pay to invest in their house. The most visible reminder of this were the stacks of bricks, cement bags, steel rods, and corrugated metal sheets that were stored near older houses (see Figure 3.1).

While a mud hut could be built with minimal monetary expense—mud, wood, and thatch were all readily available and could be collected form the forest—bricks and cement had to be purchased with money. Indeed, when it came to house building, many Guaraní people demonstrated a real knack for speculation and investment. Aware of the fluctuating value of the Argentine peso, I knew of many people who kept a constant eye on the variable prices of building materials in both Argentina and Bolivia in the hope of finding a bargain. In other words, being able to build a *casa de material* depended on the happy coincidence of low prices, the availability of cash, and a favorable exchange rate. Unsurprisingly, in my host settlement practically all the *casas de material* had been built between five and ten years prior—a time when the peso was strong relative to the boliviano, and when many men landed jobs in the oil sector.

While construction materials had to be purchased from external vendors, the work of actually constructing a house was most often performed by the men of the family who would inhabit it or by close male kin who did not expect monetary compensation. However, given the current lack of jobs among men, some of these patterns seemed to be changing and some men had started to build houses in exchange for money. On the one hand, these monetized transactions appeared to commodify kinship networks, but there was also a sense in which these payments constituted a form of reciprocity that resonated with past practices of collective agricultural labor known as *mötiro* or *minga* where individuals would compensate relatives with food for their help during busy harvest times. In this sense, although paid, builders worked at their own inconstant tempo and "employers" did not pressure their kin to get on with the work. These practices suggest that the mere exchange of money does not necessarily result in a market logic.

Unlike the peasant household described by Gudeman and Rivera (1990), Guaraní household economies are not geared toward self-subsistence and survival. Instead, in a context marked by unemployment and uncertain agriculture, house economies react to the labor market's unpredictable oscillations. Investment in the physical structure of a house offers a stable platform for improvement and durable shelter, but this investment also aims to capture the allure of progress and wealth. As a form of consumption that relies on temporary moments of wealth, house construction requires a thrifty disposition that is imbued with ethical considerations about the proper use of resources.

Indeed, for those families who still lived in mud huts and "humble houses," the very walls they inhabited and the roofs that sheltered them were a constant reminder of the resources they lacked or had squandered. Thus, Indalecio often lamented that his son, who had enjoyed several stints of oil employment, had squandered his wages on alcohol and status items, and he could now only afford to live in a mud hut with his young family. In this father's eyes, his son had failed to manage his wages in a thrifty manner that would have enabled his young family to move beyond a state of shameful poverty into what he felt was a more dignified existence. For his part, the young man found solace in expensive consumer goods, including an audio system and motorcycles, that appeared to be congealed markers of the wealth to which he had once had access. Contrary to the observations made among peasant households elsewhere (Gudeman and Rivera 1990), these expenditures were not an attempt to establish a resilient or stable household that would endure over time.[1] Instead, they constituted an appeal to the status associated with employment, typically for men.

Houses constitute long-term plans—their construction melds market and nonmarket considerations. The kind of thrifty house construction I have described relies upon wages, the quintessential scarce resource in today's Guaraní settlements, and a speculative attention to price fluctuations and exchange rates across the Argentina-Bolivia border. It is also reliant on the "mutuality" (Gudeman 2016) of kinship relations that appear to rely on commodifying market-based logics, but which simultaneously enfold intimacy, care, and reciprocity. As a project, thrifty house construction extends into the long term as an always-unfinished task that is attuned to aspirations for material progress and a kind of "expectation of modernity" (Ferguson 1999) that would break with the poverty of the past. Houses are plotted out over time, always under construction, always potentially improved. They are also markers of status, incorporating elements of style, consumption, and aspiration that are contrasted with the huts of the ancients or the poor. Thus, houses are as much about creating forms of

Figure 3.1. A house with three distinct phases of construction; in the foreground, a pile of bricks signals the intent of future construction. © Agustin Diz.

balance and mutuality as they are about ranking social values and demonstrating a family's ability to achieve desirable material wealth.[2]

In the next section I move to a different kind of house: *Casillas*, which are government-donated houses that constitute a valuable form of political patronage. By contrasting patronage with the kinds of thrift deployed for building brick houses, I want to draw attention to how the different ways in which Guaraní people access patronage, and how they go about redistributing it within their own communities, leads to a form of antithrift, imbued with its own temporality and moral force.

Community, Patronage, and Antithrift

The houses discussed above were unfinished projects, constructed over the long run and reliant on wages, kinship, and speculation. By contrast, the government-donated houses or *casillas* I will discuss here were fully formed and constituted an important form of patronage. With their white brick walls and identical format, they were instantly recognizable. As we will see, the temporality surrounding *casillas* typically operated in the short term, mobilizing and creating political solidarities beyond and within settlements, but also generating discontent and suspicion. These distinct temporal and social traits placed patronage outside the realm of thrift and inscribed them, instead, within a form of antithrift. To understand why this is so, it is helpful to contextualize *casillas* within everyday Guaraní politics.

Most of the government houses I saw during my time in the Chaco were sponsored by the Federal Program for Housing and Habitat Improvement among Native and Rural Peoples, which was approved at the national level in 2010 (Secretaría de Obras Públicas 2010). This program required the coordination of a national ministry and various secretariats and subsecretariats within it. In the Province of Salta, it was executed by the Provincial and Municipal governments, who in turn worked alongside the Provincial Institute for Native Peoples (IPPIS) and the Provincial Institute for Housing (IPV). However, as the mayor of one of the towns in the region explained to me, resources only reached the ground when political allegiances at the various levels of state were in place. The result was a complex institutional matrix, one that Guaraní leaders had to learn to navigate. Using their existing contacts, forging new ones, and applying pressure at the right points, Guaraní leaders had to find ways of convincing bureaucrats and politicians that their settlements were particularly needy; all while managing people's expectations back home.

As is the case among many indigenous societies in South America (Clastres 1989; Killick 2007), Guaraní leaders have no coercive authority and people are loathe to follow their orders. Nonetheless, the state recognizes them as official representatives when dealing with external actors, including politicians and private interests. This means leaders occupy an important brokering role (Diz 2020a). Guaraní people expect their leaders to know how to "speak well" and, increasingly, how to produce effective documents. These skills are useful in as much as followers also expect leaders to display a sense of courage and assertiveness when dealing with external actors. Ultimately, these skills and attributes allow leaders to "bring down" (*bajar*) resources for their followers. The use of the spatial metaphor of "bringing down" for describing political leadership reinforces the idea that the Guaraní feel themselves to be at the margins of an external *criollo* world of abundance: a world of nonindigenous politicians, engineers, lawyers, and company representatives that need to be pressured, spoken to, and confronted.

In the context of the *casillas* mentioned above, then, Guaraní leaders were expected to "bring down" housing modules and negotiate with the municipal government, the IPPIS, and IPV offices so that the needs of their particular settlements would be recognized. When successful, Guaraní leaders were granted a small number of houses for their settlements. Assemblies were called and the houses were allotted by lottery among the families that were deemed to be most in need—large families with no employed members and living in adobe huts were typically favored. However, the families that would inhabit the *casillas* did not always work on their own house. Instead, the construction jobs were also distributed by lottery among a leader's followers. In the settlement where I lived, the jobs were distributed among a group of unemployed young men who had self-organized into what they called a Center for Unemployed Workers (see Diz 2020b). Each house provided short-term jobs for a handful of men whose wages were paid with national government funds. In other words, these houses had the double advantage of providing new houses *and* wages.

Leaders were not always successful, however; and, even when they were, they were often accused of favoring their extended family, or worse, of accumulating and pursuing their own self-interest. In fact, such accusations were so prevalent that factional conflict was a recurring feature of life in all the Guaraní settlements I worked with (see also Diz 2020a). The cause of conflict always revolved around the apparent maldistribution of resources. Because they were the primary conduits for resources, leaders built a following by eliciting and redistributing goods among their supporters. At the community level, there was a widely held expectation of equitable redistribution and vigorous condemnation of any leaders who seemed to be accumulating for their own gain. Where a family might portion off some of its limited resources to spend on future house construction, people kept a constant eye on their leaders to ensure they did not accumulate resources for their own "personal ambitions." Leaders did not request that settlement-dwellers contribute to a communal fund, nor did the people I worked with expect "The Community" as a corporate entity to have a reserve it might draw on. Lest they be accused of selfishness or even witchcraft, leaders were expected to immediately redistribute any resources they elicited. While people recognized the ties of mutuality that ought to inform communal life, they were also acutely aware of the tensions and jealousies between households and of how fraught notions of a common good were. The constant surveillance of leaders, the moral injunction for redistribution, and a deeply held desire for equitable sharing combined to create a space of antithrift. Leaders had to redistribute in the short-term, and they did not accumulate for personal or collective gain. Politically virtuous resource management, in other words, was akin to immediate redistribution.

Casillas, then, articulated politics at two separate levels. At one level, they drew on party politics and the alignment of state institutions at the national, provincial, and local levels. As a powerfully visible form of patronage, they played an important part in formal democratic politics, particularly during election times, when nonindigenous politicians felt the need to persuade potential supporters. But on another level, they were also an important part of the less formalized internal politics of Guaraní settlements, which were marked by the injunction to redistribute. Because patronage in the form of government housing combined both scales, it sheds light on an important form of antithrift.

Contrary to house construction that was reliant on access to employment, the temporalities of electoral campaigning shaped the construction of government housing. Patronage also created a distinction between the world of *criollo* government and politicians and the Guaraní settlements that needed to find ways to elicit the wealth held by nonindigenous actors. The fact that these two worlds were ethnically distinguished palpably underscored the distance between wealthy *criollos* and poor *indígenas*. It also had political implications because the Guaraní felt that *criollos* inhabited a world of abundance from which resources could be elicited. This has had the effect of imbuing Guaraní efforts with a short-term dynamic in which they sought to acquire and elicit resources whenever a chance materialized. Additionally, there was the need for quick redistribution and the avoidance of accumulation. Combined, these two traits rendered communal economies a site of antithrift: an arena in which rapid redistribution trumped long-term planning and communal accumulation as a viable political strategy. This made sense given the dependence of Guaraní communities on external sources of wealth, particularly resources like *casillas* that materialized sporadically at electorally convenient times. Combined with widespread unemployment and unprofitable local agriculture, the lack of locally autonomous production meant that pursuing thrift was politically unpalatable. Antithrift built on an assumption of abundance, rather than scarcity, and emphasized elicitation and redistribution over production and accumulation.

Welfare, Gender, and (Anti-)Thrift

So far, I have described how the thrifty management of sporadic wages enabled Guaraní people to upgrade their houses and discussed the distribution of patronage as an instance of antithrift. In this section, I will discuss forms of welfare payments that blur the boundaries between thrift and antithrift. These welfare payments were relatively new and closely associated with the post-neoliberal government (2003–15). They were also directly related to the global commodities market, for it was from revenues derived from the soy boom that the national government financed its redistributive program.

As of 2009, Guaraní households have been receiving payments from a conditional cash transfer scheme known as the Universal Child Allowance (*Asignación Universal por Hijo*, or AUH). The AUH distributed small per-child payments to families without formal employment. Funds were managed at the national level and distributed to local welfare offices, who in turn deposited payments into bank accounts that beneficiaries could withdraw with their bank cards. In exchange for these payments, parents had to ensure that children attended school regularly and that they received periodic medical check-ups. Given the prevalence of unemployment in Guaraní settlements, practically every household in my host settlement had access to these benefits.

Policy makers envisioned the AUH as a supplementary income that was not designed to provide a living wage. Thus, in 2015, AUH payments were worth AR$670 (about US$75) per child per month, which was roughly equivalent to 10 percent of the Argentine minimum wage. A single household could claim payment for up to five children, meaning families could only earn up to about 50 percent of the wages of a full-time minimum wage job through the AUH (Alonso and Di Costa 2015: 49). While these amounts were modest by design, they had a strong impact upon the Guaraní, who had rarely enjoyed access to regular and dependable sources of cash. Although men were legally able to collect these allowances, I did not know of any Guaraní men who collected child allowances—the allowances were effectively the preserve of women.

If wages were sporadic and patronage determined by the rhythms of electoral cycles, AUH payments were monthly and dependable. Such a regular form of income was unprecedented in Guaraní settlements, and the AUH soon became one of the most crucial resources for Guaraní households. Families often used it to cover everyday expenses, especially food, but it was also often used for aspirational consumer goods. Like *casillas*, AUH payments were a government-donated resource. However, bureaucratized collection processes and individualized payments meant Guaraní leaders had no role to play in acquiring them. The tactics of elicitation, brokerage, and "bringing down" resources were superfluous in this context, and welfare payments did not feed into factional divisions. Nonetheless, these benefits were still evaluated in moral terms.

As others have noted (Morton 2015), conditional cash transfers often cast recipients in a morally ambiguous light. Unlike wages, which are paid out in exchange for work, CCTs are received in exchange for meeting simple criteria. Anxieties about people's motivation for work are common because they raise questions of moral desert (Diz 2018). Importantly, programs like the AUH have also been highly gendered. Among the Guaraní, the AUH's gendered connotations have granted women managerial control over payments, but they have also circumscribed the discretion with which women can spend them. The association of CCT payments with women and, specifically, mothers reinforced surveillance over expenditures and created a dichotomy between "good mothers," who spent their payments in a responsible manner to benefit their children, and "bad mothers," who were accused of wasting benefits and indulging in vanities. This moral evaluation was fundamentally about thrift understood as responsible intrahousehold planning aimed at future ends. Notably, it burdened women with the responsibility for long-term planning and resource management.

At the same time, people worried that the AUH could incentivize excess. For instance, the Guaraní nurse who worked in my host settlement's first aid room once admonished a group of women for having numerous children, explaining that although they would receive AUH money for each child, this money would not be enough to cover the expenses associated with child rearing. In this understanding, resources were finite, and their management had to extend into the long term. I also heard people accuse neighbors of wastefully spending most of their payments within the first few days of receiving them. In addition, the fact that AUH payments were made regularly enabled people to become increasingly in debt and often left them at the mercy of loan sharks who charged exorbitant interest rates. Finally, while a majority of my Guaraní friends and neighbors valued the AUH program as an indicator of the national government's concern for the poor, they also wondered whether the Argentine president was squandering valuable resources. Some were concerned about what would happen when the money ran out, and several even suspected that the CCT program was merely an effort to buy people's votes. Not unlike the Guaraní leaders discussed in the previous section, the sense that the president might be thinking in the short term raised the possibility of antithrift. These doubts and concerns reflected yet another instance of anxiety about recipients' and the state's responsibility to manage resources in a thrifty manner.

The AUH provides fascinating insights into the ambivalence of thrift and antithrift, and how the two can often be hard to distinguish. Here again we encounter issues of scale. Welfare was at once creating a relationship between the government personified by the figure of the president (see also Eger and Damo 2014) and between the members of beneficiary families. These monetary exchanges established relationships of mutuality that could be fulfilled through sharing and redistribution, but they also created obligations and expectations of thrifty expenditure that carried moral weight. The fact that these relationships were so strongly gendered in the Guaraní context made them all the more powerful, for they could effectively reinforce stereotypes that created two separate, and differently evaluated, realms of thrift and antithrift. In the next section I explore how these two realms come together within a particular household.

Thrift and Antithrift within a Household

The preceding three sections have schematized the three most important kinds of resources Guaraní people live with today. For each of these resources, I have shown how considerations of thrift and antithrift came into play, often in relation to ideas about temporality and scale. While I have distinguished between wages, patronage, and welfare, in everyday life most households juggled between the three kinds of resources. In as much as each resource generated different kinds of mutuality and political loyalty, they combined in powerful ways and played a significant role in the social life of Guaraní people. To illustrate this process, this section will focus on the case of Ana and Hernán's household.

Ana had had her first daughter at the age of fifteen; however, the father of her five children passed away when she was in her early thirties. Her two youngest sons attended secondary school in a nearby town, while two of her three daughters were unemployed. Her third daughter worked part-time and dreamed of joining the police force. Now in her forties, Ana had remarried. Hernán, Ana's current husband, had spent fifteen years as a migrant agricultural worker and had taken jobs all over the country before returning to the settlement and moving in with Ana. Upon his return, Hernán fell in with a logging crew and was able to support the family with the wages he earned. Soon he began investing in construction materials and upgraded Ana's wooden house. By 2012, the family lived in a unique and relatively large brick house.

But, as the amount of available wood near the settlement dwindled, Hernán was forced to find alternative ways of generating income. He joined in with a group of politically active unemployed young men and landed a short-term job as part of a highway paving crew that was hired by the municipal government during the run up to local elections. However, he soon felt he was being purposefully excluded from other job opportunities and became disillusioned with the settlement leader, whom he accused of pursuing his own selfish interests. Drawing on his experience on plantations, Hernán cleared out a patch of forest, installed an ingenious irrigation system, and planted an impressive vegetable garden. In this he demonstrated admirable resourcefulness, reusing old tools by fashioning new grips out of branches and repurposing lengths of hose that had been donated by politicians a few years back. Hernán exemplified a form of thrift that minimized expenditure (Gudeman 2001: 38) and enabled him to work with what tools and materials were readily available.

Unfortunately, the garden proved short-lived, as a forest fire destroyed it before he had a chance to collect the first harvest. By the time I arrived in the community, Hernán had cleared a new patch of forest and was in the process of sowing a large field of maize. At the same time, he was busy raising pigs, hoping to fatten them for sale at Christmas time. Despite Hernán's best efforts, a cattle herd destroyed his maize fields and diseases decimated his drove of pigs. Ultimately, he admitted to me, he wanted to make a profit, and he hoped his projects would make him rich so he would not have to work ever again.

While Hernán struggled to earn wages and found himself excluded from the patronage the leaders generated, Ana found alternative ways of supporting the household. Her youngest son was fifteen years old, which meant he was entitled to an AUH allowance for three more years. Ana was a staunch supporter of the Kirchnerista government and expressed wonder at how the president had transformed her role in the household. She also supplemented Hernán's paltry and inconstant income with a small disability subsidy she collected in the name of one of her daughters. In addition, Ana began baking bread for sale. She stayed up until the small hours of the night baking small round loaves. Over the course of a night, Ana would bake about two hundred loaves, ignoring the pain in her scoliotic back as she bent over to stoke the fire in her clay oven. By six in the morning, as women throughout the community began lighting the fires in their lean-to kitchens, children were sent to buy bread from Ana. The demand for bread was high, and Ana always managed to sell all the bread she made. At two pesos each (US$0.44 at the time), Ana made roughly four hundred pesos, or the equivalent of a monthly state-granted child allowance, every day. The work was extremely hard, but she managed to keep up the routine for two full months, sometimes making two batches of bread a day and only taking breaks when the pain in her back became unbearable. Ultimately, Ana gave up on her bread-making enterprise after Hernán, who struggled with alcoholism, found her cash and disappeared for a week.

With the money she earned from bread and welfare payments, Ana bought bricks, a bag of cement, tiles, and a porcelain toilet with which she hoped to build what she called a "first class bathroom." For this, she enlisted her unemployed uncle's help and paid him a small wage in exchange. However, Ana's in-laws felt that her ambitions to upgrade her house would lead her to neglect her children's needs. Even more damningly, Ana's mother felt she should be using the money to support her younger sister, Clara, who had a serious but undiagnosed illness and was struggling to take care of her own three young children. Ana, however, felt that Clara was an irresponsible mother and lamented how she misspent her AUH payments to go clubbing in a nearby border town instead of providing for her own children.

Ana and Hernán's toils, their daily division of labor, and the tensions they endured shed light on the internal workings of Guaraní households. The story is a complex one, with multiple layers of obligation, mutuality, and responsibility, as well as intersecting forms of income, patronage, and welfare. Hernán's variously shifting jobs, from agricultural migrant to logger, from highway paver to failed agriculturalist, accurately reflected the kinds of jobs available to men. For her part, Ana demonstrated a heroic capacity to keep the family afloat, and she succeeded in feeding the family while paying for her sons' education and guarding her resources from Hernán. It is worth noting that while Hernán's obligations to provide were restricted to his immediate family, Ana's extended family judged and laid claims on the resources she generated. Similarly, Ana evaluated her sister's use of resources along gendered lines.

We can see here how Hernán and Ana attempted to establish thrifty strategies, particularly in their work to upgrade their house. But we also see how hard they struggled to maintain their strategies and how often they had to come up with new endeavors. Party politics and communal politics came together for Hernán in the form of temporary employment; but while this created momentary loyalties, the antithrift expectations of fair redistribution rendered these political allegiances fragile. Meanwhile, Ana experienced welfare payments as a personalized act of care from the government. To the extent that thrifty accumulation and long-term planning intersected with short-term redistribution and expectations of abundance, the case of Ana and Hernán demonstrates the fundamental tensions between forms of mutuality and market logics. As individuals negotiate and grapple with the temporality and scale of various resource flows, they are able to forge social relations, while also coming up against the limits of both thrift and antithrift.

Conclusion

This chapter has considered the three most important resources upon which Guaraní people depended for their livelihoods during Argentina's post-neoliberal regime. This was a time of comparative abundance for the Guaraní, one in which resources were relatively easy to come by. However, it was also a time in which extractive employment had come to an end due to resource depletion. In this situation, wages had become relatively infrequent, but patronage and welfare had increased.

I have shown how people approached house construction in a thrifty manner by accumulating resources with a view to future construction. These construction projects were often informed by a sense of how material conditions had changed over recent years; and the construction of brick houses was felt as a move away from the poor living conditions of "the ancients." Thrifty approaches to house construction drew on speculation and careful attention to market prices, but they also built on existing ties of kinship and mutuality, thus blurring understandings of thrift as cold, self-interested calculation.

On the other hand, I have shown how government-donated housing was a particularly desirable form of patronage, and one that Guaraní leaders worked hard to elicit. Unlike wages, though, patronage did not rest on ideas of work and production. Rather, it built on an understanding of how non-indigenous *criollos* inhabited a world of abundance from which resources could be "brought down." As a result, community-level politics were a site of antithrift. The emphasis was not on communal accumulation, or even on creating a form of commons or "base" (Gudeman 2001: 27), but rather on egalitarian redistribution, which resulted in its own forms of political competition. The problem with this antithrift understanding of politics was that it generated discontent with leaders because of suspicions of favoritism and unmet expectations of equal redistribution.

Finally, I looked at post-neoliberal welfare payments and suggested that these blurred the realms of thrift and antithrift. Their regular payment created new material possibilities for many Guaraní households, and they also generated political loyalty toward the national government. The way in which these policies were designed as small contributions to the household created disciplinary pressures, particularly for women who were expected to spend resources in a thrifty manner to maximize benefits for their children. They also generated moral anxiety around questions to do with deservingness and raised concerns about whether they incentivized excess. Intriguingly, critics and pundits who decried what they saw as a populist strategy for buying off votes leveled similar sorts of accusations at the presidency. By contrast, from a developmental perspective, conditional cash transfers are often interpreted as a thrifty way of spending national resources—one that builds human capital gradually, with a view to boosting development in the long term.

Each of these resources operated at different scales, linking employees and employers in face-to-face interactions, connecting Guaraní leaders with regional and local government, and even creating loyalties between distant presidents and citizens on the ground. In moving across these scales, different resources created ambivalent ties of mutuality and obligation. Similarly, the fact that these resources had very different temporalities imbued them with socially powerful rhythms. In exploring how these resources, scales, and rhythms combined in a particular household, I illustrated how the different forms of thrift and antithrift generated tensions within and across Guaraní households. These tensions often worked along gendered lines, reinforcing women's obligations to manage the household in a thrifty manner, while simultaneously bracketing off community politics as a space of masculine antithrift.

Overall, this chapter has shed light on how people's engagements with wealth and resources constitute a movement in and out of thrift. It has also demonstrated that not all resources, not even all kinds of monetary payment, are the same and suggested that how resources are sourced, managed, earmarked, and distributed often determines their social possibilities and limits. In the Guaraní case, we find that such an approach reveals paradoxical ambiguities surrounding the analytical distinctions between thrift and antithrift. Despite a context of poverty, thrift does not emerge as the preferred strategy for economic security in Guaraní households. Rather, thrifty household management works alongside the antithrift of local politics and national welfare as people navigate the scales and rhythms of resource flows.

Acknowledgments

Estoy muy agradecido a todas las familias que, a través de su paciencia y generosidad, me enseñaron a valorar distintas formas de gestionar recursos y a imaginar alternativas políticas. I would also like to thank Catherine Alexander, Daniel Sosna, and Deborah James for their encouragement and help in writing this chapter. Research for this project was supported by the Economic and Social Research Council [grant number ES/J500070/1].

Agustin Diz is a political and economic anthropologist who specializes in Latin America and has conducted research among indigenous Guaraní settlements in Argentina's Gran Chaco region. His research focuses on labor and unemployment, energy and extractive industries, welfare policies, and democratization among indigenous populations in Latin America. Agustin holds a PhD from the London School of Economics and Political Science.

Notes

1. Thanks to Catherine Alexander for this observation.
2. Thanks to Daniel Sosna for this observation.

References

Alonso, Guillermo, and Valeria Di Costa. 2015. "Más Allá Del Principio Contributivo: Cambios y Continuidades En La Política Social Argentina, 2003–2011." *Estudios Sociológicos* 33(97): 31–62.

Clastres, Pierre. 1989. *Society Against the State: Essays in Political Anthropology*. New York: Zone Books.

Diz, Agustin. 2017. *The Afterlife of Abundance: Wageless Life, Politics, and Illusion among the Guaraní of the Argentine Chaco*. Unpublished doctoral thesis, London School of Economics and Political Science.

———. 2018. "Money from Above: Gender, Cash Transfers and Enfranchisement among Guaraní Households of the Argentine Chaco." In *Money from the Government in Latin America: Social Cash Transfer Policies and Rural Lives*, edited by E. M. Balén and M. Fotta, 114–29. London: Routledge.

———. 2020a. "'Healing the Institution': Conflict and Democratic Sovereignty in an Indigenous Community of the Argentine Chaco." *Geoforum* 117: 173–82.

———. 2020b. "'We Could Be Rich': Unemployment, Roadblocks and the Rhythms of Hydrocarbon Work among the Guaraní of the Argentine Chaco." *Bulletin of Latin American Research* 39(3): 319–33.

Eger, Talita Jabs, and Arlei Sander Damo. 2014. "Money and Morality in the Bolsa Família." *Vibrant: Virtual Brazilian Anthropology* 11(1): 250–84.

Ferguson, James. 1999. *Expectations of Modernity: Myths and Meanings of Urban Life on the Zambian Copperbelt*. Berkeley: University of California Press.

Grugel, Jean, and Pía Riggirozzi. 2012. "Post-Neoliberalism in Latin America: Rebuilding and Reclaiming the State after Crisis." *Development and Change* 43(1): 1–21.

Gudeman, Stephen F. 2001. *The Anthropology of Economy: Community, Market, and Culture*. Oxford: Blackwell Publishers Ltd.

———. 2008. *Economy's Tension: The Dialectics of Community and Market*. New York: Berghahn Books.

———. 2016. *Anthropology and Economy*. Cambridge, UK: Cambridge University Press.

Gudeman, Stephen F., and Alberto Rivera. 1990. *Conversations in Colombia: The Domestic Economy in Life and Text*. Cambridge, UK: Cambridge University Press.

Hirsch, Silvia. 2004. "Ser Guaraní En El Noroeste Argentino: Variantes de La Construcción Identitaria." *Revista de Indias* 64(230): 67–80.

INDEC. 2004. "Encuesta complementaria de pueblos indígenas" (ECPI). Buenos Aires: Ministerio de Economía de la República Federal Argentina.

Killick, Evan. 2007. "Autonomy and Leadership: Political Formations among the Ashéninka of Peruvian Amazonia." *Ethnos* 72(4): 461–82.

Langer, Erick. 2009. *Expecting Pears from an Elm Tree: Franciscan Missions on the Chiriguano Frontier in the Heart of South America, 1830–1949*. Durham: Duke University Press.

Lapegna, Pablo. 2016. *Soybeans and Power: Genetically Modified Crops, Environmental Politics, and Social Movements in Argentina*. New York: Oxford University Press.

Lavinas, Lena. 2013. "21st Century Welfare." *New Left Review* 84: 5–40.

Morton, Gregory Duff. 2015. "Managing Transience: Bolsa Família and Its Subjects in an MST Landless Settlement." *The Journal of Peasant Studies* 42(6): 1,283–305.

Peck, Jamie, and Nik Theodore. 2010. "Recombinant Workfare, across the Americas: Transnationalizing 'Fast' Social Policy." *Geoforum* 41(2): 195–208.

Richardson, Neal. 2009. "Export-Oriented Populism: Commodities and Coalitions in Argentina." *Studies in Comparative International Development* 44(3): 228.

Rival, Laura. 2016. *Huaorani Transformations in Twenty-First-Century Ecuador: Treks into the Future of Time*. Tucson: The University of Arizona Press.

Savino, Lucas. 2016. "Landscapes of Contrast: The Neo-Extractivist State and Indigenous Peoples in 'Post-Neoliberal' Argentina." *The Extractive Industries and Society* 3(2): 404–15.

Secretaría de Obras Públicas. 2010. "Resolución 993/2010: Créase el Programa Federal de Vivienda y Mejoramiento del Hábitat de Pueblos Originarios y Rurales." 5 October. http://servicios.infoleg.gob.ar/infolegInternet/anexos/170000-174999/173479/texact.htm.

Svampa, Maristella. 2015. "Commodities Consensus: Neoextractivism and Enclosure of the Commons in Latin America." *South Atlantic Quarterly* 114(1): 65–82.

4

Generous Thrift

Postpastoral Cooperation and Fortune-Making among the Torghuts of Mongolia

TOMASZ RAKOWSKI

In this chapter, I explore ethnographically how thrift appears as a social virtue in contemporary Mongolia. I use the concept of "social thriftiness" to indicate the apparently paradoxical simultaneity of shared accumulation and use of resources alongside a technology of generosity. This, as I unpack below, is only a paradox where saving (or keeping together) and giving away are perceived to be inimical. Such social thriftiness originally emerged from cooperation between pastoral families, but it continues, as I discuss, amidst the transformative potential of capitalist markets that shape the region. This form of thrift, interwoven with generosity, also serves to knit together divergent scales such as cohorts of former schoolmates, family networks, local authorities, various business networks, and state-level policies and politics. Thus, to understand the logic of thrift, we need to trace it through these different scales: within a group of yurts/households (*khot ail*); in a team of herders (*bag*, a brigade); in a settlement; in the district (*soum*); and finally, in the imagined and performed community of the Mongolian state. This kind of thrift also weaves together spheres often considered separate: the sacred, the market, and the household. In order to understand how such social thrift operates, we also need to pay attention to both Mongolia's specific economic and political context of emerging capitalism (Oyungerel 2017; Bonilla and Shadgar 2018; Bumochir and Plueckhahn 2018; Chuluunbat and Empson 2018; Waters 2018) and its particular history of collective economics (see Sneath 2003, 2006).

In the remainder of this introduction I outline, first, how anthropologists have analyzed thrift via the household economy as both distinct from the market and as part of a continuum with it, and how the ethnographic instance I explore here challenges and extends that understanding. Second, I outline the ethnographic context and my fieldwork before explaining the three key concepts of *nutag* (local homeland), *fortune*, and *life-forces*, which are central to the practice of husbanding or keeping resources together in part by generously giving them away.

The social mode of thrift encountered in Mongolia is very different from the model of the self-sufficient house economy, the typical locus of anthropological discussions on thrift. While many ethnographic studies, across post-socialist Europe as well as in Colombia (see e.g., Gudeman and Rivera 1990; Gudeman and Hann 2018), have focused on rural practices of collecting and reusing goods that create a protective cocoon in the face of rapid market reforms, in the Mongolian case we see something different. Thrifty business-making, undertaking challenges and risks through self-organization, may be considered a particularly distinct and locally emerging capitalist activity in Mongolia, produced alongside the spread of global economic forces (see Empson 2018). One could claim that in the theory of "house economy," thrift qua virtue plus practical and organizational skills are hardly transferable to larger scales. Therefore, in this frame, the very idea of social thriftiness, implying something greater than the household, might seem an oxymoron. Anthropological debates about thrift (e.g., Gudeman and Rivera 1990; Gudeman and Hann 2018; Alexander and Sosna this vol.), however, correspond well with the logic of running a yurt-household or a group of households (*khot ail*), and can then be extended beyond this local scale. The relationship between house and market economies may thus be analyzed not only as a tension between two extremes—where household self-sufficiency is a clear contrast with modern corporations (and their specialization and optimization)—but also as a continuum, described as a series of economic transfigurations that lead to modern economies (see Gudeman and Rivera 1990). In this view, the model of house economy serves as a device or force for "economizing" different socioeconomic units along the continuum. In Mongolia, thrift developed in the context of post-pastoral cooperation: a specific social art of being thrifty and generous at the same time, and thus created new socioeconomic worlds. However, this form of cooperation is deeply rooted in both earlier and ongoing cosmological realms. In the case of the Torghuts, we encounter a very particular and persistent mode of life: organizing life-forces by doing material and spiritual favors, and reciprocating them (e.g., organizing festivals and public donations). I will demonstrate how this new Mongolian business-making develops within newly created postpastoral networks.

Recently, Rebecca Empson (2018) described how cosmological realms were constantly recreated during Mongolian economic rises and falls. Drawing on the idea of making visible and disputable the larger system of exchange of hybrid qualities, entities, energies, and flows—the cosmoeconomy (a notion initially coined by Giovanni da Col on the basis of his Tibetan ethnography; see da Col 2012)—Empson has built her approach on treating relations of debt and dependency as a sort of "custodianship" played out between land, vital energies, resources, and diverse human powers and enterprises (Empson 2018: 265–66). In her view, economic and cosmological spheres overlap and cocreate one another. As she claims: "integral cosmological work goes into securing one's share and determining one's fate, so that exchange in the market and cosmological life are one and the same in the production of modern economics" (Empson 2018: 265). In this sense, the path leading from the classical Aristotelian ideal of a self-sufficient estate (or *oikos*) to the emergence of modern economy may be interestingly transformed into the question of how to move across different scales and registers in the newly emerging capitalist subjects throughout Asia. At the same time, however, economy may be analyzed in the light of local cosmologies, as, for instance, in Mette High's description of moralities that emerged along with artisanal extraction of land resources in Mongolia (High 2013).[1] Such intertwining of cosmology and economy may be understood as related to a reaction to capitalist forces and deep socioeconomic change. However, people do not merely respond using magical or spiritual means to fulfill their economic needs, nor do they psychologically retreat to the former cosmological system (and its "mechanics" of fortune and life forces [Empson 2018: 266]). Empson argues that all this is rather about producing a new capitalist form that was only triggered by rapid change. It contains noncapitalist diversity. This new socioeconomic world may be conceived of as a pluriversal sphere, containing a self-reproducing interplay of political, economic, and spiritual (cosmological) forces, which are neither activated anew, nor simply continued in the previous form (see de la Cadena 2010). This betwixt and between state of continuity and change resonates with the problem of thrift, or rather social thriftiness.

We may imagine, then, that holding the internal circulation of goods and labor within a group of households may be protecting them from the necessity of buying goods and taking part in market exchange ("holding the savings may negate market functioning," writes Gudeman in this vol.). But, in fact, at some point the house economy, through the act of "economizing," gives way to accumulation in terms of cosmoeconomic growth, which enables a kind of economic "liquidity," which does not necessarily represent only a form of "coping mechanism" or "resilience." This is especially important: this chapter goes deeper into the above, quite surprising transfiguration by setting up a social perspective on thrift in order to move beyond the notions of both a continuum and an opposition between the house (the prudent, "closed" unit) and the market economy (the capitalist, "open" system). I argue that, in Mongolia, the kinds of solidarity and mutuality that are encountered across different scalar registers are closely related to thriftiness. Thus, the art of pastoral household "economizing" (or "cosmoeconomizing") is also the skill of being thrifty, while practicing and celebrating generosity at the same time, and, paradoxically, eventually generating a profit, although this was not the primary aim.

To substantiate this argument ethnographically, I draw on my fieldwork from 2012 to 2015 in Mongolia with the Torghuts, particularly a new generation of Torghut businesspeople, coming from the Bulgan *soum* located on the southern slopes of the Altai Mountains in Mongolia.[2] This generation of former "children of herders" developed its own business enterprises in the capital city of Ulaanbaatar. In 2007, they established the Torgon Nutag Club, an activist center that collaborates with local authorities (*dargas*), supports many local initiatives and institutions like kindergartens or schools, and lobbies central political circles around the Mongolian parliament. They also launched a series of *Bürenkhairkhany takhilga* ceremonies, which are publicly performed offerings and celebrations conducted around the sacred mother-mountain in their hometown of Bulgan. Kin and former schoolmate ties enable these businesspeople to mobilize these relationships when necessary. This is part of a larger phenomenon in Mongolia: former pupils from the same cohort frequently celebrate their ties over the course of their lives and in many ways. Pupils of both sexes from the same class, who were children of local herders, usually studied together, lived together in dormitories, and finished their school years by working for the benefit of their hometown school; for example, a new path was paved in Bulgan's schoolyard by a group of former schoolmates. These ties become almost as durable as the strong pastoral, family ties, especially those between siblings, children, and their parents. However, this form of being and working together is also a celebration of a very specific form of "generous self-sufficiency," or even "generous thriftiness," that is quite close to the sociality performed in everyday pastoral activities, a complex system of cooperation that enables animals to be bred.

Thriftiness contains here both a sense of pastoral sociality and the internal circulation of exchanged labor as a generous gesture that may have an element of competition. Such forms of sociality and exchanged labor are used equally for managing collective resources, such as herds, and spiritual resources. In both cases, the effective or thrifty organization is grounded on principles of keeping together while giving away. This way of acting is embedded in a broader domain. Such local communities integrate their members through interaction with local resources. The local homeland, the *nutag*, has a broad meaning in contemporary Mongolia (Sneath 2010, 2014; Stolpe and Erdene-Ochir 2021). Groups supporting their local homelands, pastures, and settlements, such as *nutag*-committees (*nutgiin zövlöl*), have been functioning in Mongolia for several years. They have lobbied parliament on behalf of their hometowns and settlements (Sneath 2010, 2014; Shadgar 2015; Stolpe and Erdene-Ochir 2021), and often speak of managing the spiritual qualities of the locality, the "living" or "animated" landscape. Acting for the benefit of one's hometown is, in this view, also working for collective life-forces that are accumulated in the local land and responsible for fortune-making. Fortune refers to the fluid matter of life-forces in Mongolian vernacular practices that are based on the Buddhism of yellow-hat lamas, but these practices are often connected to shamanist ideas as well. These practices are related to the intertwined pastoral, symbolic, and sociotechnical systems of accumulation of wealth, good deeds, and the interplay of life-forces, as depicted in studies by Caroline Humphrey and Hürelbaatar Ujeed (2012) and by Rebecca Empson (2012). Such sociotechnical systems include knowledge of links between the use and capacity of pastures, grass and animal biology, and pastoral and veterinary techniques.

The stream of life-forces is central to ideas of natural and spiritual resource husbandry and can be understood in three distinct ways. First, it can appear as an individual accumulation of brilliance, cleverness, and courage, presented as an "air- or wind-horse" (*hiimori*), a force moving upward, radiating upon others, or as the accumulated force of *sülde* ("might," "potency"; see Humphrey and Hürelbaatar 2012: 152) of a given individual, even if they rely on external sources or objects to enhance the flow of life-forces. Second, the stream of life-forces may also appear as a moral or social force in people with strong and creative personalities, a result of their accumulation of good deeds, their organization of resources, and reciprocity in labor; in this sense it is manifested via increased material (or immaterial) benefits. In other words, such virtue is recognized as a surge of wealth or fortune called *hishig*, or *buyan-hishig*, that may be maintained or lost (Empson 2012, 2018), and which is also associated with networks of relations: relatives, friends, accumulated deeds, and the abundance of potential favors.

Finally, the stream of life-forces contributes to the "diffusion of the self" (Humphrey and Hürelbaatar 2012: 163), a being that "transcends the delimited, materially organized self and thereby creates an impersonal kind of individuation" (ibid). The *nutag* is used here in its broad sense of being a sort of condenser of various circles in the locality: local life-forces, cultivated hometown networks, the *soum*, the landscape, and the place of origin or of one's birth (the *törsön nutag*). *Nutag* thus enables people in various ways to get involved in (or to "catch") the streams of life-forces (Humphrey and Hürelbaatar 2012; Oyungerel 2013).[3] In essence, the *nutag* is a unit of vibrant social activity, in line with real political, spiritual, and economic practices (see Sneath 2010: 257, 2014: 463; Bumochir 2019; Stolpe and Erdene-Ochir 2021).

Taking these two intertwined spheres into account—the *nutag* and the very specific "mechanics" of fortune in Mongolia—I propose a sense of thrift as a cocreated act of living that is also an act of pursuing collective and political purposes based on pastoral patterns that use the *nutag*'s material and existential resources. This operation is necessary to achieve a novel insight into the rapid social, political, and economic changes that the Mongols have experienced since the 1990s. In brief, from 2011, the state budget grew significantly, but a financial crisis developed starting in 2014, causing various political perturbations. Many Mongols, especially in remote *soum*s such as Bulgan, developed new strategies for living from local or cross-border trade, transportation, building, and construction businesses. They set up small and medium-sized enterprises (Chuluunbat and Empson 2018; Ichinkhorloo 2018), which often relied on easy access to state investment orders. In 2012 such enterprises employed almost 50 percent of the workforce (Chuluunbat and Empson 2018: 425). The idea of social thrift that I suggest here allows us to understand the effects of such socioeconomic transformation as a spectrum of behaviors and organizational forms appearing over the last decade.

In the following sections, I unpack this sense of thrift in order to interpret how new generations of Torghut businesspeople of Mongolia cooperate and exchange roles in their management of collective enterprises. I focus on how they create their new economic networks, and how they operate according to their former pastoral idioms of self-organization and interchangeability, while creating a social hub, the *Torguud Town*, in Ulaanbaatar. Also, I refer to their complex and strong bonds with their own *nutag*: the Bulgan *soum*. Their participation in and organization of festivals and donations for local institutions represent in this way a collective thrifty management of local goods, both economic and spiritual. I argue that thanks to the preservation and distribution of local life-forces, a different understanding of postpastoral cooperation may appear, which is particularly "thrifty," closely related to the complex way in which goods and resources are brought together, held together, supported, and protected, and at the same time distributed with generous gestures.

Torguud Town and Postpastoral Cooperation: Keeping the Business Together

The residents of the Bulgan *soum* experienced the economic collapse of the 1990s and early 2000s, and then, since 2012–13, the rapid infrastructural, financial, and economic development that came with structural and economic changes in Mongolia. These transformations were triggered by the growing mining industry and the sale of a large quantity of state bonds, which triggered a kind of financial crisis from 2014 onward. During the socialist period, the Bulgans were engaged in herding and cultivating vegetables and fruit. Processing plants and cooperative workplaces were also created at this time. Between 1990 and 1996, state herding cooperatives (*negdels*) collapsed, the orchard station and irrigated fields deteriorated, and the local power plant gradually fell apart. This is when small businesspeople and traders began to appear in the town, trade on the border with China intensified, and the Bulgans gradually started to do business in Ulaanbaatar. Many of the best-known Mongolian businesses in the capital city, alongside many smaller companies, were created by Torghut businesspeople. Bulgan itself started to develop significantly after years of collapse: the establishment of orchards and gardens in semidesert lands sped up, while rapid (sometimes violent) fencing and taking of new lands was based on a local, Mongolian form of land possession,[4] and went along with the internal migration of Bulgan inhabitants from remote pastures to the center of the *soum*.

The Torghut businesspeople used their former pastoral and family-based networks and collectives to shape their new businesses. In other words, their activities were rooted in historical phenomena, a prerevolutionary and then socialist system of sharing pastures. This was related to a specific way of organizing informal connections and entanglements between herders and the local administration in Mongolia (see e.g., Sneath 2003, 2006). I mostly encountered the new, young generation of sons and daughters of shepherds and employees of state-owned cooperatives. They were a group of Torghuts, mostly from the Bejlijn group, who, after finishing school, started trading on the border, importing goods from Russia, establishing stores and warehouses, and, after a few years, running their own businesses in the capital. They built a five-story block of flats in Ulaanbaatar with apartments, offices, shops, and restaurants, which they call *Torguud Town*, that became a meeting point in the capital for the Bulgans. This Torghut estate is the first step in following thrift and sharing goods.

I entered Torguud Town in the autumn of 2014 with my friend, twenty-two-year-old Bold. The system of sharing goods clearly shaped a very specific environment. When we arrived after a two-day road trip from Bulgan, before we even managed to leave the car, "brothers" from the dorm suddenly appeared, took our backpacks, bags, and parcels off our shoulders, and carried everything up to an apartment on the fifth floor. When we came down, Bold greeted everyone with great familiarity, addressing everyone as auntie/sister (*egch*) or uncle/brother (*akh*), or if they were younger than him, younger brother/sister (*düü*). This was where Bulgans stayed when they came to Ulaanbaatar, and where they worked together. They organized goods for sale to China, and (usually within smaller groups of siblings or schoolmates) shared equipment, cars, and looked after each other's premises. The most thriving businesspeople helped the young to get settled; they also hosted people visiting from Bulgan and organized medical care.

The social network was dense. Bold's uncle, Galsan, one of the creators of Torguud Town, ran a shop that he leased from his brother, who had built the tower block and had his company on the first floor. Apartments above were made available to relatives from Bulgan—young families, students coming to study in Ulaanbaatar—whereas offices and companies occupied two central floors located below. This was where members of the same group worked: the wife of one of the most successful vendor-businessmen, Batnasan, worked in a company run by Galsan, located right next door. On the ground floor, next to Galsan's shop, was his cousin Tsogt's canteen, where relatives of theirs worked. A year later, the venue had been completely renovated and now "belonged" to Ganbat, one of the most dynamic and smart Bulgan businessmen, although, once renovated, it was Ganbat's daughter and sister who actually ran it.

Thus, this place brought together Bulgan circles in Ulaanbaatar, even though other Ulaanbaatar residents were unfamiliar with the name Torguud Town. It was where a sort of social "internal circulation" of goods and relations operated. In the apartment blocks around the Torguud Town building there were Torghut services, businesses, hairdressers, pawnshops, shops, canteens, and bars with pool tables. Several young Torghut women, all of them Bold's cousins or acquaintances, worked in a *guanz* (food bar) located in the central part of the building, and about five young Torghut women worked at the cash register in a small shop called the Lord Market, run by Galsan. At the same time, the dorm apartments housed groups of five to six people, brothers and sisters from Bulgan, who studied in Ulaanbaatar. There was also a more "secret" passage in the back, which Bold and I used freely, that led from the canteen to the office and residential part of the building; Torghut families, construction workers, and their children lived in "dormitories" (i.e., apartments granted to the Bulgans by Tsogt and others). Bold lived in such a dormitory, Tsogt's apartment, along with his two brothers, his son, and a cousin. Bold studied aviation engineering, his brothers studied law and economics, his cousin studied computer science, while another cousin was a nurse. The nurse was Ganbat's daughter, there with her husband and daughter and Tuya—the youngest sister of "the brothers" (Ganbat, Davaa, Nyamaa)—who had just returned from Japan and was now learning English and looking for a job. Downstairs was another dorm housing "brothers" from Bulgan, and again, private apartments occupied by the coowner (i.e., Tsogt's relatives). They all slept on the floor on mats, and periodically exchanged places in their flats. When I lived with them and "the brothers," we slept on the floor of the largest room. Every day there were different people sleeping there, as some returned while others left; the nurse, for example, vacated her room, but then came back for two weeks.

I was frequently told in Ulaanbaatar that the Torghut are especially "cohesive," that they "cooperate and support one another," operating through kinship and acquaintanceship structures. Usually the Bulgan businessmen I worked with, just like their parents, recited their ten or twelve brothers and sisters by age, listed what they did, and immediately corrected any mistakes with a smile. However, focusing only on Torghut, or general Mongolian, kinship ties and patterns, while important,[5] would be to omit a dynamic, functional, and human dimension of the Bulgan Torghut structures of self-organization, as shown in the description of Torguud Town. On a social, economic, and even spiritual level, Torghut groups of brothers and sisters acted through their relationships with their siblings and through schoolmate networks in a specific context of "internal circulation" of goods and resources.

That pattern of cooperation seemed to be an extension of the organization of the self-sufficient yurt, or teams of closely collaborating yurts (*khot ail*), which may also be understood as a distinct economic-cosmological, symbolic system (Szynkiewicz 1981: 56–79; Wasilewski 1977). However, I use a neologism here—the verbs "to brother" and "to sister"—to suggest the way they operated, self-organized, developed their businesses, or just swapped their roles in various situations. This "brothering" and "sistering," understood as a technique of swapping/replacing (Mongols use an idiom here, *akh düüsekh*, meaning literally "brothering"), is thus at once an economic act, a form of sudden, reactive togetherness, and the specific art of replacing one person with another. Thus, when we were driving with yet another brother of this family, Dawaa, who had just bought a new Istana bus to use for his livelihood, his nephew appeared suddenly at a petrol station located at the outskirts of town and took over the driving; it turned out that his uncle Dawaa did not have the driving license required in the city. When Galsan, Bold's uncle who ran the Lord Market shop located at the bottom of Torguud *Town*, was away on his trips, his nephew, who had just finished his studies, regularly replaced him. In this manner, a kind of collective, thrifty navigation of property, goods, and investments becomes evident. A pastoral form of ownership, which originated in the former pastoral land use and took the form of "temporary possession" (*ezemshil*: Empson 2018; Plueckhahn 2019; see also Sneath 2003; Pedersen and Højer 2008; Endicott 2012), makes possessions also collective and only temporarily assigned to a particular family. Generally speaking, these forms are drawn from family-based informal ties, a sociotechnical, informal system of the common use of goods and land (Sneath 2003); but they also involve an interplay of interests and leave some room for extortions, shifting borders, and even the quiet seizure of territory. To put it differently, this interplay is directly related to the complex way in which such uses are organized around collective and spiritual resources managed thriftily. Therefore, the big, new, off-road vehicles (Toyota Land Cruisers) in which they drove me from the Bulgan *soum* and the city to various places were almost always collective property, although they would be registered by one of the brothers. They served both for prestige and for practical purposes; usually several brothers went in together to buy big expensive cars, and then used them to take the whole family to Bulgan.

These cars, of course, enabled fast transportation, which was crucial for the Torghut business; thus Ganbat, one the most reputed vendors, traded in his car for a new one three times during my five-year fieldwork, despite living in a modest, one-story brick house in Bulgan. This example also shows why, in running their businesses, they usually assumed that they simultaneously affected several people. The thrifty system of collectively managing ownership here, with a certain flexibility, owes a lot to a system of land use that can be negotiated or delicately "shifted" between neighboring herders using distinct pastures in each season (Potkański and Szynkiewicz 1993: 44–46). Thus, in the case of Bulgans, we find a form of collective management associated with fast-growing businesses and a wide range of activities, which is also related to a constant susceptibility to failure—which happened both in Ulaanbaatar and in Bulgan during my stay. However, since these were essentially family- or schoolmate-based activities, the risk of failure was mitigated or managed through the exchange or swapping of one person for another. Thus, the considerable degree of business diversification went hand in hand with risk-taking; this can be easier to comprehend precisely when the activity is collective and based on a virtue of interchangeability and, in this way, specifically thrifty cooperation.

De-animalization and the *Nutag*: Keeping Goods Together

The creation of postpastoral cooperation was also connected to activities performed by Torghut businessmen for the benefit of their local homeland, the *soum* of Bulgan. Their endeavors were visibly related to the cosmology discussed above and to images of the life-forces contained in the place of origin (Humphrey and Hürelbaatar 2012); and they were supported by recreated traditions of celebration and political mobilization around the *nutag* (Sneath 2010, 2014). In this case, however, celebrating the place of origin also took the form of the Torgon Nutag Club, mentioned earlier; it was organized by activists who were directly related to the *Torguud Town* founders. Businessmen from the club, aside from founding this block, also organized support for the *soum* during the 2000s, when a disastrous hard freeze (*zud*) and harsh winds decimated herds, and they built and funded a "park of glory," called Torgon Nutag Park, in the middle of Bulgan. They also started to organize and fund local sacrificial ceremonies in Bulgan called *takhilga* (*Bürenkhairchany takhilga*, a celebration centered around the mother-mountain, Bürenkhairchan). In every office run by Torghuts in Ulaanbaatar, there is a picture of this sacred mountain in the middle of the Bulgan settlement. The most important ceremony, centered on worship of the mother-mountain, was held biennially. The club decided, however, that the ceremony of celebrating and "feeding" the mountain would take place not in the spring (which was proposed by the local lamas, and would be in line with the lunar calendar), but in September, after haymaking and the movement of livestock to autumn pastures, when all the businesspeople could travel from Ulaanbaatar to Bulgan.

On this occasion, a column of Toyota Land Cruisers, decorated with the club emblems and packed with businesspeople and their families, arrived at the *soum*. The group had crossed the entire territory of Mongolia by car and was greeted at the town gate by residents and *soum* officials. Over the next few days, groups of men traveled around to other holy mountains located in the area that were connected with particular Torghut subgroups; several dozen people climbed the other local sacred mountains, where they tossed rice and grain into the air, sprinkled milk and vodka, and recited prayers. There were joint prayers with hundreds of participants at the foot of Bürenkhairkhan, and a new hall was opened in the local House of Culture. Then the local community gathered for the festival (*naadam*). There were horse races (including Torghut pacers), wrestling competitions, concerts lasting many hours, speeches, and award ceremonies, including ones for the best shepherds, businessmen, teachers, and officials. Horse racing and wrestling awards were funded by individual businessmen, who, in addition to medals, awarded the winners framed diplomas with the amount of the cash prize written on them.

Such activities for the benefit of *a nutag* are, as I mentioned, a broader phenomenon in contemporary Mongolia, where regional, *soum* based communities, integrating their members, have functioned actively over the last two decades (Sneath 2010, 2014; Shagdar 2015; Stolpe and Erdene-Ochir 2021). In many cases, they were organized into groups lobbying parliament on behalf of their hometowns and settlements, usually under the

Figure 4.1. Torgon Nutag businessmen and the Bulgans: an informal gathering during the *naadam*. © Tomasz Rakowski.

Figure 4.2. Torguud Town, Ulaanbaatar. © Tomasz Rakowski.

label of *nutag*-committee. The Torgon Nutag Club and the *Torguud Town* founders are similar structures, though less formal. Establishing and then running the business, and then the club, was quite a spontaneous action, albeit bound to the *nutag*, which increased, on the one hand, the "internal circulation" of businesses (people coming from Bulgan to set up their new businesses in the capital), and on the other hand, the possibility for prestigious deeds oriented toward *nutag* life and the celebrations held in the remote *soum*.

Reinforcing the *nutag* and thereby acting on the businessmen's attachment to the life-forces contained in the landscape could make the flow of fortune more accessible. However, acting for the benefit of the *nutag* also took the form of competition in donating, supporting, and endless striving for visible reinvestment of their incomes in the local social, economic, and spiritual environment. In this way, generosity became another form of being thrifty, and vice-versa, which could also be understood with regard to the postpastoral exchangeability in carrying out business.

This endeavor of reinvesting goods and energies in the local *nutag*, and at the same time making it public, was especially visible in one particular celebration: the fiftieth anniversary of the Bulgan kindergarten, which serves as an example of the Torghut (and general Mongolian) idiom of the production of the thrifty as well as generous "public good." In the 1990s, this kindergarten almost fell apart—out of thirty employees, only nine remained

Figure 4.3. Businessmen's vehicles at the bottom of a sacred mountain. © Tomasz Rakowski.

Figure 4.4. *Takhilga* sprinkling and blessing at the top of the mountain. © Tomasz Rakowski.

because after the herds of animals were privatized, many people "went into the steppe" in order to start building up their own flocks of animals.[6] Only a few children remained to attend classes in the small, dilapidated building. When a new director, Tömörjargal, took over the management in 2000, she convened parent meetings and announced what she would need to run the kindergarten. Several parents immediately installed a boiler and central heating in the old building, and then for several years the parents partly covered the cost of the children's board. The director held organizational meetings and individual talks with the parents who participated in the refurbishment, and she helped arrange for the building materials.

When the director decided in 2012 to organize a festival for the fiftieth anniversary of the founding of the Bulgan kindergarten, and to collect funds for retrofitting the building, she turned for help to the employees, parents, *soum* residents and authorities, and businesspeople from the Torgon Nutag Club, as well as to the people from the *nutag*-committee and *aimag* (province) authorities. Preparations took two years; the employees sewed costumes, prepared a school play, and two kindergarten teachers performed as lead singers on the stage (even agreeing early on not to get pregnant). At meetings with Torgon Nutag Club and the *nutag*-committee, Tömörjargal was promised donations, while *darga*s, using funds from the *soum* budget, tripled the stakes for horse racing competitions in five age categories and for traditional wrestling. Offices, hospitals, and schools also promised to donate funds for kindergarten purposes. Employees and parents organized the fundraising themselves and managed to collect large sums, which helped build a fence and a playground. There was also a gala concert that lasted several hours, with well-prepared actors from among the kindergarten children and teachers. On this occasion, the fundraising results were announced: who donated and how much, with precise amounts displayed by a projector on a side wall of the concert hall. The amounts also appeared on public noticeboards, at the commune office, and at a bus stop. On this occasion *darga*s, officials, teachers, and directors of institutions dressed in festive *deel*s (Mongolian caftans), some with decorations pinned to them, and solemnly sang the anthem with their right hands placed over their hearts. All this was largely a continuation of the old socialist assemblies from the time of the Mongolian People's Republic; the next day the festival began, which was attended by as many as a thousand people.

As is typical, it was difficult to distinguish the extent to which it was the local *soum* that organized this support and fundraising or "private investors" such as members of the Torgon Nutag Club, the group of entrepreneurs from Ulaanbaatar. What matters is that this action did not take place in simple opposition to state conditions, in response to the state's failure to fulfill its basic duties or to its excessive control. Moreover, for the celebration of the kindergarten's fiftieth anniversary, the residents collected the required sums in an almost impromptu manner; as mentioned above, the event included spontaneous and quasi-official fundraising, and lists of donors hung on the notice board in front of the *soum* office. Director Tömörjargal received expensive gifts for furnishing children's classrooms, and generous residents and parents were awarded medals and gratitude certificates. It was emphasized several times that in order to achieve success, obtain funds, and organize a big celebration, one has to publicly announce all the plans to parents, employees, and authorities, but above all, one must organize a kind of solemn feast, *nair*, which, as Oyungerel (2013: 133) pointed out, is the basic way of building desired relations in postpastoral Mongolian society. Tömörjargal told me: "You can't hide what you want to do; you have to say clearly that you need such and such an amount of money, and you have to invite officials to lunch, to dinner. This is how it needs to be done, especially in the *soum*." These meetings, during which toasts were made, funds declared, and stakes topped, took place in a hotel restaurant designed and equipped under the Mercy Corps project (USAID funding) owned by a member of the Torgon Nutag Club, and where officials, *darga*s, businessmen, and teachers also gathered.

Such events entrench and embody the idea of cooperation, but also demonstrate the ability to form informal networks and act on the fringes of official regulations and institutions; certain individuals can use this to become powerful in the eyes of others, achievers aware of their value (see Sneath 2006; Humphrey 2012). A particular manifestation of social force also comes to the fore through the organization of public donations and doing favors for the local government, which can generate specific ties that can be mobilized as privileges. People gravitate around strong, intelligent (*aztai*), and creative personalities, who are understood to have abundant resources of life-forces, proven by their publicly manifested fortune. This public manifestation of life-forces is a moment of intense "taming" or "harnessing" of fortune, making it manifest (Empson 2014), but this fortune is also based on demonstrating a specific way of building one's prosperity by doing something concrete or keeping things together in cooperation with family, friends, and peers (Oyungerel 2013). Moreover, it creates a play of life-forces, allowing the winners to capture the moment of "self-ascending" energy flow (the movement upward, *ööröö öödlökh*) and the flow of prosperity (Oyungerel 2013: 115).

Yet, what is really crucial is that these activities slowly transform into the sphere of the *political*; it is not merely a way of acting through a grassroots social organization. The activities around the fiftieth anniversary of the kindergarten took place on the edge of decisions taken by the current *dargas* after a long period of systematic financing of the kindergarten from the surplus budgets of 2010–12, during which time the number of children increased annually by about thirty. In this sense, only an individual who could accumulate the sense of fortune publicly, thus proving his abundant life-forces, holding onto those forces while at the same generously distributing them through "magnificent" deeds, could get into politics. Likewise, public donations for the *nutag* and the local government were similarly considered "being in the right place." The right man in the right place, they say, would be Batnasan Otgoo, a member/head of Torgon Nutag Club. Once he had accumulated sufficient life-forces, he became much more powerful and louder than "thousands of mouths": in 2016, he became a Member of the Mongolian Parliament.

Therefore, initially these donations, fundraising drives, and collaborations may be conceived of as "thrifty solidarity," a form of self-help, stemming from Mongolian systems of local support.[7] In this manner, we see the expanding sphere of *the political*, initially rooted in the specific life and organizations of the local *soum* communities and then expanding across scales, finally reaching the state. However, in order to explain it in more detail, I need to return to the very intimate relation that Mongolian *soums* have with the state, which is created not only through collective, informal actions usually related to the *nutag*—or to *nutagism*, as it was called by Tuya Shadgar (2015)—but also related to pastoralism, animal husbandry, the fact of being a herder, and finally, to the animals.

Here we need again to use a notion of thrift, a keyword to unlock the meanings and, therefore, the forces that are "kept together." In Mongolia, having large, productive herds and being a successful herder is an excellent example through which a certain dynamic of thrift in its transformed sense appears. The reinvestment of goods and deeds is also related to keeping flocks of animals, and even to a more profound image of being a good herder, which on various levels means also being a good citizen. That is because breeding herds well, keeping the animals safe and well fed together, requires a mastery of self-sufficiency on every plane: thrifty cooperation within a group of *khot ail* that involves exchanging labor when breeding animals, "placing" herds with other families, exchanging weanlings in order to enable neighbors to milk animals (*saakhalt* in the past), taking care of animals when moving with big herds, joint production of felt, and many other joint activities. At the same time, such successful breeding fulfills the requirements of the state, both now and in the socialist and prerevolutionary periods. This imagination also goes along with a more general feature of pastoralism, mentioned by Gudeman (this vol.) as "being thrifty." Keeping animals, he argues, is an action that keeps "the base for future use" and yields milk, the "no-cost food," as well as breeding animals, which "augments the base" with relatively little expenditure of labor. Still, being a good herder in Mongolia is equivalent not only to being a skillful, and in this sense also "thrifty," master/manager, but also a "good" and territorially bounded citizen of the state (Bristley 2016). It is essential that herders in Mongolia still receive medals from the state, and those who have been so honored keep them at home with pride. Moreover, as Joseph Bristley (ibid.) demonstrated, the relationship with animals takes the form of a "shepherd-citizen," while the relationship between being a citizen of a local territory (*hoshuu*, formerly "banners") within the state and being a master shepherd also has historical continuity in areas of Inner Asia. Successful herders receive diplomas as "best breeders" (in the *aimag*, *Ajmagiin Sain Malczin*, or even, like Baatarsüren, in the whole country, *Ulsyn Aimagiin Malczin*), for the accomplishment of high productivity, rearing numerous herds.

Thus, people kept large herds in Mongolia for prestige, for the continuity of working with animals, or because of the desire to maintain wealth and "fortune with the animals" (*malyn hishig*; see Empson 2012). Moreover, in almost every nonpastoral Bulgan household—in the *soum* center—we encountered children of our hosts' relatives who were camping outside the center, looking after large herds that belonged to those living in the center. Similar stories recurred, such as the story of a taxi driver (and singer) Nasaaand, his wife Altan, who was a meteorological station worker at the airport, both of whom worked in the center; or the family of the clerk Bat.

They all had close pastoral families (or simply contracts with the families of shepherds) whose children they took in for the school year. Another case was the story of the businessman Tulga, of Torgon Nutag Club, who, along with his parents, kept large herds of up to a thousand animals, which were taken care of by a hired family. Until recently, three of his brothers were also engaged in pastoral care; they gradually moved to trade and business, just like their other brothers and sisters. In all these cases, however, all these people emphasized that it was good to have "your own animals": the best meat and cheese were your own, so that from autumn until spring you did not have to buy anything, and there was something to hand over for the winter to your relatives, "the young in the city," which provided support to the students. This seems to have been particularly important for a new generation of Torghut businessmen as well, such as Tulgafor, for whom maintaining herds was a bond with his family, parents, and all that was related to the past, as well as a testimony to the very strength of success in the form of accumulated, enduring prestige and a proper place in the hierarchy. Owning a herd also indirectly showed that he had strong pastoral skills acquired in childhood.

However, this move toward new occupations, trade, business, and finally supporting children's education in Ulaanbaatar, while still relying on certain life-forces or prestige drawn from breeding animals, was a little paradoxical. On the one hand, people in Bulgan retreated from maintaining herds, especially after the hard freezes, and this may be conceived as a broader withdrawal from pastoral work; nowadays more than half the *soum*'s inhabitants are no longer engaged in pastoralism. On the other hand, this transition toward new professions and efforts to provide an excellent education for children closely corresponds to keeping large herds of animals, or having at least a link to them, through their relatives. Also, private journeys undertaken by people from the towns and *soum* centers to their former pastures, herds, relatives, and, thus, to the *nutag* have become very popular across Mongolia, as witnessed by testimonies of these journeys on social media. In this sense, pastoralism and the skill of "thriftiness" were keys to understanding ongoing transformations. These mechanisms and virtues were now taking their new forms, such as collective support for kindergartens and the self-organizing struggle to educate the children so that they could finally find a job outside pastoralism.

Conclusion

It is clear from the ethnography above that new activities and a new system of work in trade and business emerged after people left their pastoral way of life, or at least significantly reduced the extent to which they lived on animal husbandry. However, having said this, I echo Sławoj Szynkiewicz's (1993) observation that "building a new society again" for Mongolia's nomads was related to the fact that prerevolutionary pastoralist systems of cooperation could adapt to the socialist, *negdel* cooperatives, and then again to a market economy when many people began to live on their privately owned flocks. However, this "thrifty" cooperation, the art of managing adequate numbers of herds and the whole "sociotechnical system," was largely related to the ability to respond to cyclical hard freezes and severe conditions in winter and early spring. Hard freeze catastrophes are regular natural disasters with which shepherds have been familiar for several hundred years and for which they were continually getting prepared (Szynkiewicz 1993; Sneath 2002, 2003).

We can look at this long-established system of cyclical, long-term grazing and the fast transfer from one camp to another as a system that developed in the past, but that has been substantially continued today, even though manifested through different activities, such as doing business in the capital city, celebrating the creation of new institutions, or taking part in the "educational race." However, in the sense of the cosmoeconomic approach, it is not only a matter of a continuation or a reaction to the harsh competition experienced within the new capitalist regime. My ethnography shows a new generation of people who still rely on their pastoral background and the art of cooperation, but who take on very different activities: seeking other jobs, migrating to Ulaanbaatar, reinvesting their funds in the *nutag*, and establishing new enterprises, shops, and restaurants. Such new practices may be understood as a continuation of the social, moral, and economic practices of pastoral self-organization, but then also as a form of the present cosmoeconomy and the complicated way of dealing with new economic conditions.

What appears to be a new practice is, in fact, "transfigured" pastoral self-organization, where thrifty actions now extend beyond the scale of the pastoral households (*khot ail*) to serious business in the city, and finally into political action. These collective "postpastoralist" trade ventures were, therefore, based on a familiar system of self-help, as enacted in the markets of Ulaanbaatar, and centered around the *Torguud Town*. The celebrations in the *nutag* and the forces coming with the investment in festivals and local events of *takhilga* can only be understood by acknowledging such transfigured social mechanisms, centered around work, goods, and land tenure, flexible exchangeability, and a sort of "generous thrift."

Thus, to sum up, the contemporary art of being socially thrifty, combining keeping resources together with generously giving them away, has been created at the intersection of earlier pastoral forms of cooperation and the new economic environment. The latter has largely driven the retreat from pastoralism, together with the local moods and policies of de-animalization, as well as the devastation of hard freezes. The final cause that has precipitated new-for-old forms of social thriftiness is the attempt to take on the commercial-cum-educational challenge against huge capitalist markets, spurred on by the visible success of the "youth from the city." The notion of thrift acts as a keyword to understand profound transformations in present-day Mongolia. Social thriftiness, as illustrated here by the Torghut, unlocks the logic of cosmological and political drives to "economize" both private and public goods in Mongolia, managing them collectively by simultaneously keeping together and generously giving them away.

Acknowledgments

I wish to thank Catherine Alexander and Daniel Sosna for their support and encouragement in the production of this chapter, and their thorough work on consecutive versions of the text. I am also very grateful to Daniel for inviting me to the great seminar on thrift in anthropology, which was held in Pilsen back in 2018, and which initiated my writing on thrift. Besides, special thanks go to Patty Gray, who carefully proofread the final version. My warmest appreciation goes also to the Torghuts for their great hospitality, openness, and friendship. Finally, I am grateful to my dear colleague Oyungerel Tangad for her support, and for our work together in Mongolia.

Tomasz Rakowski, an ethnologist and cultural anthropologist, is an Associate Professor at the Institute of Ethnology and Cultural Anthropology, University of Warsaw. He is also a medical doctor specializing in accident and emergency medicine. He is the author of two ethnographic monographs, multiple edited volumes, and peer-reviewed articles. Recently, he published *Hunters, Gatherers, and Practitioners of Powerlessness: An Ethnography of the Degraded in Postsocialist Poland* (Berghahn Books, 2016, 2019) and *Przepływy, współdziałania, kręgi możliwego: Antropologia powodzenia* (Fundacja Terytoria, 2019). He is especially interested in postsocialist transformations, vernacular forms of socioeconomic development, and social art and experimental methodology in anthropology.

Notes

1. This is also the case of oil extraction and the Christian ontology of "doing good" described by Mette High in the contemporary United States (see High 2019).

2. I conducted a large part of this fieldwork in collaboration with Dr. Oyungerel Tangad, a Mongolian-Polish ethnologist based at the Polish Academy of Sciences.
3. This term may also be defined more precisely as "a site for pasture, used by a family or a group of families." It can refer to "either one particular seasonal pasture or to the set of four seasonal pastures" (Potkański and Szynkiewicz 1993: iii–iv). It may also be treated as a very particular place, a condensation of life-streams in the place where somebody was born, meaning the soil or the stone where the yurt stood at the time of one's birth, and from where a clod was often taken to be attached later to a newborn's cradle. The Mongols are told to roll on this piece of land in order to acquire a surge in *hiimori* (Humphrey and Hürelbaatar 2012: 161; see also a beautiful film, *Zud*, directed by Marta Minorowicz 2016).
4. This is a form of temporal lease and land tenure (see Endicott 2012; for more on "temporary possession" [*ezemshil*] in Mongolia, see Empson 2018 and Plueckhahn 2019) that is different in herders' land tenure versus private companies'/citizens' land tenure, and may last for years or decades; it is usually regulated and administered by the local government, which issues a "certificate of possession" (*ezemshih erhiin gerchilgee*).
5. The kinship structure is predominantly based on a patrilineal and patrilocal principle, in paralineage groups, and was analyzed in detail by Sławoj Szynkiewicz (1981).
6. In Mongolia during the 1990s the total number of livestock increased, as did the number of people working with animal husbandry, reaching almost half of the total workforce (Sneath 2003: 442).
7. As in the case of *idesh* (i.e., the widespread phenomenon of herders providing meat for their relatives living in the cities, which is usually returned later in various forms of help to the herders' families).

References

Bonilla, Lauren, and Tuya Shadgar. 2018. "Electoral Gifting and Personal Politics in Mongolia's Parliamentary Election Season." *Central Asia Survey* 37(3): 457–74.

Bristley, Joseph. 2016. "Animalising Territory: Boundaries, Herding, and the Economy in Pastoral Mongolia." Paper presented at the International Union of Anthropological and Ethnological Sciences Congress, Dubrovnik, 4–9 May 2016.

Bumochir, Dulam. 2019. "Nationalist Sentiments Obscured by 'Pejorative Labels': Birthplace, Homeland and Mobilisation against Mining in Mongolia." *Inner Asia* 21(2): 162–79.

Bumochir, Dulam, and Rebekah Plueckhahn. 2018. "Capitalism in Mongolia—Ideology, Practice, and Ambiguity." *Central Asia Survey* 37(3): 341–56.

Chuluunbat, Narantuyan, and Rebecca Empson. 2018. "Networks and the Negotiation of Risk: Making Business Deals and People among Mongolian Small and Medium Businesses." *Central Asia Survey* 37(3): 419–37.

da Col, Giovanni. 2012. "The Poisoner and the Parasite: Cosmoeconomics, Fear, and Hospitality among Dechen Tibetans." *Journal of the Royal Anthropological Institute* 18(s1): S175–95.

de la Cadena, Marisol. 2010 "Indigenous Cosmopolitics in the Andes: Conceptual Reflections Beyond 'Politics.'" *Cultural Anthropology* 25(2): 334–70.
Empson, Rebecca. 2012. "The Danger of Excess: Accumulating and Dispersing Fortune in Mongolia." *Social Analysis* 1(56): 1–16.
———. 2014. "An Economy of Temporary Possession." Malinowski Memorial Lecture, London School of Economics, 22 May 2014. Podcast. Accessed 18 January 2019. https://www.lse.ac.uk/lse-player?id=2461.
———. 2018. "Claiming Resources, Honouring Debts: The Cosmoeconomics of Mongolia's Mineral Economy." *Ethnos* 84(2): 263–82.
Endicott, Elizabeth. 2012. *A History of Land Use in Mongolia: The Thirteenth Century to the Present.* New York: Palgrave Macmillan.
Gudeman Stephen, and Chris Hann, eds. 2018. *Oikos and Market: Explorations in Self-Sufficiency After Socialism.* New York: Berghahn Books.
Gudeman, Stephen, and Alberto Rivera. 1990. *Conversations in Colombia: The Domestic Economy in Life and Text.* Cambridge, UK: Cambridge University Press.
High, Mette M. 2013. "Polluted Money, Polluted Wealth: Emerging Regimes of Value in the Mongolian Gold Rush." *American Ethnologist* 40(4): 676–88.
———. 2019. "Projects of Devotion: Energy Exploration and Moral Ambition in the Cosmoeconomy of Oil and Gas in the Western United States." *Journal of the Royal Anthropological Institute* 25(1): 29–46.
Humphrey, Caroline. 2012. "Favors and 'Normal Heroes': The Case of Postsocialist Higher Education." *HAU: Journal of Ethnographic Theory* 2(2): 22–41.
Humphrey, Caroline, and Ujeed Hürelbaatar. 2012. "Fortune in the Wind: An Impersonal Subjectivity." *Social Analysis* 2(56): 152–67.
Ichinkhorloo, Byambabaatar. 2018. "Collaboration for Survival in the Age of the Market: Diverse Economic Practices in Postsocialist Mongolia." *Central Asia Survey* 37(3): 386–402.
Minorowicz, Marta, dir. 2016. *Zud.* Berlin: Zero One Film.
Pedersen, Morten A., and Lars Højer. 2008. "Lost in Transition: Fuzzy Property and Leaky Selves in Ulaanbaatar." *Ethnos* 73(1): 73–96.
Plueckhahn, Rebekah. 2019. "Rethinking the Anticommons: Usufruct, Profit, and the Urban." Society for Cultural Anthropology "Fieldsites" Editor's Forum. Accessed 9 September 2019. https://culanth.org/fieldsights/rethinking-the-anticommons-usufruct-profit-and-the-urban.
Potkański, Tomasz, and Slavoj Szynkiewcz. 1993. "The Social Context of Liberalisation of the Mongolian Pastoral Economy: Report of Anthropological Fieldwork." PALD Research Report No. 4. Brighton, UK: Institute for Development Studies.
Shadgar, Tuya. 2015. "Homeland Association and the Production of Informal Power in Mongolia." *Emerging Subjects Blog*, University College London. Accessed 14 May 2016. https://blogs.ucl.ac.uk/mongolian-economy/2015/11/05/homeland-associations-and-the-production-of-informal-power-in-mongolia/.
Sneath, David. 2002. "Mongolia in the 'Age of Market': Pastoral Land-use and the Development Discourse." In *Markets and Moralities: Ethnographies of Postsocialism*, edited by Ruth Mandel and Caroline Humphrey, 191–210. New York: Berg.
———. 2003. "Land-Use, the Environment and Development in Post-socialist Mongolia." *Oxford Development Studies* 31(4): 441–59.

———. 2006. "Transacting and Enacting: Corruption, Obligation and the Use of Monies in Mongolia." *Ethnos* 71(1): 89–112.

———. 2010. "Political Mobilization and the Construction of Collective Identity in Mongolia." *Central Asian Survey* 29(3): 251–67.

———. 2014. "Nationalizing Civilisational Resources: Sacred Mountains and Cosmopolitical Ritual in Mongolia." *Asian Ethnicity* 15(4): 458–72.

Stolpe, Ines, and Tumen Erdene-Ochir. 2021. "*Nutag* Councils as Post-Socialist Resilience Cultures in Mongolia." In *Horizons of Future in Post-Utopian Mongolia*, edited by Ines Stolpe and Judith Nordby, 49–114. Berlin: EB Verlag.

Szynkiewicz, Sławoj. 1981. *Rodzina pasterska w Mongolii*. Wrocław: Zakład Narodowy im. Ossolińskich.

———. 1993. "Mongolia's Nomads Built a New Society Again: Social Structures and Obligations in the Eve of the Private Economy." *Nomadic Peoples* 33: 163–72.

Tangad, Oyungerel. 2013. *Scheda po Czyngis Chanie: Demokracja po mongolsku*. Warszawa: Wydawnictwo Trio.

———. 2017. "Cultural Aspects of Democratization in Mongolia: The Ethical Perspective." *Ethnologia Polona* 37(1): 133–44.

Wasilewski, Jerzy S. 1977. "Symboliczne uniwersum jurty mongolskiej." *Etnografia Polska* (21)1: 98–116.

Waters, Hedwig A. 2018. "The Financialization of Help: Moneylenders as Economic Translators in the Debt-Based Economy." *Central Asia Survey* 37(3): 403–18.

5

Discretio and the Golden Mean

Working Out Frugality and Thrift in Two Czech Postsocialist Monasteries

Barbora Spalová

Since 2000, a few monasteries in the Czech Republic have been reestablished after their almost complete suppression in the eighteenth century and then being rendered illegal during the socialist regime. In monasteries that follow the Rule of Benedict (hereafter the *Regula*), the monks and their employees have had to reinterpret what it means to be a monastic community in the twenty-first century that follows an ancient, sixth-century rule. In this chapter, based on fieldwork in two monasteries, I focus on how they were working out the best response to the *Regula*'s directives on frugality and thrift, which might, at first sight, seem to be at odds with other moral imperatives associated with care for people, land, and the monastery itself. I explore below how the monastic communities worked out this tension between economic and spiritual logics in practice by at once distinguishing between different domains (spiritual and economic), scales (e.g., the individual soul, the monastic community, regional stewardship), and publics (guests, pilgrims, the local secular community, the public-at-large), uniting them through a shared adherence to a sense of the golden mean.

This process of reinventing monasticism in the postsocialist Czech Republic uses the very monastic spiritual technique of *discretio* (Czech: rozlišování, English: discernment). The word discretion, discernment, or discrimination is used in Christian Scriptures in the sense of distinguishing between good and evil (Heb. 5, 14). St. Benedict, Jan Cassian, and other early monastic authors blended this biblical discernment of spirits, *discretio spirituum*, with the Hellenic tradition. The Greeks had long proposed the idea of virtue in terms of moderation, defining "the good as the mean between two extremes (*aurea mediocritas*), an avoidance of excess and of all things being done in due proportion" (Wortley 2011: 637; see also Wilk's discussion of balance in this vol.). *Discretio* in monastic praxis is the discernment or understanding of what leads to God and what moves one away from him; it is finding and fulfilling the will of God without exaggeration or deficiency. It is the practice of spiritual discernment and measured decision making. "Discretio makes possible the golden mean, but not the mean of mediocrity" (Luislamp 1998: XLII).

To trace this notion of discernment and the golden mean through frugality and thrift in contemporary monasticism in the Czech Republic, I first introduce the historical context, the theoretical frame, and how thrift and frugality are defined in the Rule of St. Benedict, before moving on to explore how these ideas were discussed and played out in two monasteries.

More than seven hundred Central European monasteries were suppressed by the Enlightenment Emperor Joseph II from 1780 to 1781. The few remaining ones had to adopt "socially useful activities," which changed the face of monasticism across the region (Winter 1945; Jonveaux 2018b; Jewdokimow 2018). Perhaps we could say that a certain thriftiness was behind the emperor's actions in choosing to support or allow only those monastic orders that could demonstrate a secular "return." The economic life of surviving monastic communities was later further endangered by the land reforms of the first Czechoslovak Republic (1918–38), which reduced Roman Catholic church land properties; 16 percent of their land was sequestered and given to farmers. The real break in monastic tradition in Czechoslovakia came on 13 April 1950, under the new communist regime, after St. Bartholomew's night of consecrated life. That night all male monasteries were seized by the army and secret police, all their property confiscated, and the brothers imprisoned in internment monasteries.[1]

Female monastic orders shared the same fate, although some were allowed to care for handicapped people (Koura et al. 2014); the communist authorities apparently sharing with the enlightenment utilitarians a degree of indulgence toward orders providing socially useful activities. The male consecrated life was completely illegal until 1990. Many monastic communities could only emigrate and find asylum in another monastery to save their community. The Velvet Revolution in 1989 brought to power former dissidents such as Václav Havel but also the Catholic activist Václav Benda. The Enumeration Act in 1991 swiftly followed, which returned two hundred convent buildings to the communities but not their economic base, such as lands, forests, ponds, farms, and breweries. It took another twenty years before the Act on church property restitution and compensation was adopted in 2013. The churches, including monasteries, received 56 percent of their former land properties, and they are entitled to receive fifty-six milliards CZK, more than two milliards EUR, over the next thirty years as financial compensation. This Act started the process of the progressive separation of church and state in the Czech Republic and was the historical context for my research.

Here, I have chosen to focus on two of the eight Czech monasteries of the Benedictine tradition in which I carried out fieldwork as part of a small team (described in the acknowledgments below). During our visits, we conducted interviews with different members of the monastic communities: priors, cellarers, novice directors, and monks or employees responsible for a specialized economic field (especially forestry and food production). We also interviewed the guests of the monasteries, parishioners, tourists, as well as neighbors such as mayors, cultural managers, local activity group managers, foresters, and farmers. Another important source of knowledge was informal discussions in monastic shops and guesthouses, as well as observations. Such participant observation gave us experience, however limited, of monastic time and space, of monastic rhythms. To understand the image of monasticism in media coverage, we analyzed the mainstream newspapers, radio, and television production from 1993 (or 1996)[2] until 2018 (Spalová et al. 2016). In this text, I use terms from the book *Liquidation of the Church* (de Groot 2018), such as the "public-in-contact" (usually indicating employees, pilgrims, regular or irregular guests, friends of the monastery, and parts of the Church membership, especially other monks and nuns) and "public-at-large" (the secular neighborhood, tourists, and Czech society at large, the latter represented mostly by media coverage of its opinions and standpoints), to distinguish the level of proximity and understanding of monastic cosmologies among these two heterogeneous groups.

To understand the monastic conceptualization of frugality and thrift, the relation to work, and the ideal of a balanced life, I draw on moral anthropology or, more specifically, the anthropology of values (Dumont 1980; Graeber 2001). Heinich (2017) identifies measure, attachment, and judgment as the main forms of attribution of value. For example, the value of a monastic product can be measured and priced, but it can also have another kind of value, thanks to the attachment of the buyer to the producing monastic community. The "value of value" is therefore certainly different when it is the abbot who judges the work of a monk versus when it is a merchant who buys his work. Still, value is a concept that connects the spiritual scale, where certain values or virtues, defined in the *Regula*, lead to monks' salvation, to the economic scale, where the monastery produces different kinds of values: means for sustainability and eventually profits, which may be used for charitable aid. Fourcade's (2016) discussion of value as a concept that connects ethics and economics is helpful here. The difference between values on the moral/spiritual scale and values on the economic scale is in the potential of different values for the self-constitution of moral subjects. If a monk discerns the will of God in the question of how frugal his life should be, it makes him God's disciple. If he decides the same question with the help of the monastery's balance sheet, it might constitute him as a good manager, but it does not necessarily touch his moral subjectivity. It is this connection between values in action and cosmologies of monastic worlds that I trace in order to understand the ethical condition (Lambek 2015) of monastic frugality and thrift. Even if the monastic worlds would rather be considered as "total institutions" with a given hierarchy of values, where spiritual values encompass the economic ones, I want to show that there is still enough place for the morality of freedom (Robbins 2012: 119) through the means of spiritual discretion. However, first I turn to how thrift and frugality appear in the *Regula.*

Frugality and Thrift in the Rule of St. Benedict

Let us hear first the words of the *Regula,* which are cited every day in monastic communities, and which are the most important source for the reinterpretation of tradition in contemporary monasteries.

Frugality (in Czech *střídmost,* etym. from mean, middle) is present here as one of the virtues necessary for a monk or nun to achieve peace and to develop *the instruments of good works* (Rule of St. Benedict [hereafter RB] 4), such as obedience, silence, and humility: "Let there be chosen from the brotherhood as Cellarer of the monastery a wise man, of settled habits, temperate and *frugal* [*lat. sobrius*], not conceited, irritable, resentful, sluggish, or wasteful, but fearing God, who may be as a father to the whole brotherhood" (RB 31, 1). Frugality-as-temperance is presented here as a sign of man fearing God; it is both a condition and a consequence of an intensive, good spiritual life. Therefore, it is important to underline that frugality here is a spiritual value, as well as the work (*labora*) itself: "Idleness is the enemy of the soul; and therefore the brethren ought to be employed in manual labor at certain times, at others, in devout reading" (RB 48, 1). Work was considered, during the time of St. Benedict, a humiliating activity for slaves, but it is valued here as a weapon against the vice of idleness.[3]

Thrift (in Czech *šetrnost, šetření,* etym. from to carefully observe, take care of something) is addressed in the *Regula* only indirectly as the quality of using money and other resources carefully and not wastefully: "Let him regard all the utensils of the monastery and its whole property as if they were the sacred vessels of the altar" (RB 31, 10). Thriftiness as careful management of the monastic resources appears in the *Regula* also as an example of how obedience, self-discipline, and humility should be practiced. The *Regula* anticipates quotidian life very specifically:

> When anyone is engaged in any sort of work, whether in the kitchen, in the cellar, in a shop, in the bakery, in the garden, while working at some craft, or in any other place, and she commits some fault, or breaks something, or loses something, or transgresses in any other way whatsoever, if she does not come immediately before the Abbess and the community of her own accord to make satisfaction and confess her fault, then when it becomes known through another, let her be subjected to a more severe correction. (RB 46, 1–4)

The problems of thrifty, careful management are here described as typical situations in monasteries, but they are not primarily problematized because of the loss or damage of the property; it is rather because of the possible (and actually not unusual) temptation of hiding the sin and engaging in self-justification. Again, thriftiness here is not the goal; it is just a means by which to achieve a peaceful life in the monastery and the spiritual growth of individuals.

Frugality and Thrift in Two Different Monasteries

To compare how thrift and frugality are lived and understood in contemporary monasteries, I chose male monasteries, one Cistercian and one Trappist. The orders differ slightly in their spirituality. Both are reformist, seeking the original strict observance of the *Regula*. Thus, the Cistercians branched away from the Benedictines in the eleventh century, and the Trappists, in turn, moved away from the Cistercians in the seventeenth century to renew the tradition. However, historical differences between the places and communities are even more important.

Vyšší Brod, a Cistercian monastery, was founded in 1259 by Wilhering in Austria and is a few kilometers from the Czech-Austrian border. It survived the abolition of monastic orders by Joseph II, but, as with all the other monasteries, was closed down in 1950 by the communist regime, which used the buildings for farming, later establishing a secular museum of monastic culture in the complex's Gothic core. The rest of the community escaped to Austria and continued in the monastery of Rein, near Graz. In 1990, two of the old monks returned to Vyšší Brod and started afresh, slowly building a new community, which today has five monks and two postulants. With a new prior, and while maintaining intensive contact with the Heiligenkreuz monastery in Austria, where the novices from Vyšší Brod accomplish their novitiate, the community started to become more and more traditionalist in the sense of practicing the exclusively Latin Tridentine liturgy. It eventually became an important place for Lefevbristes[4] and other traditionalist networks in the Czech Republic, Austria, and Germany, as well as France, Italy, and the Netherlands.

In 2014, a considerable number of forests (about 3,500 hectares), as well as fields and ponds, were restored to the Cistercians thanks to the restitution law. The monastery founded a company, Bernardinum, to take care of this property, which quickly became the main source of its income (50–90 percent, depending on investments and changes on the timber market). They also rented out their farmlands, developed fish farming (5–25 percent of their income), sold the water and electricity from their water turbine (4–10 percent), and ran tourism and pilgrim businesses (1–15 percent). Around thirty thousand visitors per year are attracted by the huge national heritage complex, one of the largest baroque libraries in the Czech Republic, with fine Gothic pieces of art. The monastery employs about thirty lay people to work in the forests, as guides in the monastery, and as managers.

Nový Dvůr was founded in 2002 from Sept-Fons in France as the first Trappist monastery in the Czech Republic and the first new monastic foundation after six hundred years. Situated in a sparsely populated area of the former western Sudetenland, the monastery is isolated from the world by the ring of forestland around the buildings that they bought as a "natural enclosure." Its spirituality can be labeled as neo-fundamentalist and strictly contemplative. This proved attractive for many relatively young postulants.

Figure 5.1. Monastery of Vyšší Brod. Photo by Jan Schlitz. © Jana Schlitzová.

Figure 5.2. Nový Dvůr monastery. © Tereza Sedláčková.

The community has around thirty monks and novices altogether. The ideal of a simple concentrated life was also expressed by the minimalist architecture of their newly built complex. The community's income came from the production of organic cosmetics (50 percent), biocertified mustards (40 percent), forestry products, and cow and sheep breeding (10 percent). Only monks worked in all these branches because they did not want to employ outside workers, in order to preserve the monastic space intact. With the help of monastic market networks, they mostly sold their products in France, Germany, the United States, and Canada.

When discussing the economic management of the monasteries, or just the daily life of the communities, I often noticed that my interlocutors needed to exercise some moral judgments to discern the right measure or golden mean of frugality in the quotidian life. The topic reappeared in the legitimizations of thriftiness and generosity in the monastery's economic management. By analyzing these situations, I reveal the limits of frugality and thriftiness (see the Introduction to this vol.) in contemporary monastic worlds.

I first came, as a researcher with my team members, to Vyšší Brod in spring 2017. The prior took us to his office, gave us about fifteen minutes of a very general talk about Cistercians, and then called Mr. Franz, the curator of the Vyšší Brod museum and art gallery, who showed us the artistic beauties of the monastery. We could not stay in the guesthouse because, the prior said, "it is too sober"; and we could not eat in the monastery, as they did not provide meals for guests. The prior expected that, as researchers from a secular university, we were only interested in history and art.

When we returned in November the same year, the monastery's lands had been completely dug up. When the monastery started its forestry enterprise with the restored forests, the monks built a new wood-burning boiler house, and now they were installing heating pipes to the many buildings of the monastery complex. The director of the Bernardinum Company guided us through the mud of the construction and showed us the works with great enthusiasm. The prior then explained: "It was necessary, because electric heating is terribly expensive and, in addition, the old Gothic and Baroque buildings will not heat up enough using electric heating. In winter it was only thirteen degrees [°C] in the cells. The Cistercians do follow strict observance, but we would like to have at least sixteen degrees" (Prior of Vyšší Brod, November 2017). This story is typical for monasteries of the Benedictine tradition, because Benedictinism is not an ascetic order;[5] even if the knowledge and practice of desert ascetics inspired St. Benedict when writing the *Regula*, all the communities must ask and find for themselves the right moral measure of frugality. Such discretion and negotiation took place on many levels. First, there was the constant work of the monks' community, and especially of the superiors, to discern the golden mean in frugality, which would serve each monk to achieve the purpose of his life. This negotiation was based on interpretation of the *Regula* and the specific tradition of the given community, taking the historical place and moment into account. Monastic frugality is also a value for the publics with whom they are in contact, such as guests and pilgrims, a way to see how the lived ideal can help them in their everyday Christian lives. It pushed the monks to reflect on the morality of their frugality and to perform it for this audience. And there was also the public-at-large represented by the local secular neighborhood as well as the media that was focused on church property restitution or the historical heritage held by the monasteries. The public-at-large was mostly convinced that monks should live in poverty (the difference between contemplative and mendicant orders is known only to the public-in-contact), and if they did have some money, it would be moral only if they invested it in the maintenance of the (national) historical heritage.

The criteria of such discerning and searching for moral frugality in the sense of the golden mean, avoiding both extremes of asceticism and intemperance,[6] were explained to us by the prior later when I directly asked what frugality meant for them:

> Saint Benedict says: no uselessness, just what you need—a roof over your head, a chapel or a church where you will serve the Holy Mass. We do not need anything extra; we have robes, we do not go on holiday, we have a kitchen here, basic food. We must have a livelihood, nothing luxurious. The monk must not own any property;

> we have no property other than what we have in common. And at the same time, *we should have requirements that would really stand up before God.* And then the monastery must have it [i.e., the monastery must have enough money to cover such expenses], like a dentist. The dentist also costs a lot of money today. (Prior of Vyšší Brod, April 2019)

Not needing "anything extra" in Vyšší Brod meant considerable renunciation of comfort: a cell with a bed and table (and now sixteen degrees of warmth), no Internet, daily work in the monastic enclosure, three meals, rising at 4:00 a.m. If a monk had a wish or requirement, it became a space for spiritual discernment as to whether this wish would be acknowledged by God or not. Every such discernment then helped to create and form the moral self of the monk in dialogue with God. The *Regula* intends that frugality should be lived not primarily as an economic value, but as a spiritual one. Many choices in the monastery were routinized, and the monks had "only" to obey the established moral order. This is the realm of morality of reproduction, in Robbins' words (Robbins 2012: 118). However, there remained considerable leeway for a morality of freedom (Robbins 2012: 119) in situations when the monks had to make a moral choice. It might be argued that monastic life in the Czech Republic is not yet sufficiently established; but the morality of freedom is inherent to the *Regula*. The established order should provide the monks with a firm structure that enables them to freely navigate their spiritual seeking without getting lost.

Our first experiences in Nový Dvůr, the Trappist monastery, were quite different. It was March 2017, and we were driving around in circles on ever-worsening roads deep in the snow before we discovered a stone cross delimiting the sacred space of the monastery. After a final hill, we enjoyed the view of an impressive, white building in the middle of nowhere. There were no cars in the parking lot; the place was gravely silent. We rang the bell of the guesthouse. After a considerable while, a smiling and speaking (we were surprised because strict silence is usually applied in this monastery) monk came and brought us to our rooms. The guesthouse was rebuilt from a former sheep pen, divided into two parts, one for men, one for women. Each of us received a beautiful, single room with a huge window opening to the meadows and forests, a Bible, and a statuette of the Virgin Mary. We also received a list of prayers with a notice that Matins at 3:15 a.m. was only for men, because it was an intimate space for monks and, according to the brother who received us, "it could be too early for women." We came to a later prayer time in the church. As one of our team wrote later:

> I see this image very clearly. We sit in the church of the Trappist abbey of Nový Dvůr and the brothers pray the vespers. The day comes to an end. I feel very physically how the church sinks into silence. While monks sing and their deep voices vibrate in my chest, the light coming to the gleaming white church from outside slowly fades.

> I observe it. The white color everywhere around me becomes first slightly blue, then grey, then finally disappears in the darkness. The only object standing out from the gloom is the statue of the Virgin on the column at the altar. The simple but kind face on the white column shines from the dark. Her golden crown seems to be a star in the darkness, a vessel on the troubled sea of the days. (Jan Tesárek's fieldnotes, March 2017)

I cite these fieldnotes to show the impact of the building, which was designed to glorify God and to create a profound spiritual effect in worshippers with or without a Christian background. The building was rather expensive, but the community judged this investment to be moral, because beauty was, in their perception and experience, a special value. The monks, as well as the visitors, felt *attached* (one of the forms of attributing value defined by Heinich 2017) to the building of the monastery and to the feelings, experiences, and situations mediated by the building. The beauty expressed by the materiality of the monastery should communicate the simple beauty of the contemplative life, the simple beauty of God.

Over the course of three days, we were served wonderful meals in the guesthouse (the cook was one of the French monks, and guests received better meals than the brothers, according to the rules of hospitality; see below), we enjoyed the rhythm of the monastic life (especially as women who only attended at 6:00 a.m. for Lauds), and we experienced silence.

Figure 5.3. Beauty of consecrated life presented on the website of Nový Dvůr. Photo by a Nový Dvůr monk. Republished with the kind permission of the Nový Dvůr monastery.

At the end of our visit, we had an interview with Father Prokop, a former sociologist, who gave us a basic outline of the quotidian life of the monks: "Nobody can pray all day. You need the work, especially the physical work outdoors. For young monks, the best is to work with animals, because the sheep will not say what they need. You must observe them carefully and understand. And it is also a perfect school for young monks to learn community life" (Father Prokop, March 2017). Work is presented here not as economic activity, but as a balancing activity to prayer and as training for community life. "The monk has to open the eyes and take care," emphasized Dom Samuel, abbot of Nový Dvůr, whom we met two years later to discuss the economy of the monastery. We were rather impressed by the spontaneity of his explanation:

> We know that one monk in our monastery costs 800 EUR per month, which seems to be quite a lot for a Trappist monk. But it includes the running of the guesthouse, the hospital, the church, the school for novices. . . . If you live in a family, you don't have to pay for the running of the hospital. Without these costs, it would be only 320 EUR per monk per month (Dom Samuel, March 2019).

The fact that the abbot knew precisely how much they spent for the everyday life of a monk proves that the right, balanced frugality is an important value discussed in the community. He wanted to legitimize for us why they were spending so much (when the average monthly wage in the Czech Republic in 2018 was 1,027 EUR). He also wanted us to know that they had only three cars for thirty monks, did not eat meat except for fish twice a week, and ate eggs once a week.[7]

The problem of what constitutes a moral (favorable for spiritual life) standard of living is as old as monasticism itself. A French monk from the Bellefontaine monastery, Bertrand Rollin, OSB, wrote in 1975: "To keep the ability to control our standard of living is at the same time the consequence and the condition of the spiritual atmosphere of all of us and every member. We have to bear this witness" (Rollin 2013: 175). Later, during our interview, Dom Samuel developed the main topic—what I call the moral standard of living—into its relational and spiritual consequences. We asked why they chose to sleep in the common dormitory when contemporary Trappist monasteries usually respect the individual needs of monks by providing them with cells:

> If we would have to build thirty cells, it would cost five million, while the dormitory cost only one million. It's not easy; one must learn not to snore, not to wake up the others. I snored a bit in December; the brothers banished me from the dormitory, so I slept in the office, on the ground, because I didn't want to take a room in the guesthouse" (Dom Samuel).

Frugality becomes here the space for respect toward others, for self-humiliation, for obedience. It is not only a question of the approved standard (which is frugal) but a question of the individual acceptance and performance of the standard without making individual adherence to the standard a norm for others (even if it is the abbot who speaks). The *Regula* is very careful about individual abilities and differences, as in its famous section: "'Everyone has her own gift from God, one in this way and another in that' (1 Cor. 7:7)." It is therefore with some misgiving that we regulate the measure of others' sustenance. Nevertheless, keeping in view the needs of the weak, we believe that a *hemina*[8] of wine a day is sufficient for each. But those to whom God gives the strength to abstain should know that they will receive a special reward" (RB 40, 1–4). The norm is a guideline through which both the weak and the strong can be accommodated; crucially, it is not an absolute but a relative norm. The monk should be as frugal as he can; more would be inappropriate for him and immoral for his superior to ask of him. Frugality is a value in monastic life if it leads practitioners to connect with God. It can be valuable as training in self-control, it leads to the "simple life," and it also has potential for a peaceful life in community because it can be lived as a form of respect for others, as personal humility, and as obedience to the hierarchy. But as a norm, it should respect individual capacities and needs. As described above, moral frugality emerges through *discretio* in the relationships between the monastic community, their public-in-contact, and the public-at-large, as well as from the relations inside the community: between superiors and monks, between monks of different maturity, and especially between monks and God.

Management of the Monastery: Thriftiness and Generosity

The economic management of Vyšší Brod, the Cistercian monastery, was in the charge of a prior with a theological education and rather conservative ideas on the economy ("we will invest only when we have saved up enough money; we don't take credit, we cannot put a strain on future generations"). He managed the forests in cooperation with the employees of the company Bernardinum, especially with the forest engineer, Mr. Dušek, who was experienced in the global timber trade. It brought some moral clashes and negotiations, as well as an effective differentiation of their roles. The forest engineer was responsible for profit-making (and had to prove his successful management in capitalist terms to the supervisors from the neighboring Austrian monastery in Schlägl). The prior was responsible for the moral limits of this profit-making: no work on Sunday (not even tourist visits to the monastery), well paid and secure jobs for employees, benefits for local people, and no profit to be made from pilgrims and believers coming to the monastery for feasts and other occasions, especially believers with big Catholic families. The value of balanced forest management emerged precisely from these negotiations, which also included collective deliberation about what sustainable management of the forests means. Practically, that meant reinvesting about 30 percent of the profits in the forest; maintaining and educating a stable team of workers; managing the forest according to the high standards of the Forest Stewardship Council (FSC) in order to obtain their certification; and selling the timber for correspondingly higher prices.

In February 2019, the Supreme Court of the Czech Republic reopened the question of monastic property and decided to take back 2,000 hectares of monastic forests (from the total of 3,500 ha), arguing that the restitution in 2013 had not been legitimate. The monastery appealed this verdict. I went to Vyšší Brod in April 2019 to see how they were managing this situation. Mr. Dušek was very worried about it; he planned to scale back the company and tried to restructure the portfolio of services it offered. Then I discussed it with the prior, who was disgusted by the judge's verdict, saying that she had "old-style thinking" (meaning communist thinking). He seemed to be persuaded that they would win the appeal. During our discussion in the rooms of the Bernardinum Company, one of the foresters it employed, who would remain employed even if "his" forest became state property again, came into the room. The prior greeted him and said: "We will win it, Mr. Skočdopole, we do believe!" Mr. Skočdopole smiled, but evidently was not assured. When he left, the prior explained to me that he did not want to release these people: he had invested in the team, and it would be better to pay them for the year or two it would take before they got the forests back than to build the team again; they had families to support.

I cite this moment as an example of the unusual economic behavior that illustrates the different framing of the monastic management lived by the prior versus the people experienced in the secular management of a company. The difference was often not significant, but there were still different values, different time frames, and a different placement of trust: in the Providence of God or in the state.

In 2019, the monastery was still recovering from the devastation of the communist era. Income was used to maintain (and eventually to develop slowly) the business and to cover the minimal needs of the small community, but mostly to repair the complex of buildings. The moral imperative to repair and maintain all that had historically belonged to the monastery was strongly internalized by the monks, but it was also expected by the broader society: the mayor and town inhabitants spoke about it in interviews, sponsors gave money almost exclusively for restoration work, politicians used it as the only common-sense argument for why the church should receive any money. Even if it is hard to find a new use for a historical windmill or pharmacy, the moral pact between the community and the public-at-large that it should be repaired and ideally also somehow used was hard to break. However, the exorbitant cost of the restoration work[9] unbalanced the management of the monastery, which invested a disproportionately large amount of its income in the renovation.

Figure 5.4. Restoration of the altar in the Vyšší Brod monastery. © Marek Liška.

The management of Nový Dvůr, the Trappist monastery, was fully in the hands of the monks who created the company Labora to produce and sell monastic products (mustards, cosmetics, mutton jerky). Jonveaux (2011: 435–55) describes this economy as charismatic; the prices of the products reflect the charisma of their producers: the monks are rare, chosen by God, spiritual virtuosos. The monastic shop webpage says: "Discover our products: it will be a joy for you and your relatives, and you will support the life of the monastic community by your purchase."[10] When I first heard that a community of thirty monks living in a huge complex supported themselves through the production and sale of mustards, I could hardly believe it. Moreover, the monks worked only about five to six hours per day, because they spent more time praying, while young monks spent half of this work time studying; being such a young community, therefore, made it all the more economically difficult. Only a few monks were employed in profitable production, which requires expertise, and even those monks did not work every day in the laboratories, because they also needed to work outdoors to achieve the "right balance of the monastic life," as Father Prokop explained to us during our first meeting. To survive and even make some profit, you must live thriftily; it was thus sensible for the individual lives of the monks to be governed by the virtue of frugality, and for frugality to be exercised in the management of the building. Maintenance work was done by the monks, heat was provided by burning wood from their forests, they produced part of the food, wasted nothing, shared everything, and worked effectively. As Dom Samuel told us: "We don't have much time for work, everything should be done as quick as a flash."

Thanks to this combination of thrifty living with a charismatic economy that relied on global monastic networks, they were able not only to survive, but even to generate some surplus. Thirty percent of this surplus was then designated "to people in need":

> . . . to our monasteries, for example in Africa, or to an organization helping socially excluded people in the neighboring village Dobra Voda, or to families close to us. Now, as there was a financial crisis, we too lack a few million in our budget,[11] but we keep giving to the families because it is important to them. Brother Theofan can wait for a new digger, but those families can't. (Father Prokop, March 2017)

The monastery received donations, but these were designated only for construction: the complex was not yet ready, as new parts, such as the guests' chapel, were still being built.

Management of monasteries should cover the costs of frugal community life and the costs of "services" provided by the monasteries to the broader society: in Vyšší Brod the "service" consisted mostly in maintaining and keeping partly open the national heritage complex, while in Nový Dvůr it was more about social aid to neighbors and receiving guests. Thriftiness can be morally applied to the needs of community, but not so much to the "services." And even in the realm of the needs of the community, thriftiness has some clear moral limits.

The Limits of Thriftiness

The monks more or less took for granted that they should live frugally and thriftily, and this was also a response to public expectations. Perhaps for this reason, in exchanges with us, they placed more emphasis on the limits of frugality and thriftiness. I conclude the ethnographic sections of this chapter with an overview of the spheres where thriftiness would be immoral because these delimitations reveal the hierarchically organized landscape of lived monastic values. First and foremost, thriftiness was inappropriate within the sacred sphere, when God was being glorified, but this was also the case when considering social justice, receiving guests,[12] maintaining heritage, or acting as stewards of the region.

The Sacred Sphere

The glorification of God is the main and eternal purpose of the monastic institution and the central preoccupation of monks, which lasts after death and even beyond the end of the world. Work and all economic activities were introduced into monastic life to enable the monks to pray constantly, and they are subordinated to this higher purpose in the *Regula* as well as in the contemporary practice of both monasteries. The most significant example is the celebration of the Divine Liturgy, which is the central point of every day in monastic communities. In Vyšší Brod, even if they did not have enough money to heat their cells to more than thirteen degrees in the winter, they would pay a professional orchestra to embellish the liturgy for their feasts. The director of the Prague Conservatory, Mr. Churáček, a great admirer of baroque sacred music who came regularly to Vyšší Brod to play the organ during the masses, said: "Five, six times a year I plan some bigger festivities, where I get professionals. The monastery will help us economically because Father Justin said *we do not spare money when it concerns the Lord God*. . . . I think the same and very much like it" (Mr. Churáček, organist, May 2019). In Nový Dvůr, the mass, especially Sunday mass, can be the reason why some monks do not work during the preceding days, because they are rehearsing Gregorian chants for the special occasion. Simple, clear beauty in liturgy, architecture, the arrangement of the surroundings, or even the beauty of the handmade paper used for letters from the abbot to friends of the monastery—everything should translate the beauty of the Lord and his Order.

Social Justice

"To relieve the poor" is one of the basic "instruments of good works" cited in chapter IV of the *Regula.* The monastery is responsible for the poor: "the cellarer will have to render an account for all these on the Day of Judgment" (RB 31, 9). The poor no longer usually sit at the church door, but they still come, and they are helped by the monastic community; in Nový Dvůr, it is through regular financial support of families in trouble, while in Vyšší Brod, they support the people in need by providing them wood for free.

The story of the organization Český Západ (Czech West) helping the Roma inhabitants of the village Dobrá Voda was also an expression of this vocation for charity. When the community of monks started to build the monastery in Nový Dvůr, they realized that just a few kilometers away, Roma families lived in an abandoned house in an area without work or the possibility of mobility. As they are not a pastoral order, they founded the secular, nonprofit organization Český Západ to assure social services, and called upon the Order of Oblates of the Immaculate Mary to provide pastoral care. In 2019, Český Západ was financed mostly by state grants for social work, but the Trappists also continued to help them financially.

Receiving Guests

"Let all guests who arrive be received like Christ," says the *Regula* (RB 53, 1). Both monasteries received guests, and neither realized financial profit from it: In Nový Dvůr the balance of income and expenses of the guesthouse was around zero; in Vyšší Brod the expenses were higher.[13] Both also served meals for guests. In Nový Dvůr, the guesthouse accepted the families and friends of brothers; male seekers of seclusion for prayer, contemplation, and silence; groups coming for spiritual retreats; and from time to time, also some researchers. In Vyšší Brod, the guests were mostly faithful families coming to celebrate Easter, Pentecost, or Christmas, or male seekers of traditionalist spirituality.

What interested us were the explanations for why it was impossible to make a profit on guests. In both monasteries, the men who were seeking their vocation to live with them were charged either nothing or very little. A similar view was taken of families, especially those with many children. It was moral to cover the expenses connected with the stay of guests, but anything else should be freely donated by guests.

Maintaining Heritage

The monasteries were also limited in their potential economic growth by the shared commitment to maintain the heritage of their predecessors as described above. At first sight, it can look like thrifty behavior to keep and use everything that they have inherited in order to hand it on to the next generation. But in reality, it is often the main economic burden. Especially in Vyšší Brod, it consumed all the surpluses of the budget to maintain the buildings, even though the community, which was ten times smaller than before World War II, hardly used them all. The commitment to maintain and eventually develop the heritage of the community caused the monks to embrace the historical monuments as well as the surrounding land; therefore, the monastic management of fields and forests became known globally as having a high ecological standard, which also inspires secular society (Hervieu-Léger 2017: 615–50).

This monastic commitment should be understood within the framework of a special monastic temporality that overarches the centuries of more or less continuous functioning of the monastery in that same place, and that connects this worldliness to the eternal horizons of Parousia, the Second Coming of Christ to the world. But what is conceived in such a monastic framing as their community heritage may also be seen as national or European or even planetary heritage when regarded on different levels or perspectives or scales. On the economic scale, "heritage" could bring in some income; but it also complicated the situation through numerous norms and obligations that were often in conflict with the internal norms and values of the monastery (for example, the monastery could get money from the state to repair the altar, but they could not then move the altar to another chapel where they could use it more frequently).

Acting as Stewards

The last sphere that relativizes the thriftiness of monastic management is the embedded position of the monastery as a steward of the region. This position comes from the special Benedictine vow of stability, which means that a monk entering a particular community lives there for his whole life. Stability necessitates a special economy (Spalová and Jonveaux 2018) and responsibility for the region and local society. It is internalized by the communities and also expected by people living nearby. Thus, it seems to be "natural" that the monastery would employ local people, giving them good wages and other benefits, and that it would be a place of prosperity, investing money in the local market, place, and society.

Conclusion: The Ethical Condition of the Monastic Balanced Life

Contemporary monasticism is particularly concerned with the balanced life: frugal, but not too much, not for everybody in the same way; thrifty, but not too much, not in every sphere of monastic life in the same way—the Christian golden mean achieved by practicing *discretio*. These efforts to find, through spiritual discernment, the right measure and right limits for the everyday life of the monks and nuns, as well as for the life of long-lasting monastic communities, are the first step. For the second step, the monks and nuns need to embrace these limits, voluntarily and somehow happily submitting to them. The second step is crucial for the reflected authenticity of the monastic life as well as for the plausibility of monasticism in the eyes of the public-in-contact. It is this morality of freedom that makes it authentic.

Frugality, as a means to achieve self-control over the monk's body, becomes interpreted more as the possibility of self-fulfillment through the simple life leading to peace and God. The autonomy of the individual is rediscovered in the *Regula*. An individually calibrated frugality for every monk or nun is valorized by the intensity of the individual spiritual life, while it also makes peace and respect possible in the monastic community.

The same connection functions on the level of thrifty management of the monastery. It is important for the community to control and to assure that their needs are met in the short- and long-term, but this exercise also allows the community to invest its surpluses in charitable work or in the maintenance of heritage. Limiting the needs of the monastic community also means opening it to the needs of others.

The monks and nuns were living according to a text from the sixth century, but they were also children of their time (and space). The balanced life lived in harmony with surroundings was one of the contemporary phases of the genealogy of Christian instructions on how to live a good, moral life. It was important in the dynamics of the monastic community, because men and women usually entered the monasteries to achieve a balanced life and therefore to be able to meet God; yet it was also something that the visitors to the monasteries expected. These inner and outer expectations helped to create the ethical condition for a monastic balanced life in which individual frugality and collective thrifty management and generosity have their place. Monastic worlds provide us with an example of frugality that is subordinated to the more prominent religious values (salvation of souls) and encompasses less important values like economic sustainability or profit. The Benedictines think that such an order of values is something needed in the contemporary world. To conclude with the words of a Benedictine sister:

> Clearly the whole world needs Benedictinism again, it needs a mindset that cares for the tools of life "as if they were vessels of the altar." We need a sense of balance, of sufficiency, of stewardship, and a sense of the eternal presence of God. We need a life lived in harmony with the seasons, the sun, the self, and the other. (Chittister 2006)

Acknowledgments

This chapter draws on the project "Dynamics of the Church's moral economy in the Czech Republic and Slovakia in the context of restitutions and the separation of church and state," financed by the Czech Science Foundation, no. 19-08512S. I am deeply grateful to Catherine Alexander and Daniel Sosna for their support and for opening my scientific and other horizons when writing the text. Thanks also to Isabelle Jonveaux, who introduced me to the realm of the sociology of monasticism and shared the fieldwork with me. Thanks to my colleagues from the Institute of Sociological Studies who were involved (and opened to enchantment) in our monastic research collegium: Marek Liška, Tereza Picková, Tereza Sedláčková, and Jan Tesárek. Thanks to the brothers and sisters, other research participants, and God for their patience with the researchers and for much inspiration.

Barbora Spalová studied ethnology and social anthropology in Prague. She does research in the field of anthropology of religion, particularly the anthropology of Christianity. She is also involved in border studies and memory studies. She lives in the Czech-Polish-German borderland. She is the editor-in-chief of the qualitative research journal *Biograf.* She works at the Faculty of Social Sciences, Charles University Prague.

Notes

1. Operation K (for male religious orders) and Operation Ř (for female orders) were planned several months in advance by the Czechoslovak secret police with the aim of discrediting the Catholic Church. On 5 April 1950, ten senior representatives from different orders were sentenced to death or life imprisonment as pro-Vatican spies. That same night, 2,376 brothers and 4,262 sisters were taken to "centralization monasteries" (i.e., labor camps).
2. We used the Newton Media database, which covers some media providers from 1993 and others only from 1996. We searched using the names of the monasteries as keywords. We analyzed content units for Vyšší Brod and for Nový Dvůr.
3. Later, between the eleventh and thirteenth centuries, manual work was further valued as an opportunity to practice humility, according to a new interpretation of the *Regula* during the monastic reform, which give birth to the Order of strict

observance: Cistercians (Le Goff [1999] 2014). Today, work is mainly valued as a counterbalance to prayer, as a means to achieve a balanced life.

4. Lefebvriste is the popular name for the members and sympathizers of the Society of Saint Pius X (Latin: *Fraternitas Sacerdotalis Sancti Pii X*), also known as the SSPX, or the FSSPX, which is an international priestly fraternity founded in 1970 by Marcel Lefebvre, the French archbishop. The Fraternity aims to protect the church from modernist influences introduced, according to them, by the Second Vatican Council.
5. In the words of a contemporary Benedictine scholar: "We strive for the love of God, not for the ascetic exercise" (Luislamp 1998). Also, Jonveaux (2018a) documents the very free and individualistic, partly reluctant, relationship of contemporary monks and nuns to the ascetic tradition. She reflects on the decline of ascetic practices in religious institutions and the rise of secular asceticism (diets, fasting, body cleansing) in western societies.
6. The opposite of frugality in the words of the *Regula* is *crapula*, meaning excessive intemperance, indulgence, mostly in the sense of eating and drinking (it is mentioned in the chapter "On the measure of food," RB 39). The *Regula* calls here upon the authority of the Gospel: "See to it that your hearts be not burdened with over-indulgence" (Luke 21:34).
7. It is important to say that they did not include in these figures the money they spent on construction. Construction is possible thanks to gifts from the mother monastery or other Trappist monasteries, as well as individual givers, but it is not a part of the budget that is funded by income produced by monks.
8. A *hemina* is an ancient Roman measure equivalent to about a third of a liter or ten ounces.
9. Of course, the Cistercians were not the only investors in the restoration of the complex. In 2002, the Association for the Support of the Cistercian Monastery Vyšší Brod/Hohenfurth was founded in the neighboring Austrian city of Linz, and it has helped to finance the restoration work up to the present. Also, the municipality and the Czech state began investing in the restoration of this national monument at the turn of the millennium.
10. See the Nový Dvůr monastic shop webpage at https://www.novydvur-obchod.cz/ (last accessed 1 November 2021).
11. He meant they had sold less than usual because of the financial crisis.
12. This is mandated by the demand of hospitality in the *Regula*.
13. This is not the only possible monastic model. Some monasteries, also in the Czech Republic, turned their guesthouses into regular commercial hotels (Břevnov, Broumov), while others kept them as monastic accommodation, but still used them as an important source of income (Venio). In Italy, most monasteries have both: touristic hotel and monastic guesthouse.

References

Chittister, Joan (OSB). 2006. "A Benedictine Consciousness Whose Time Has Come—Again." In *Listening to the Earth: An Environmental Audit for Benedictine Com-*

munities, edited by William L. Bartlett, Margarita Dangel (OSB), Pat Lupo (OSB), and Annette Marshall (OSB), VII–VIII. Erie, PA: Lake Erie-Allegheny Earth Force.
de Groot, Kees. 2018. *Liquidation of the Church*. London: Routledge.
Dumont, Louis. 1980. "On Value." *Proceedings of the British Academy* 66: 207–41.
Fourcade, Marion. 2016. "The Fly and the Cookie: Alignment and Unhingement in 21st-Century Capitalism." *Socio-Economic Review* 15(3): 661–78.
Graeber, David. 2001. *Toward an Anthropological Theory of Value: The False Coin of Our Dreams*. New York: Palgrave Macmillan.
Heinich, Nathalie. 2017. *Des valeurs: Une approche sociologique* [Values: Sociological Approach]. Paris: Éditions Gallimard.
Hervieu-Léger, Danièle. 2017. *Le temps de moines: Clôture et hospitalité* [Time of Monks: Enclosure and Hospitality]. Paris: PUF.
Hervieu-Léger, Danièle, and Bertrand Hervieu. 1983. *Des communautés pour les temps difficiles: Néo-ruraux ou nouveaux moines* [Communities for Difficult Times: Neo-rurals or New Monks]. Paris: Le Centurion.
Jewdokimow, Marcin. 2018. *Klasztor w perspektywie socjologicznej: W poszukiwaniu nowego ujęcia* [Monastery in Sociological Perspective: Searching for New Roads]. Warszawa: Wydawnictwo naukowe UKSW.
Jonveaux, Isabelle. 2011. *Le monastere au travail* [Monastery at Work]. Paris: Bayard
———. 2018a. *Moines: Corps et âme* [Monks: Body and Soul]. Paris: Les éditions du Cerf.
———. 2018b. *Mőnch sein heute: Eine Sociologie des Mőnchtums in Ősterreich im europäischen Dilaog* [To Be a Monk Today: Sociology of Monasticism in Austria in European Dialogue]. Würzburg: Echter.
Koura, Petr, David Lorenc, Jan Stříbrný, Jaroslav Šebek, Vladimíra Vaníčková, and Stanislava Vodičková. 2014. *Diktatura versus naděje: Pronásledování římskokatolické církve v Československu v letech 1948–1989* [Dictatorship versus Hope: Persecution of Roman Catholic Church in Czechoslovakia 1948–1989]. Praha: Ústav pro studium totalitních režimů.
Lambek, Michael. 2015. *The Ethical Condition: Essays on Action, Person, and Value*. Chicago: University of Chicago Press.
Le Goff, Jacques. [1999] 2014. "Práce" [Work]. In *Encyklopedie středověku* [Dictionary of Middle Ages], edited by Jacques Le Goff and Jean-Claude Schmitt, 515–24. Praha: Vyšehrad.
Luislamp, Pia. 1998. "Spiritualita Řehole Benediktovy" [The Spirituality of the Rule of Benedict]. In *Regula Benedicti*. Praha: Beuroner Kunstverlag & Benediktinské arciopatství sv. Vojtěcha a sv. Markéty v Praze–Břevnově.
Mumford, Lewis, and Langdon Winner. 2010. *Technics and Civilization*. Reprint ed. Chicago: University of Chicago Press.
Palmisano, Stefania. 2015. *Exploring New Monastic Communities: The (Re)invention of Tradition*. New York: Routledge.
Robbins, Joel. 2012. "Cultural Values." In *A Companion to Moral Anthropology*, edited by Didier Fassin, 117–32. Malden, MA: Wiley-Blackwell.
Rollin, Bertrand (OSB). 2013. *Ako dnes žiť Regulu sv. Benedikta* [How to live the Rule of st. Benedict today]. Sampor: Mnísi z rehole svätého Benedikta.

Spalová, Barbora, and Isabelle Jonveaux. 2018. "The Economy of Stability in Catholic Monasteries in Czech Republic and Austria." *Annual Review of Sociology of Religion* 9: 269–96.

Spalová, Barbora, Jan Tesárek, Tereza Drábková, Aneta Hemerová, and Zuzana Pešková. 2016. "Redefinice smyslu zasvěceného života" [Redefinition of the Aim of Consecrated Life]. *Dingir* (1): 15–20. Full version, last accessed 14 April 2019, is available at http://dingir.cz/cislo/16/1/redefinice_smyslu_zasveceneho_zivota.pdf.

Tesárek, Jan, and Barbora Spalová. 2021. "Other Time: Construction of Temporality in Contemporary Benedictine Monasteries." In *(Trans)missions: Monasteries as Sites of Cultural Transfers*, edited by Monika Brenišínová and Lenka Panušková, (in press). Oxford: Archaeopress.

Weber, Max. (1905) 2013. *The Protestant Ethic and the Spirit of Capitalism*. Translated by Stephen Kalberg. New York: Routledge.

Winter, Eduard. 1945. *Josefinismus a jeho dějiny: Příspěvek k duchovním dějinám Čech a Moravy 1740–1848* [Josephinism and Its History: Contribution to Religious History of Bohemia and Moravia 1740–1848]. Praha: Jelínek.

Wortley, John. 2011. "Discretion: Greater than All the Virtues." *Greek, Roman and Byzantine Studies* 51: 634–52.

Zerubavel, Eviatar. 1980. "The Benedictine Ethic and the Modern Spirit of Scheduling: On Schedules and Social Organization." *Sociological Inquiry* 50(2): 157–69.

6

Regimes of Asceticism

Austerity and Thrift in a Spiritual Economy

DAROMIR RUDNYCKYJ

On a rare rainy day in Cilegon, Banten, in the mid-2000s I sat in the grandstand of the stadium of Pelita KS, the soccer team representing Krakatau Steel, with several hundred of the company's workers. The occasion was the annual address delivered to the state-owned enterprise's employees by the CEO, Daenulhay. It was an opportunity to update employees on the company's fortunes in the past year, but also to try to motivate them toward greater productivity in the future. The address came at a precipitous time. Indonesia was in the throes of a broad-scale political and economic transition that had wide-ranging ramifications for the company and, according to some, could threaten the very survival of the state-owned enterprise.

In a steady drizzle, sheltered by an umbrella, the CEO stood under a large banner proclaiming the coming year as the "Year of Cost Competitiveness" and delivered a speech emphasizing the importance of thrift to ensure the survival of the company, especially under increasing pressure from steel producers outside Indonesia. In dire tones Daenulhay invoked the specter of the extraordinary growth of Chinese steel production ominously intoning, "They will soon be able to produce almost three hundred million tons per year, and we only produce two and a half!" His voice rising, he continued, "I want to remind you of the possibility of the demise of the company!" The remedy to these challenges, he said was both "hard work" and "cost competitiveness." He then explained to the assembled workers that cost competitiveness meant avoiding wasteful practices at the company, obeying budget limits, and treating the company's resources like they would treat their own. In so doing, he linked across scales from the individual households of company employees to the enterprise as a whole. If the company achieved cost competitiveness, he enjoined, "God willing, Krakatau Steel will continue to exist!"

After Daenulhay delivered the message, a document "officially proclaiming 2004 as the year of cost competitiveness" was brought to the stage. In the unrelenting drizzle three figures, Daenalhay, Amir Sambodo (the chairman of Krakatau Steel's board of directors), and Jilfikar (the vice-chair of the company's newly formed labor union, Serikat Karyawan Krakatau Steel), leaned over a small table and signed the ceremonial document. Amir Sambodo then produced two medals commemorating the "Year of Cost Competitiveness" and ritually pinned them to the chests of Daenulhay and Jilfikir. Later, Hari, an employee I had come to know well, told me he had heard that Daenulhay had made an agreement with the Minister of State-Owned Enterprises, Laksamana Sukardi, to reduce purchasing costs by 25 percent.

Such injunctions toward cost competitiveness may not sound inspirational, but the recurrent injunctions toward belt-tightening, parsimony, and thriftiness made sense in context. In the mid-2000s Indonesia was emerging from a devastating economic crisis and tumultuous political transformation. Suharto, who had assumed power in the wake of an aborted military coup in 1965 and served as president for thirty-two years, was finally compelled to step down in 1998 in the wake of widespread political unrest and social discord. Following the 1998 Asian Financial Crisis, the Indonesian government had teetered on the brink of bankruptcy. In a final act of public humiliation, Suharto had been forced to accept a $40 billion loan from the International Monetary Fund (IMF), memorably signing the loan documents under the watchful eye of the then IMF president, Michel Camdessus. These events had caused no shortage of consternation among managers at Krakatau Steel. Part of the bailout requirements were cuts to subsidies for marginally profitable and loss-making state-owned enterprises, such as Krakatau Steel. These demands opened up a new, unprecedented chapter in the history of Krakatau Steel. Whereas for years the company had been able to count on generous state subsidies, suddenly a new landscape brought into being new imperatives to cut costs. Part of the rationale for such corporate austerity was to enable the firm to compete with larger steel producers elsewhere in Asia who had achieved much greater economies of scale and, therefore, threatened to overwhelm Krakatau Steel's comparatively meagre output. Furthermore, fear spread around the company that cost-cutting and austerity would mean increased precarity for workers, as threats of mass layoffs loomed.

While today cost-cutting is often taken for granted as the common sense of market-oriented economics, it is not intrinsic to all capitalist enterprise. This chapter seeks to show how cost competitiveness and the imperative toward thrift, frugality, and austerity that it conveys are characteristic of a particular formation of capitalism: a capitalism to which the sociologist Max Weber referred as premised on "worldly asceticism" (Weber [1920] 2001). Weber showed that what was distinctive about capitalism as it emerged in the North Atlantic was that it relied on an ethics of frugality and self-abnegation, which was quite foreign to forms of capitalism that had emerged in other parts of the world.

In recent years, austerity has become an apparently incontestable response to economic crisis (Bear 2015; Doxiadis and Placas 2018; Knight 2015). Although austerity has a long genealogy in sites from Ceausescu's Romania to Latin America during the 1980s (Canak 1989; Edelman 1990; Verdery 2004), since the global economic crises that kicked off in 2007 and 2008, it has swept across much of Europe and North America as well. Susana Narotzky identified austerity as a form of neoliberal "expert" knowledge that has had wide-ranging impacts on populations through insistence on budgetary control (Narotzky 2019). Indeed, austerity is often constitutive of the neoliberal insistence on the extension of economic rationality to domains not previously represented in economic terms (Foucault 2008; Rudnyckyj 2017). In this chapter I seek to develop a longer genealogy of austerity by illuminating how it draws on an earlier premium on frugality, thrift, and self-denial born in the Protestant Reformation. In so doing, I show how injunctions to austerity and thrift were constitutive of what I have identified as a "spiritual economy" (Rudnyckyj 2010). In so doing, I seek to illustrate the generative resonances between thrift and austerity highlighted by Alexander and Sosna in the introduction to this volume. Building on Weber, I argue, in part, that the moral overtones embedded in injunctions to frugality and cost-cutting rely on the same set of logics in corporations and households as they do in the state. As Weber has shown, in capitalism there is an ethical imperative that represents frugality as a moral good. It is this ethical imperative that makes balancing budgets both in households and firms, and at the broader scale of the state at large, something hard to question in capitalism.

For Weber, worldly asceticism laid down the conditions of possibility for "the spirit of capitalism": an historically peculiar set of dispositions that married the compulsion to thriftiness with an imperative to accumulation. This chapter considers Weber's arguments regarding the origins of this ethic in Protestantism, before describing efforts to recast worldly asceticism as an Islamic virtue. Drawing on ethnographic fieldwork at Krakatau Steel, the chapter shows how self-styled spiritual reformers sought to instill ascetic values by recasting practices such as cost competitiveness, anticorruption, and increased production as divinely ordained and evident in sacred texts, such as the Qur'an and the sunnah, and in the history of Islam.

The chapter concludes that ascetic regimes become effective insofar as they are made to appear as incontestable ethical values.

Cost and Worldly Asceticism

This chapter seeks to show how the injunctions to cost competitiveness and thrift evident at Krakatau Steel illustrate a feature of capitalism that Weber identified as worldly asceticism. Weber argued that worldly asceticism was the outcome of two distinct rubrics for how to live a life that were characteristic of reformist Protestantism: the notion of the calling and the doctrine of predestination. In seeking to diagram the origins of worldly asceticism, Weber turns first to the work of Martin Luther and the doctrine of the calling that Luther formulated. Weber writes that "the fulfillment of duty in vocational callings became viewed as the highest expression that moral activity could assume. Precisely this new notion of the moral worth of devoting oneself to a calling was the unavoidable result of the idea of attaching 'religious significance' to daily activity" (Weber [1920] 2001: 40). Critical here is that Luther's doctrine of the calling meant that one could fulfill one's moral duty by everyday work in the world. Thus, one did not have to immerse oneself in religious practice to live acceptably to God, but rather one could fulfill one's otherworldly obligations simply through pursuing one's worldly vocation.

The calling had wide-ranging implications for moral life and distinguished Protestant ethics from Catholic morality. Weber explains that "the conception of the calling thus brings out that central dogma of all Protestant denominations. . . . The only way of living acceptably to God was not to surpass worldly morality in monastic asceticism, but solely through the fulfillment of the obligations imposed upon the individual by his position in the world. That was his calling" (Weber [1920] 2001: 40). In Catholicism, worldly occupations had no spiritual merit and religious practice reached its apogee in "ascetic withdrawal from the world." Thus, Catholic morality viewed the contemplative life of monastic orders sealed off from the profane realm of worldly affairs as the highest form of ethical life that an individual believer could attain. Protestantism overturned this moral order by carrying asceticism "out of monastic cells into everyday life" (Weber [1920] 2001: 123). Thus, whereas ascetic practice formerly was the sole provenance of monasteries, by reconfiguring worldly activity as a legitimate form of moral action, the notion of calling paved the way for the ethic of worldly asceticism that undergirds notions of thrift, austerity, and cost competitiveness today.

Nonetheless, the calling was not sufficient in its own right to transform asceticism into a moral pillar of capitalism. After elucidating the centrality of the calling to the Protestant ethic, Weber turns to the next doctrinal innovation that precipitated the ethic of worldly asceticism: the doctrine of predestination formulated initially by John Calvin. According to Calvin, God designated before the creation of the world who would be among the members of the elect who would reach heaven and who would be consigned to eternal damnation. Furthermore, human sin or merit is irrelevant to the possession of grace since that would subject God's decrees to human influence (Weber [1920] 2001: 59–60). One might think that the notion of predestination could lead the followers of Calvin to a life of fatalism and debauchery under the presumption that the odds favored damnation over salvation. However, Weber reasons that precisely the opposite occurred. Rather than embracing hedonism, Calvinists turned to an austere lifestyle. Under the doctrine of predestination, everyday existence only became tolerable if one was able to convince oneself of one's own salvation. In Weber's words, one had an "absolute duty to consider oneself chosen and to combat all doubts as temptations of the devil, since lack of self-confidence is the result of insufficient faith, hence of imperfect grace" (Weber [1920] 2001: 66–67). Any doubt about whether one was saved was taken as a sure sign that one was not one of the chosen for election. This led to a regime in which worldly activity was taken as the most suitable means to attain confidence of salvation because Calvinists held that "God helps those who help themselves" (Weber [1920] 2001: 69). Whereas for Catholics good deeds might be performed haphazardly, for the Calvinist they became part of a rationalized, methodical, and systematic approach toward life, such that the Calvinist could create his or her own conviction of salvation (Weber [1920] 2001: 70). Ultimately, predestination leads to "rational planning of the whole of one's life in accordance with God's will" (Weber [1920] 2001: 100). The systematization of life creates an austere form of practice in which one exercises extreme self-discipline, monitors oneself constantly, and views all luxuries as potential temptations.

The notion of the calling and the doctrine of predestination come together to combine the Puritan notion of "worldly asceticism" (Weber [1920] 2001: 102–25). According to this ethos, an individual was compelled to follow a secular vocation with almost spiritual devotion. The compulsion toward intensive worldly activity inextricably led to the accumulation of money. However, Protestant moral views presented obstacles to spending the proceeds of one's vocation. Consumer purchases were frowned upon as sinful. Donations to the church were inhibited due to the rejection of icons among Protestant sects. Finally, donations to the poor were eschewed because poverty was generally attributed to either laziness or divine disfavor (or both). The outcome of all this was that Protestants were led to invest their capital, leading them to produce even more capital, a cycle that accelerated capitalist development (Weber [1920] 2001: 116). A testament to the insights in Weber's arguments is the number of scholars over the past century who have taken issue with it (McCloskey 2010; Tawney [1926] 2015; Troeltsch [1912] 1958).

According to Weber, worldly asceticism lays the foundation for the spirit of capitalism in which the Protestant values of self-denial and austerity take an economic cast. Invoking the writings of Benjamin Franklin, a key figure in the early history of the United States, Weber argues that values such as frugality become prized due to their economic benefit. He writes that according to the spirit of capitalism, "Honesty is useful, because it assures credit; so are punctuality, industry, frugality, and that is the reason they are virtues" (17). As capitalism accelerates, frugality becomes critical to commercial success so that the "old leisurely and comfortable attitude toward life gave way to a hard frugality in which some participated and came to the top, because they did not wish to consume but to earn, while others who wished to keep on with the old ways were forced to curtail their consumption" (Weber [1920] 2001: 30). Thus, as Weber's example of Franklin illustrates, according to the spirit of capitalism, frugality is just as critical in the domestic life of the household as it is in the public world of commerce.

Weber finds the precedent for this capitalist emphasis on frugality in Puritan values, such as the Puritan abnegation of anything that might incite pleasure. He writes that the Puritan "toleration of pleasure in cultural goods . . . always ran up against one characteristic limitation: they must not cost anything. Man is only a trustee of the goods which have come to him through God's grace. He must . . . give an account of every penny entrusted to him, and it is at least hazardous to spend any of it for a purpose which does not serve the glory of God but only one's own enjoyment" (114). Thus, a consciousness of cost, in which one is understood to be responsible to account for "every penny" comes to be an indispensable component of worldly asceticism, which provides the groundwork for the subsequent spirit of capitalism. One of Weber's great insights was to show how worldly asceticism, and the ethics of individualism, austerity, thrift, and abstinence which it contains, became embedded in the spirit of capitalism. Indeed, worldly asceticism is a central value for North Atlantic life at large (Kalberg 2001; Parsons 1989).

From a Moral Economy to a Spiritual One

While worldly asceticism is a prevalent value in the North Atlantic, it could not be said to have deep roots in Southeast Asia. Although colonized by the Calvinist Dutch for over three hundred years, it would be a stretch to say that anything like the spirit of capitalism was a widespread cultural value in Indonesia. As a number of scholars have observed, the prevailing economic ethic in Southeast Asia was what they identified as a "moral economy." In James Scott's classical formulation, the moral economy was characterized by a norm of reciprocity and a moral right to subsistence that was inherent to peasant society in the region prior to the era of "high colonialism" that took root in the latter-half of the nineteenth century (Scott 1976). Although Scott's account focuses on mainland Southeast Asia, as several scholars have shown, versions of a moral economy are evident across the region (Adas 1980; Peletz 1983; Scott and Kerkvliet 1977). Indeed, in his magisterial two-volume history of Southeast Asia, *Southeast Asia in the Age of Commerce*, Anthony Reid identifies patron–client relations based on loyalty and obligation as the predominant socioeconomic tie in premodern and early modern Southeast Asia. (Reid 1988: 121, 129–36).

The moral economy is characterized in large measure by patron–client ties, in which clients commit to loyalty toward patrons and accept a measure of apparently exploitative relationships (Bubandt 2006). In return, they understand that the authority will guarantee the subsistence of the people in the event of widespread famine or hardship (Thompson 1971). Thus, in the classic patron–client exchange, the client provides a disproportionately large share of their annual agricultural produce to the patron in return for the commitment, on the part of the patron, that he or she will guarantee the subsistence of the patron in the possible event of crop failure (Scott and Kerkvliet 1977). My ethnographic work confirmed a tension between the patron–client relations characteristic of Scott's moral economy and the more individualistic ethics characteristic of capitalism and amplified by neoliberalism.

As Marc Edelman notes, the "proliferation of the term [moral economy] into an overly capacious, catchall category runs the danger of rendering it simultaneously clever and meaningless" (2012: 63). Nonetheless, the concept has been extremely useful in Southeast Asian studies for identifying the different economic ethics that prevailed in the region prior to the onset of colonialism and those that emerged thereafter. In this chapter I refer to the conceptualization of moral economy strictly in the narrow sense developed by Thompson and Scott: the notion that actors (in this case, peasants) are not motivated by economic calculation and are instead motivated by concerns of justice and fairness. Thus, they accept what on the surface ap pear to be exploitative economic arrangements (giving the patron an unfair share of their harvest) with the implicit understanding that their subsistence security will be guaranteed in the event of future hardship or famine. This is the relationship at the core of both Scott's and Thompson's use of the notion of a moral economy, which is decidedly opposed to the spirit of capitalism. The spirit of capitalism, according to Weber, refers to the moral obligation of the subject to increase his or her capital (Weber [1920] 2001: 16). The pursuit of profit is opposed to Thompson's and Scott's notion of moral economy because it is not premised on market exchanges but relations of reciprocity. For example, in Scott's analysis, Southeast Asian peasants have no interest in maximizing profit, but rather in ensuring their security in the event of famine (Scott 1976: 4–5). Patron–client networks precipitated a specific form of economic subjectivity, characterized by avoidance of risk, deference to authority, and reliance on superiors. Furthermore, it did not produce the type of ethical dispositions characteristic of capitalism and premised on savings and reinvestment. As Scott and Reid point out, the subjects of a moral economy are typically fatalistic: accepting their lot in life, spending whatever surplus they had beyond the tribute they were obligated to pass on to their patron, and seeing little point in reinvestment to improve their positions. These dispositions conflict dramatically with the entrepreneurial impulses that emerged out of worldly asceticism. Whereas worldly asceticism hatched capitalist ambition in its embrace of frugality and thrift, those embedded in a moral economy saw little point in such self-abnegation.

Networks of Patronage

The tension between the fatalist ethics of the moral economy and the impulse to thrift in worldly ascetism were visible in the predicament faced by Krakatau Steel and the new imperative to "cost competitiveness." At Krakatau Steel, the end of the authoritarian Suharto regime did not only portend the arrival of a new, more democratic political order. It also meant the transformation of an economic order, largely embedded in a broader moral economy, that had held sway at state-owned firms such as Krakatau Steel since the 1970s. The company was both embedded in and the vehicle for overlapping patronage networks that undergirded the moral economy that operated at the company.

Perhaps most notable was state patronage. For years Krakatau Steel had been able to depend on consistent infusions of state development funds under the import substitution industrialization prong of Indonesia's New Order development strategy (Arndt 1975; Rock 2003). In the 1970s, Krakatau Steel's construction had been underwritten by the profits of the state-owned oil company Pertamina. Pertamina's swashbuckling CEO, Ibnu Sutowo, readily spread the proceeds of Indonesia's 1970s oil boom as he loaded debt upon the company. Krakatau Steel was no stranger to such largesse. The initial rationale for state support was in part premised on the notion that Krakatau Steel would produce the metal pipes indispensable to Indonesia's burgeoning oil and gas sector (Purwadi et al. 2003). But even after the company was unable to meet Pertamina's demands for infrastructure technology, the company continued to receive generous state support. Several long-time factory employees wistfully recalled the 1970s and Sutowo's support for the company.

Even after Sutowo was unceremoniously dismissed in 1978, Krakatau Steel continued to benefit from state patronage. In the 1980s, with the support of Suharto's charismatic Minister for Research and Technology, B. J. Habibie, Krakatau Steel and a number of other state-owned companies had been designated "strategic industries." These firms operated under the Strategic Industries Supervisory Agency (Bahana Prakarya Industri Strategis or BPIS) alongside other companies that produced airplanes, ships, and armaments. As strategic industries, these companies did not operate solely according to profit imperatives. Steel, like weapons, ships, and airplanes, was designated as critical to the country's modernization imperatives. Habibie embraced the notion of "leap-frog development," which held that Indonesia could advance rapidly to the status of a developed nation by

Figure 6.1. A Krakatau Steel employee walks past a mosque adjacent to the Krakatau Steel complex. The direct reduction plant is in the background. © Daromir Rudnyckyj.

adopting the technological developments that had taken place in industrialized countries, thus skipping several steps of what were taken to be stages of economic growth (Rostow 1960). Habibie ensured that Krakatau Steel received steady infusions of state funds to modernize aging facilities and to build new ones (Staff 1996). Habibie had been educated in West Germany and had maintained strong contacts with industrial and engineering firms in the country, and German consultants and advisors were common at the factory at this time. During the 1980s and 1990s, Krakatau Steel came to occupy an iconic position in the nation, receiving frequent visits from President Suharto and other official dignitaries, particularly for the inauguration of new mills.

In addition to state patronage, the company itself operated as a sort of patron. This was most evident in the fact that it offered permanent, salaried positions that were well-compensated, especially by local standards. One foreman in the slab steel plant at Krakatau Steel explained to me that "the social was the most important and profit was secondary," but "now profit is number one and the social mission is number two." He asserted that this "social mission" was premised upon what he called "dense work" (*padat karya*), which refers to a pattern of hiring more workers than necessary to conduct normal business operations. Another employee described the company's rationale not as a "pure business" but rather to "support the livelihoods of the masses." These tendencies are broadly visible in Indonesia and speak to the values that undergirded the moral economy at Krakatau Steel and elsewhere in Indonesia. The notions of "dense work" and "supporting the livelihoods of the masses" evoke patterns of "work spreading" that Geertz observed as characteristic of rural Indonesia during the 1950s and 1960s (Geertz 1963). Geertz argued that rural life in Java was premised on an ethic of "shared poverty" in which small-scale agriculturalists accepted their status and lacked the motivation to improve their livelihoods. The work spreading evident at Krakatau Steel also evoked employment patterns not only in Central and Eastern Europe under various developmentalist imperatives, but also in other countries whether overtly socialist or not (Alexander 2002).

The company also offered benefits beyond only jobs. One former employee I interviewed still held a house in the vast housing complex that Krakatau Steel had built. Although he had retired years before, he had held on to the house despite the company's demands to move out. Several adult children, who were not company employees, were also living there. The house was large and had an expansive yard, but it was visibly in need of extensive repairs. Although he lacked the money to make the repairs, he had resisted moving out, fearing that he would be unable to afford anything comparable on the open market. Likewise, the company had its own

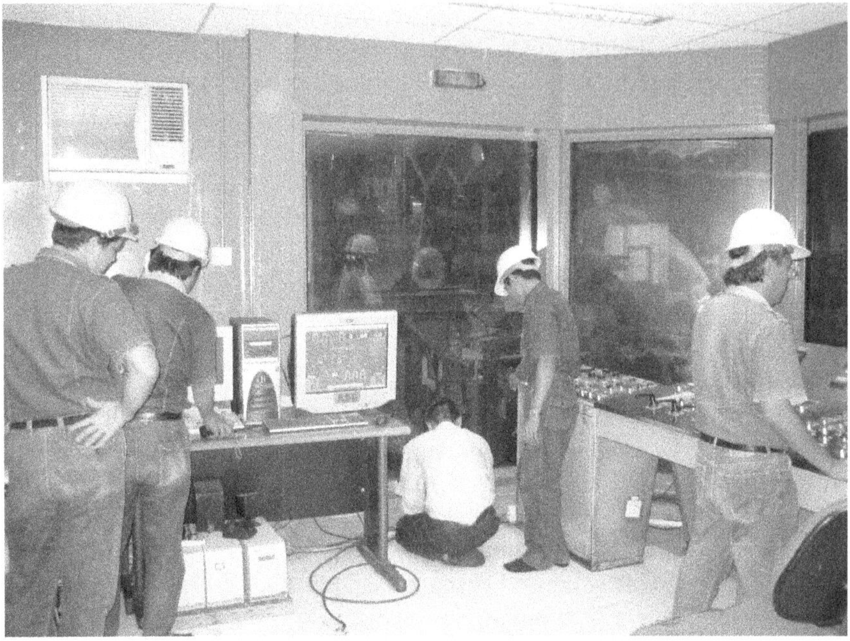

Figure 6.2. A control room in the cold-rolling mill. © Daromir Rudnyckyj.

hospital, which was widely acknowledged to be the best in the region and provided high quality health care to employees.

Nonetheless, the factory's patronage of employees was subject to contestation. One plant manager told me that management consulting firm Booz, Allen, and Hamilton performed an audit of employment at Krakatau Steel and concluded that at least 1,500 employees out of a total workforce of roughly 6,000 were superfluous. Furthermore, other managers cited the practices of work spreading as a rationale for poor job performance at the company, claiming that employees at the company lacked motivation because they knew they were superfluous.

In sum, two overlapping patronage networks showed how the values of the moral economy undergirded life at Krakatau Steel. State patronage meant Krakatau Steel did not have to operate according to a strict calculus of profit and loss, but could rather rely on consistent infusions of funds from the central government to cover any potential shortfalls. In turn, the company essentially served as a vehicle for redistributing this surplus, as the company hired more employees than necessary to conduct its operations. Not only that, but the company also provided employees with resources necessary to sustain their livelihoods, such as shelter and health care. However, by the mid-2000s it was clear that the largesse of the moral economy of state patronage was no longer tenable. Whereas Krakatau Steel had long been able to rely on state patronage to fund modernization of older facilities and expansion, a new regime of austerity was in the process of implementation. At the national level, former President Suharto had been forced to consent to the terms of the IMF bailout. How would the new regime of austerity be implemented? How could employees who had become accustomed to the guarantees of the moral economy be inculcated into the brave new world of worldly asceticism?

Training Asceticism

The new corporate commitment to "cost competitiveness" illustrated by the vignette with which I opened this chapter was one technique through which austerity was introduced. But managers went even further: they sought to create a new ethical regime in which virtues such as accountability and thrift were recast as Islamic values. This new ethical regime was prompted by a wide range of challenges to which this worldly asceticism

Figure 6.3. A drawing in the cold-rolling mill exhorting employees to make Krakatau Steel a "World Class Company" rather than being content with its status as a "Regional Class Company." Note the fatherly bearing of the central figure. © Daromir Rudnyckyj.

was seen as a solution. First was a reduction on tariffs on imported steel, which meant the factory would have to compete with larger and more efficient steel producers elsewhere in Asia. Second was the evaporation of state largesse in the form of generous subsidies. Third was the introduction of liberal reforms that offered unprecedented opportunities for unionization. Finally, both managers and workers reported that corruption was rife at the company. This was seen as both an obstacle to competitiveness and a sign of how out of step Krakatau Steel was with international practices. Stories in the Indonesian press asserted that the company was in danger of going bankrupt (Akbar 2003). Corporate managers sought to redress these issues by inculcating an ethics of worldly asceticism among all members of the company hierarchy.

The vehicle for eliciting practices of worldly asceticism was an ingenious project of what they called "spiritual reform" created by a private, Jakarta-based company, the ESQ Leadership Centre (Ginanjar 2001). The main vehicle of the "Emotional and Spiritual Quotient (ESQ)" training was a three-day-long employee training session that combined Islamic practices and American management science to enhance productivity and foster discipline. The brainchild of a charismatic Indonesian businessman, Ary Ginanjar, the program used evocative high-tech media that centered on a Microsoft PowerPoint presentation and featured graphs, charts, tables, and a steady stream of bullet points, as well as entertaining film clips, vivid photographs, and popular music with a driving bass line and catchy lyrics. The program relied on a diverse array of popular media, websites, and academic journals, drawing as much on Hollywood blockbusters and the research of Harvard business professors as on Qur'anic passages and episodes from the life of the prophet. The air conditioning in the room was turned all the way down, creating a disconcerting chill in contrast to the sweltering tropical heat outside. The combination of sights, sounds, and feelings was designed to elicit retrospection and self-inquiry among the participants.

The five pillars of Islam were recast as recipes for corporate success in what participants called a new "era of globalization." For example, the fourth pillar of Islam, the duty to fast during Ramadan, was taken as a broader injunction for self-control and refraining from temptation. Based on this principle, ESQ sought to inculcate a constraint on worldly desires to ensure other-worldly salvation. ESQ trainers told the participants that fasting was a divine sanction for learning self-control, abstinence, and discipline. Furthermore, the prophet Muhammad was recast as a model CEO and participants were enjoined to follow his lead through exhibiting both hard work and commercial aspiration.

The gripping climax of ESQ included a simulation of events that take place during the annual *hajj* pilgrimage to Mecca. Most compelling for participants was a recreation of the circulation around the *kaaba*, the central shrine in the main mosque in Mecca. A cardboard replica of the *kaaba*, about the size of an SUV, was placed in the center of the room and participants proceeded in rotation around it chanting, in Arabic, "there is no God but Allah." Participants also reenacted the stoning of *jamrat al-aqabah*, in which pilgrims hurl rocks at three representations of the devil, by launching small wads of paper at three demonic images elaborately illustrated on flip charts. The site offered a graphic window into how Islam was deployed to meet the challenges of corporate restructuring in the context of global economic integration.

One assistant trainer, Zulfikir, described in schematic terms how an ethics of worldly asceticism was elicited by the training. The first day was conceived of as what he called "ice breaking and conditioning" in which techniques were deployed to enable participants to open up to the possibility of "changing themselves" through the methods of ESQ. On the second day, after the participants had been "broken down," they were "reprogrammed" by being confronted with existential questions that were intended to affirm their identities as Muslims. These included where are you from, where are you now, and where are you going? He said that by posing

Figure 6.4. A sign in the slab steel plant reading "Work Is Worship." © Daromir Rudnyckyj.

these questions participants were encouraged to reflect on their own lives and recognize practices that are not compliant with Islam. Participants were instructed not to "worship" material goods, property, or their employment status. They were called on to atone for pursuing material concerns to the exclusion of according to the will of Allah.

On the third day, Zulfikir told me that participants were "built back up anew." Techniques to practice self-control over material desire and emotional outbursts were introduced. Finally, the concept of "total action" was introduced through the simulation of several of the rituals central to the *hajj* pilgrimage. Total action referred to taking responsibility for one's acts and becoming "proactive" in one's work and home lives. This was a key lesson for employees of an institution that had been governed by the logic of a moral economy. In the overlapping regimes of patronage that had governed the factory for most of its three decades in existence, it had been rigidly hierarchical. Workers were expected to wait for orders from above, rather than acting of their own initiative. Spiritual reform was designed to transform passive objects of this hierarchical system into proactive subjects who made decisions based on their own judgment.

In an interview I held with him during a break in one of the training sessions, Ary Ginanjar illustrated the ethics of worldly asceticism by asserting a "link between productivity and spirituality." He said that one of his goals was to increase honesty among employees and thereby to ensure the "safety of the cash flow." He evoked the imperative to austerity and reinvestment that Weber suggested in his diagnosis of the religious roots of worldly ascetism, exclaiming, "If they [the employees] don't worry about money all the time, they will work harder, become more productive, and by doing so earn more money." He further asserted that, in ESQ, a central message was that even though one's boss might not see what an employee is doing, "God sees everything." The implication was that by being subjected to a regime of surveillance, employees would become more self-disciplined.

Cost Competitiveness and the Spiritual Economy

The link between worldly asceticism and Islamic piety resonated widely with Krakatau Steel employees. While I was waiting for a training to begin one morning, I struck up a conversation with Shafil who worked in the Marketing Department and was attending ESQ for the first time. He told me that the goal of the event was to change employee attitudes toward work. Emphasizing the notion in ESQ that proper Islamic practice should be dedicated to self-denial, he said, "Work is not about material things, but about . . . one's self-improvement." Thus, he emphasized the message that employees should not see their labor at the company as merely a means to survival, but should see it instead as a means for spiritual self-cultivation. He asserted that by accentuating the immaterial, ascetic dimensions of work, ESQ would actually "improve productivity . . . make better workers, make better employees," and finally, "release the potential" of Krakatau Steel employees. Another employee, Rosmawati, also evoked how the ethics of worldly asceticism emphasized in ESQ would raise both spirituality and productivity, saying, "It reminds us what we live for: to go to heaven. Islam teaches that we must attend to both the worldly and the afterlife. Time for work and time for prayer must be balanced. This is how we prepare to enter heaven."

Employees specifically connected the ascetic ethics that were a central feature of the ESQ training to corporate productivity, often framing these in terms of costs savings. Hari, a worker in the hot strip mill, said the goal of ESQ was to "raise productivity and efficiency. . . . We will be better if we follow all the commands of Allah and all the prohibitions are avoided." State and corporate patronage had tolerated and perhaps even fostered corruption, but he remarked that since ESQ had been introduced, "bad suppliers no longer supply the HSM." He then provided me with abundant examples of corruption that been rampant in the mill: "a piece of equipment that actually cost 140,000 rupiah,[1] would be sold for 14 million!"[2] Moral values were explicitly linked to cost competitiveness for the company. Furthermore, he professed profound personal change after he had attended ESQ, attesting to much greater vigilance on behalf of the company. He said, "False cylinders were delivered, but we reported it. This proves our concern is for the factory."

Framing spiritual change in terms of cost competitiveness was common, especially when invoking what employees referred to as corruption. Hari brought up an issue that I had heard discussed by one of his colleagues as well. He claimed that oil pipes for all the hydraulic systems in the hot strip mill had leaks, but no one bothered to fix them. The reason was that managers were taking a cut of all the oil sales, which "could be as high as 1 billion rupiah per month!" Examples of corruption, large and small, illustrated the attempt to implement values of worldly asceticism in the company through ESQ. Hadi said that the training "makes us aware of corruption [and] implements honest behavior." Taking corruption as a sign of a lack of fortitude, he said that the ethics of ESQ could enable the company to better compete, telling me that "by helping the weak we can raise the productivity of people around us who need help."

Another employee, Tasrif, illustrated how his experience with ESQ had transformed the fatalism of moral economy that previously held sway at the factory for a new more entrepreneurial capitalism. Tasrif illustrated the link between cost competitiveness and the broader emphasis on thrift that had taken hold at the factory. Several months prior to our conversation he had been working overtime to meet a delivery deadline in the hot strip mill. He was at work on a Saturday and one of the lines in the mill was undergoing maintenance. Suddenly, the second operational line broke down. Tasrif said he felt a duty to ensure that the order he was working with would reach the customer in time and thought he should simply turn on the other line. Such a decision would normally be made only by a manager, but he had tried to contact his superiors by phone, but they were unavailable. Weighing his options, he unilaterally decided to restart the line under repair. He attributed his action to "spiritual motivation," explaining that if he had not made the spur of the moment decision, the company would have lost four thousand tons of production over the two-day weekend. Taking this decision was "high risk," he said, "but [it was] successful and saved the company 10 billion rupiah!"[3] Although some employees criticized the cost of ESQ, for which Krakatau Steel paid 2 million rupiah[4] for each employee, Tasrif invoked his actions and said that the training actually "brought returns greater than the 2-million-rupiah cost. An employee who changes his attitude toward work might save more than 2 million!" Thus, the new spiritual regime was justified in terms of cost, as supporters of ESQ, such as Tasrif, argued that the benefits of ESQ far outweighed its costs.

Conclusion

Efforts at Krakatau Steel to move from a regime characterized by soft budgets and strong state support to market discipline evokes accounts of factories elsewhere, especially in Central and Eastern Europe (Alexander 2002; Dunn 2004; Rajkovic 2017). What is distinctive here is the manner in which Islam was deployed to facilitate this transformation. As Weber demonstrated, values such as frugality and thrift were embedded in religious virtues, particularly Protestantism's penchant for austerity. The unknowability of a distant and inscrutable God created a society of self-control in which Protestant believers recurrently monitored themselves to avoid even the slightest whiff of temptation. As Spalová notes in her contribution to this volume (chapter 5), these values are also evident in the Catholic monasteries in the Czech Republic today. Coincidentally, these values become central to the spirit of capitalism and the society to which it gave rise, one centered on the notion that increasing one's capital was an undeniable sign of one's moral probity. Although frugality, thrift, and self-abnegation no longer held religious or spiritual connotations, they were still constitutive of the subjects of modern capitalism.

Such values were largely foreign to Southeast Asia historically, where the fatalist and reciprocal ethics of the moral economy held sway. In Indonesia, only a narrow group of elites put much stock in ascetic values (Geertz 1960). State-owned firms such as Krakatau Steel were embedded in patronage networks in which calculations of cost were not paramount. Nonetheless, political and economic changes laid the conditions of possibility for a regime of austerity in which state patronage evaporated. The company sought to change from a regime governed by and through patronage to one that operated under the presumptions of cost competitiveness. Suddenly, managers and employees were presented with the challenge of implementing an ethics of frugality and cost accountability, and religion emerged as a compelling means of intervention. However, this did not entail anything like a wholesale conversion to Protestantism, but a reinterpretation of Islam that emphasized the religion's ascetic values. In this matrix, cost competitiveness was reframed as a problem of religious practice. Thus, an imperative toward thrift began to take hold among factory managers and workers as they sought to ensure the company's survival in the context of increasing competition from the outside.

In recent years austerity has become an ever more pervasive value (Knight and Stewart 2016; Muehlebach 2016). Particularly in the aftermath of the 2008 financial crisis, political leaders around the world have argued that the appropriate response to crisis is belt-tightening. We will all have to get used to doing more with less, or so we are told. This chapter has sought to show that injunctions to austerity are only possible because we live under an ethical regime in which frugality, thrift, and cost-cutting are seen as moral virtues. Contemporary invocations of austerity are premised on the positive moral valence attached to worldly asceticism and its attendant ethics of frugality, self-control, and discipline described by Weber. Although these invocations operate at a much broader scale from enterprises and firms to the nation-state, they rely on the same logic that takes thrift to be a moral good. The imperative that sees cutting costs as a moral good relies on the same set of logics in corporations and households as it does for the state. The ethics of capitalism sees thrift as a moral good and makes balancing budgets at the scale of the household or firm *and* at the scale of the state difficult to challenge. Such telescoping of scale has a long history in the West. As Foucault noted, the exercise of state power has long been conceived of along the same lines as leadership in a household. In his famous lecture on governmentality, he wrote: "To govern a state will therefore mean to apply economy, to set up an economy at the level of the entire state, which means exercising towards its inhabitants, and the wealth and behavior of each and all, a form of surveillance and control as attentive as that of the head of a family over his household and his goods" (Foucault 1991: 92).

This is likely in no small measure what made the likes of Angela Merkel so convinced of the probity of her criticism of Southern Europeans: a moral logic that presumed household budgets operate in fundamentally the same way as those of the state. And this is precisely what has made austerity so hard to challenge. The positive moral valence attached to thrift and frugality, to cutting costs, meant countries such as Greece could not spend their way out of recession as Keynes would have suggested. Rather, they were forced to cut budgets under austerity regimes. This was only possibly because of the moral logic that undergirds capitalism: Greeks were viewed as profligate and (therefore) morally deficient because they were doing capitalism wrong—too much spending and not enough saving.

Max Weber's generative work on the relationship between Protestantism and capitalism offers a window into the origins of the worldly asceticism that undergird these notions of austerity and thrift. Nevertheless, it is only by looking at examples such as efforts to introduce Islamic spiritual reform in Indonesia that we can truly grasp the reach of worldly asceticism. In the stunning conclusion to *The Protestant Ethic* Weber wrote, "No one knows who will live in this cage in the future, or whether at the end of this tremendous development entirely new prophets will arise, or there will be a great rebirth of old ideas and ideals, or, if neither, mechanized petrification, embellished with a sort of convulsive self-importance" (Weber [1920] 2001: 124). It would seem that spiritual reformers such as Ary Ginanjar and his ESQ program represent the rise of a new prophet; but ultimately, it would seem that he is expanding the cage, not providing an alternative to it.

Acknowledgments

This research was made possible by the kindness of the employees and management of Krakatau Steel. I extend my deepest thanks to them. I also offer my sincere thanks to Ary Ginanjar and his staff at the ESQ Leadership Center for patiently addressing my entreaties. This research was made possible with material support from the Wenner-Gren Foundation for Anthropological Research, the International Dissertation Research Fellowship Program of the Social Science Research Council, the University of California's Pacific Rim Research Program, Fulbright-Hays, and the University of Victoria.

Daromir Rudnyckyj is Professor of Anthropology at the University of Victoria where he directs the Counter Currency Laboratory and is co-PI for the Futures of Money project. He is also President of the Society for the Anthropology of Religion. His research addresses globalization, capitalism, religion, finance, development, Islam, and the sociotechnics of money. He is the author of *Beyond Debt: Islamic Experiments in Global Finance* (University of Chicago Press, 2019). His first book, *Spiritual Economies: Islam, Globalization, and the Afterlife of Development* (Cornell University Press, 2010), was awarded the Sharon Stephens Prize by the American Ethnological Society. He is the coeditor, with Filippo Osella, of *Religion and the Morality of the Market* (Cambridge University Press, 2017).

Notes

1. This was approximately equivalent to US$14.
2. This was approximately equivalent to US$1,400.
3. This was approximately equivalent to US$1 million.
4. This was approximately equivalent to US$200.

References

Adas, Michael. 1980. "Moral Economy" or "Contest State"? Elite Demands and the Origins of Peasant Protest in Southeast Asia." *Journal of Social History* 13(4): 521–54.

Akbar, Faidil. 2003. "Krakatau Steel Terancam Bangkrut [Krakatau Steel Is Threatened with Bankruptcy]." *Tempo*. Accessed 25 October 2019. https://bisnis.tempo.co/read/13471/krakatau-steel-terancam-bangkrut.

Alexander, Catherine. 2002. *Personal States: Making Connections between People and Bureaucracy in Turkey*. New York: Oxford University Press.

Arndt, Heinz W. 1975. "P.T. Krakatau Steel." *Bulletin of Indonesian Economic Studies* 11(2): 120–26.

Bear, Laura. 2015. *Navigating Austerity: Currents of Debt Along a South Asian River*. Stanford: Stanford University Press.

Bubandt, Nils. 2006. "Sorcery, Corruption, and the Dangers of Democracy in Indonesia." *Journal of the Royal Anthropological Institute* 12(2): 413–31.

Canak, William L. 1989. *Lost Promises: Debt, Austerity, and Development in Latin America*. Boulder, CO: Westview Press.

Doxiadis, Evdoxios, and Aimee Placas. 2018. *Living under Austerity: Greek Society in Crisis*. New York: Berghahn Books.

Dunn, Elizabeth C. 2004. *Privatizing Poland: Baby Food, Big Business, and the Remaking of Labor*. Ithaca: Cornell University Press.

Edelman, Marc. 1990. "When They Took the "Muni": Political Culture and Anti-Austerity Protest in Rural Northwestern Costa Rica." *American Ethnologist* 17(4): 736–57.

———. 2012. "EP Thompson and Moral Economies." In *A Companion to Moral Anthropology*, edited by Didier Fassin, 49–66. Malden, MA: Wiley & Sons.

Foucault, Michel. 1991. "Governmentality." In *The Foucault Effect*, edited by Graham Burchell, Colin Gordon, and Peter Miller, 87–104. Chicago: University of Chicago Press.

———. 2008. *The Birth of Biopolitics: Lectures at the College De France, 1978–1979.* Houndmills: Palgrave Macmillan.
Geertz, Clifford. 1960. *The Religion of Java.* Glencoe: Free Press.
———. 1963. *Agricultural Involution: The Process of Ecological Change in Indonesia.* Berkeley: University of California Press.
Ginanjar, Ary. 2001. *Rahasia Sukses Membangun Kecerdasan Emosi Dan Spiritual Esq* [Secrets of Success in Developing Emotional and Spiritual Intelligence Esq]. Jakarta: Penerbit Arga.
Kalberg, Stephen. 2001. "The Modern World as a Monolithic Iron Cage? Utilizing Max Weber to Define the Internal Dynamics of the American Political Culture Today." *Max Weber Studies* 1(2): 178–95.
Knight, Daniel M. 2015. "Wit and Greece's Economic Crisis: Ironic Slogans, Food, and Antiausterity Sentiments." *American Ethnologist* 42(2): 230–46.
Knight, Daniel M., and Charles Stewart. 2016. "Ethnographies of Austerity: Temporality, Crisis and Affect in Southern Europe." *History and Anthropology* 27(1): 1–18.
McCloskey, Deirdre N. 2010. *Bourgeois Dignity: Why Economics Can't Explain the Modern World.* Chicago: University of Chicago Press.
Muehlebach, Andrea. 2016. "Anthropologies of Austerity." *History and Anthropology* 27(3): 359–72.
Narotzky, Susana. 2019. "Austerity Lives in Southern Europe: Experience, Knowledge, Evidence and Social Facts." *American Anthropologist* 121(1): 187–93.
Parsons, Talcott. 1989. "A Tentative Outline of American Values." *Theory, Culture & Society* 6(4): 577–612.
Peletz, Michael. 1983. "Moral and Political Economies in Rural Southeast Asia." *Comparative Studies in Society and History* 25(4): 731–39.
Purwadi, Dibyo Soemantri, Alfuzi Salam, Purwo Djatmiko, Sulaeman Ma'ruf, and Zainal Muttaqien. 2003. *Sejarah P.T. Krakatau Steel: Memelihara Momentum Pertumbuhan* [The History of P.T. Krakatau Steel: Maintaining Momentum for Growth]. Yogyakarta: Pustaka Raja.
Rajkovic, Ivan. 2017. "For an Anthropology of the Demoralized: State Pay, Mock-Labour, and Unfreedom in a Serbian Firm." *Journal of the Royal Anthropological Institute* 24(1): 47–70.
Reid, Anthony. 1988. *Southeast Asia in the Age of Commerce, 1450–1680.* New Haven: Yale University Press.
Rock, Michael. 2003. "The Politics of Development Policy and Development Policy Reform in New Order Indonesia." In *William Davidson Institute Working Papers.* Ann Arbor: University of Michigan Business School.
Rostow, Walt W. 1960. *The Stages of Economic Growth: A Non-Communist Manifesto.* Cambridge, UK: Cambridge University Press.
Rudnyckyj, Daromir. 2010. *Spiritual Economies: Islam, Globalization, and the Afterlife of Development.* Ithaca: Cornell University Press.
———. 2017. "Subjects of Debt: Financial Subjectification and Collaborative Risk in Malaysian Islamic Finance." *American Anthropologist* 119(2): 269–83.
Scott, James C. 1976. *The Moral Economy of the Peasant: Rebellion and Subsistence in Southeast Asia.* New Haven: Yale University Press.

Scott, James C., and Ben Kerkvliet. 1977. "How Traditional Patrons Lose Legitimacy: A Theory with Special Reference to Southeast Asia." In *Friends, Followers, and Factions: A Reader in Political Clientelism*, edited by Steffen W. Schmidt, 439–57. Berkeley: University of California Press.

Staff. 1996. "Krakatau Steel Expands in a Big Way." *Metal Bulletin Monthly* 5: 77.

Tawney, Richard H. (1926) 2015. *Religion and the Rise of Capitalism: A Historical Study*. London: Verso.

Thompson, Edward. 1971. "The Moral Economy of the English Crowd in the Eighteenth Century." *Past and Present* 50: 76–136.

Troeltsch, Ernst. (1912) 1958. *Protestantism and Progress: A Historical Study of the Relation of Protestantism to the Modern World*. Boston: Beacon Press.

Verdery, Katherine. 2004. "Anthropological Adventures with Romania's Wizard of Oz, 1973–1989." *Focaal* 43: 134–45.

Weber, Max. (1920) 2001. *The Protestant Ethic and the Spirit of Capitalism*. London: Routledge.

7

Saving and Wasting

The Paradox of Thrift in a Czech Landfill

Daniel Sosna

One Monday morning in October 2014, I arrived early at the Pureland landfill in West Bohemia where Peter, a landfill worker, was walking to the deposit area. I joined him. Because it was very cold and windy, he decided we should go inside their trailer to sit on a sofa and warm ourselves. When we opened the door, the radio was playing. Since we were the first people in the trailer that day, I was surprised the radio was on. Peter was perplexed when I asked him whether the radio had been on during the entire weekend and responded: "Of course, it was. We never turn it off. We just reduce the volume when necessary." This was not the answer I expected from somebody who spent the last fifteen years carefully recovering things from the landfill. The landfill workers' informal activities were concerned with saving objects and scrap from the morass of waste, sometimes carefully repairing broken things or crafting new objects from salvaged bits and bobs. But often the same workers would leave water taps and electrical appliances running, appearing to be deliberately wasteful. If we consider such actions through a "resource management" lens, this seems paradoxical. How can we explain such behavior, which is by turns thrifty in terms of saving resources and wasteful in terms of squandering them? At the very least, this highlights that "thriftiness" is something more than a singular habitus guiding all kinds of action at once.

In this chapter, I move beyond the familiar resource management explanation of thriftiness that is concerned with the well-being of individuals and societies via saving (Smiles 1876: 14). By resources I mean parts of the environment as well as social worlds that become what they are via their relation to humans (Kaneff 2018: 5–6) or other organisms. Since waste is increasingly perceived as a resource (Lane 2011: 396; Alexander and Reno 2012: 4), it provides a stimulating space for rethinking thriftiness. I explore through my ethnography the meaning of "thrifty actions" for the landfill workers, as well as what might seem to be their opposite: "squandering." An action that appears to be motivated by thriftiness turns out to have many different meanings, echoing Geertz's (1973: 6) wink and blink example, in which an action means different things in different contexts or to different observers. I demonstrate that one action may carry several layers of meaning simultaneously. The workers rarely associate a single meaning with their thrifty, generous, or wasteful actions. To borrow Gibson-Graham's (2014: S148–49) words, thick description helps resist the temptation to create a "strong theory," a reductionist and all-embracing project destined to fail in accounting for the complexities of economic practices. Instead, an ethnographer attends to nuances and a plurality of meanings to make a link between small facts and large issues.

Accordingly, I approach the actions of thrift as inherently plural, crossing different scales. Thus, the workers understand their actions as ways of creating, maintaining, or resisting different kinds of social relations across the domains of kin and domesticity, friends, work colleagues, and finally, the more formal relationship between employee, employer, and the state. Zooming in and out shows that thrift can hardly be fully understood within a single scale, such as that of individual decision-making; it requires an analytical movement across scalar registers. As I discuss below in my ethnography, this leads me to conceptualize thrift, alongside exchange and indeed wastefulness, as relational. This analytical perspective stems from the conviction that relations lie at the center of the anthropological project, especially "anthropology's willingness to move between conceptual and interpersonal relations in its descriptions of social life" (Strathern 2005: 9–10). Such a perspective enables me to explore thrift not only as it emerges through relations among persons, but also as it is situated in relation to concepts such as saving, care, pleasure, wastefulness, or generosity.

Further nuances are found in the ways the workers describe their salvage operations, which, to an extent, shifts the analysis from this relational aspect to focus on the affective labor of hunting for likely scraps and objects, and the subsequent repair or crafting of new objects. All these activities can be intensely pleasurable in and of themselves (see Alexander et al. 2009: 21), despite whether the recovered object ends up playing a part in the social lives of the workers. Working with waste can be surprisingly satisfying, despite being generally underappreciated from the outside. Sanchez (2020) argues that satisfaction arises from action that has a transformative capacity. Whenever an actor's labor affects "the transition of objects between different regimes of value," it generates satisfaction (Sanchez 2020:

81). This explains why satisfaction emerges not only during the building of things but also during their disassembly or even destruction. The pleasure of scavenging relates also to "futural orientations" (sensu Bryant and Knight 2019). In the case of the landfill workers, anticipation and hope are the orientations most relevant to the affective dimension of their work. Anticipation is based on previous experience, actively "pulling the future toward the present" (Bryant and Knight 2019: 28), which encourages the workers to prepare themselves for future loads of garbage coming from known sources. Hope relates to workers' dreams of a surprising treasure that might come to the landfill, a special moment for which they wait a long time. Their hope is an attempt to "bring particular 'otherwises' into actuality" (Bryant and Knight 2019: 134). Economies of affect, however, are not just about individual emotions. As Richard and Rudnyckyj (2009: 59) argue, affect unfolds through social relations and provides a useful tool for understanding the mutual constitution of subjects. In this relational model, affect is not so much a consequence of transformation but has its own capacity to create relations and transform.

Anthropologists who have discussed how people manage their resources have focused on thrift as a practice that enables the continuation of households (Gudeman and Rivera 1990; Gudeman 2012; Gudeman and Hann 2015), even in conditions of unequal power relations (Wolf 1966). Others have explored what might be seen as contrasting practices, such as the generous distribution of resources to sustain social relationships and build hierarchies (Mauss 1990; Wiessner 2002), or various forms of nonproductive expenditure or even destruction designed to release an excess of energy and enable people to escape the pressing order of things for a moment (Bataille 1985), especially where people have been marginalized (Wilk 2006). Less attention, however, has been paid to the fact that these different practices coexist in communities and in the lives of people who may shift between different forms of engagement with resources or even combine their seemingly contradictory notions in their practice. Miller (1998: 137) demonstrates, in his research on shopping, that thrift may serve as a justification for wasteful spending. He goes even further to argue that neither spending nor saving by themselves have the potential to explain thrift, because it only becomes meaningful as a vehicle for transforming the former to the latter. This phenomenon is slightly reminiscent of the debates about exchange in which Weiner (1992) argued that a theoretical obsession with giving prevented anthropologists from recognizing the importance of keeping. As she says, "The motivation for keeping-while-giving is grounded in such heroic dynamics—the need to secure permanence in a serial world that is always subject to loss and decay" (Weiner 1992: 7). In other words, there should be balance in the world. If one admits the relevance of both keeping and giving, then it makes sense to explore the relations between saving and wasting. Not only do acts of generosity and wasting often require previous saving; there is also a potentially rich space for their conceptual relations.

Although discussions about thrift are often tied to the notion of limited or finite resources, there are spaces where resources appear to be abundant. The constant flow of waste streams into landfills creates conditions of abundance for those who can recognize the "productive afterlife of waste" (Reno 2015: 558) or engage with the "vitality of waste" (Millar 2018: 32). This provides an arena for the examination of transformations of value through the activities of various waste pickers, sanitation workers, or urban miners (Nagle 2013; Rakowski 2016; Reno 2016; Millar 2018; O'Hare 2018). Their acts of care, saving, or wastefulness have an intimate relationship to the concept of property, because social relations and the rights as well as duties associated with the discarded objects shape these acts.

Following Maine's (1861: 178) idea of a "bundle of rights and duties" tied to individuals capable of exercising them, property relations then can be seen as "social relations between persons with respect to things" (Hann 2005: 111). These relations, however, do not necessarily have to be constricted by a notion of individual property subjects. Property relations may be ambiguous, and claims might be overlapping, because of frictions between the individualized and collective notions of personhood. As Verdery (1999) demonstrated, property may become fuzzy, especially in postsocialist contexts where individualized and exclusive notions of ownership merge with the collective notion of property and associated values of common good. This also means that such fuzziness leaves space for negotiation and creativity in attributing rights and duties related to property. In waste and discard studies, one can trace the various ways persons relate to each other with respect to waste, and how that mobilizes rights or duties contingent upon the perception of waste. It is surprising that the concept of property has received limited attention in waste and discard studies (Lane 2011: 398) given the ubiquity of various informal practices that erode or contest formal property rights. One of the notable exceptions is Alexander and Reno's (2012: 22–24) work on economies of recycling, in which they demonstrate that understanding property relations with respect to waste matter requires leaving the comfortable space of production and exchange. Discard, storage, reclamation, repair, or care may lead to alternative property relations that intermingle with the earlier property relations. This points to temporality as a critical analytical dimension because resources are often "palimpsests of former, present and potential things, momentarily coalesced into a form to which property rights may be asserted" (Alexander and Reno 2012: 23). This way of thinking about property relations shows its relevance for the paradox of saving and wasting because it enables us to trace all the different strands of meaning that make social action meaningful.

In this chapter, I explore the paradox of saving while wasting among Czech landfill workers in West Bohemia. Workers' acts of value recovery are paramount in their everyday lives at work. Informal saving and recovering value from waste takes not only a significant portion of the workers' official working time that is supposedly devoted to other activities, but it also provides the basis for their self-perception. At the same time, the workers can be careless and wasteful in management of the resources provided by their employer. In what follows, I tease apart the various ways the workers think, act, and talk about the acts of recovery, and explore the different logics behind workers' wastefulness. I argue that property relations and materiality are critical for understanding the contradictory practices of landfill workers.

Managing Municipal Solid Waste

One cold morning in Spring 2015, I was sitting inside the small trailer for landfill workers in the Pureland landfill writing notes. Jindra and Karel, two landfill workers, left and approached the edge of the landfill to have a look at the trucks coming through the gate. Suddenly, they decided to run down to where the fresh waste was being deposited. When I reached them, they were walking with their high boots up to their mid calves through the soft pile of fresh garbage made up of various large plastic bags and paper boxes. They were tearing apart the bags, opening the boxes, and examining the contents. It was clear this garbage did not come from households. Jindra explained that it was from one of the large supermarkets in the city, which periodically sends unwanted goods to landfill. This kind of waste was of interest because it could contain anything from cheese that had passed its sell-by date to electric drills. Both workers reused discarded plastic bags to collect their finds, and in about half an hour they returned to the trailer with their treasures. Such scavenging was a typical activity for the landfill workers who, in addition to their formal duties, engaged in activities that turned unwanted things into valuable ones (cf. Reno 2009). There are multiple reasons for the retail sector wasting goods that are still edible and usable (for details, see Alexander and Smaje 2008: 1,291). Such commodities may lose their monetary value for the retailers, but when they reach the landfill as waste, the workers recover new forms of value.

The Pureland landfill, where I undertook my ethnographic research from 2014 to 2017, is a place where such value transformations took place. The landfill is located in West Bohemia in a former quarry (see Figure 7.1). The landfill, run by a company that I call "Warm," employed four landfill workers who managed the waste, three officers at the gate who monitored and weighed the incoming trucks, and the manager. Contrary to common expectations that landfill work is unattractive and only for those who do not have other choices, these employees remained in their jobs for many years because of various benefits, most notably the slow pace of work, a relaxed environment, opportunities for scavenging, and overall stability. As Nagle (2013: 23) and Reno (2016: 5) note, waste generation is a constant, and so too is the need to manage it. Therefore, apart from one officer, other employees had worked there between eleven and twenty-seven years. Moreover, even the landfill workers who were in everyday intimate contact with dirty matter were far from being at the bottom of social hierarchy. Rather, they represented an unlikely combination: a former carpenter; a plumber and petty entrepreneur; an army officer; and an agricultural worker. In addition to the benefit of scavenging to generate extra money, there were also more subtle motivations for staying at the landfill that I began to recognize over time. Scavenging is like a game, full of hope, excitement, and satisfaction. Once someone experiences the constant hope that something valuable might appear, it becomes almost addictive.

Workers' scavenging was intertwined with their formal jobs, which primarily entailed the monitoring and distribution of waste within the landfill. They often performed scavenging within the frame of their official duties,

Figure 7.1. Front loaders and garbage truck at the landfill. © Daniel Sosna.

which was a common practice among various kinds of workers during socialism (Wedel 1992: 76). For example, on the way to pull a garbage truck from the mud or to spray the surface with landfill leachate,[1] the workers at the Pureland landfill walked and examined the grounds and piles of trash for potential finds. Once they transported the finds to their working area near the container, they either started processing or repairing the things immediately, or did so later when there was nothing else to do.[2] These activities were satisfying for the workers, because they could use their knowledge and skills to not only repair and reassemble things, but also take them apart and imagine their new value. As Sanchez (2020: 81) argues, such satisfaction grows from one's ability to affect the transition of objects between different regimes of value. Since the workers had to repair their working tools or components of their front loaders from time to time, it was hard to draw a clear line between their formal and informal activities. For outsiders visiting the landfill, everything seemed to be naturally part of the workers' job. Informality disappeared for any observer, including the landfill manager and the workers themselves. They became so accustomed to scavenging that they did not distinguish it from their official work. This corresponds well with the model in which the informal resides inside the networks of official production (Bear 2013: 378). This mutually constitutive nature is demonstrated in the Pureland landfill when the manager "closes his eyes" and ignores scavenging as long as the workers fulfill their formal duties. The company benefits from such tolerance because it acts as downward pressure on workers' wages. It is expected that the workers recover extra value via their informal activities. At the same time, the workers need a formal job that stabilizes fluctuations in waste streams for their scavenging.

Salvaging Things: Pathways to Value Recovery

In October 2014, I was helping Slávek, one of the landfill workers, move a set of wooden windows in the landfill. The windows were in surprisingly good shape, unbroken, and only moderately worn (see Figure 7.2). The windows were a bit old-fashioned, but otherwise were perfectly functional. The day before, a truck driver from a company that specialized in building reconstructions had deposited them in the landfill. Fortunately, Slávek had carefully helped with the deposition to prevent any damage. The windows were moved closer to the workers' container, where most of the processing, repairing, and storage of things of potential value took place. The windows complemented nicely the cinder blocks and cement that Slávek had already collected from the landfill and transported home during the previous

Figure 7.2. Windows salvaged by Slávek. © Daniel Sosna

months. All these items constituted materials for his future new garage; it just required patience to accumulate the material he needed from waste delivered to the landfill.

Initially, workers' thriftiness seemed straightforward: they were saving things from waste, which was for their own benefit in terms of the money they saved by not needing to buy those things. They often talked about the early 1990s as a golden age when "one did not need money at all" (*člověk vůbec nepotřeboval peníze*) because everything could be found in the landfill.[3] During the 1990s, there were no official scrapyards for household devices, and the overall fascination with Western consumerism caused rich waste streams to flow to the landfills. The notion of the workers' thrift in terms of saving money can be understood as economizing or resourcefulness directed toward reaching certain goals in the future (Smiles 1876: 20; Lastovicka et al. 1999: 88); this corresponds well with thrift conceptualized as calculative reason including forethought. Moreover, the consequences of scavenging extended the scope of thrift beyond the workplace to have an impact on household expenditure.

Later, I began to recognize that thriftiness was more complex, with different layers of understanding assigned to salvage acts by the workers. One of these layers was to salvage things in order take advantage of relations with others. Some of the things the workers collected were meant to be shared, given as gifts, or sold. Thus, things such as pliers, knives, hammers, and brooms were shared among the workers in the sense described by Widlok (2016: 87), who emphasizes shared demands that fit neither the logic of reciprocal obligations nor commodity exchange. For example, when a worker found and repaired a hammer, he used it himself, but it was possible for others to use it as well without any obligation. When salvageable things could not be used on the site, or if there were already plenty of them, there were other routes to salvage them. Things such as sporting equipment, electric devices, books, or tools were given as gifts to relatives, friends, or acquaintances. Discarded food that was still edible (see Alexander and Smaje 2008) was either consumed on site or taken home, where it was often given as gifts to relatives. Such events were common after floods or fires, which, while disastrous for shop-owners, enabled the landfill workers to accumulate large quantities of packaged food or drink for further exchange. Although gift giving was the most natural way to use things scavenged at the landfill, the interaction could also follow a quasi-commodified logic (cf. Alexander 2009a: 236) when especially valuable things were exchanged for money with acquaintances. The price depended on the receiver's generosity and could be low, and the workers maintained the attitude that "they will give me what they will give me" (*dá mi co mi dá*), but the transaction would be thought of in monetary terms. These exchanges demonstrate that a strict separation between gifts and commodities is not always possible (Appadurai 1986: 13; Parry and Bloch 1989: 8–9; Miller 2001). It is rather a continuum; some practices incline more toward the gift, while others are closer to the commodity logic of exchange.

While whole things were exchanged primarily as gifts, broken parts or undifferentiated pieces followed a different trajectory. This was the case of scrap metal, which represented a special and well-developed part of the informal economy at the landfill. Scrap metal was omnipresent and attracted a lot of attention. The landfill workers continuously scanned the surface of the landfill for the presence of wires, bars, pipes, or broken metal parts. They also extracted metal parts from composite objects and cut them into smaller pieces for ease of storage and further transport. Different types of metal were categorized and collected into separate containers to maximize their exchange value. Recovering the value of scrap metal was mainly a question of selling it for money. Scrap metal was collected, sorted, processed, and transported to a center for metal collection, where the workers received cash. All this happened as an open secret among the employees, including the landfill manager, who was doing a favor for his subordinates (Henig and Makovicky 2017). I never encountered any sign of shame among the workers over the fact that these informal practices were not entirely legal.[4] It was perceived as a perk of the job, a natural practice that went without saying; it was not perceived as theft (see Pawlik 1992: 79–81; Alexander 2009a: 236). The landfill workers understood these opportunities as natural and inherent to their jobs. As Slávek described it: "We collect waste. Why not? Look, it's here and nobody cares. Otherwise, we would crush it with the loader. We're here every day; it can get really cold or hot; we have to spray the damned landfill water[5] and who knows what this crap [*svinstvo*] does to us. Yeah, who cares, right? And the salary we get . . . you don't wanna know. At least we can collect some stuff." Not only Slávek, but also others felt it was their moral right to scavenge and keep the things they salvaged, because they saw their salaries as inadequate, and this was a way to rectify the injustice. They talked without hesitation about their personal preferences in scavenging, the kinds of recovered objects their relatives and friends liked or did not like, projects they had accomplished using materials from the landfill, or how they outsmarted custom officers with their fictive destructions of confiscated goods. The notion of theft never appeared.

Another dimension of workers' thriftiness stemmed from a conviction that "somebody might need these things" (*někdo by ty věci mohl potřebovat*). It was reminiscent of Mr. Leli from Bohumil Hrabal's novel *The Snowdrop Festival*, who kept seemingly useless things in his shed, such as multiple left boots or leaking water containers, "just in case." The workers in the Pureland landfill used their large container to store finds that nobody on the site or anywhere else needed. For workers accustomed to being patient, it made perfect sense to hoard these things: one never knew who might need them in the future. Although the workers recognized that such accumulation might have been advantageous for them, they were not driven by greed. It was primarily the feeling that "it would be a pity to leave them here [i.e., discarded things]" (*byla by škoda to tady nechat*). Being passive witnesses of value loss was simply considered careless when workers' friends and acquaintances could potentially benefit from the stored things in the future.

Scavenging, however, is not just about the things being rescued, but also about the pleasure of the activity itself. The landfill workers unanimously agreed they like the constant search for things. Indeed, this enjoyment did not evaporate over the two decades that Karel and Jindra, the most senior workers, spent on the site. The hope that something unexpected and valuable might appear in the garbage was a strong motivator for walking through the soft and smelly matter, regardless of weather conditions. As Slávek said when he was leaving his job: "I will miss it here. One always searches for something." Reno (2016: 120) interpreted the enjoyment of scavenging as a way of weakening the divide between home and market as well as subverting existing norms and laws. Although this subversive dimension of enjoyment existed among the Czech landfill workers, there were other dimensions. Excitement from scavenging was like mushroom picking, which is almost a national sport in the Czech Republic: it is considered an exciting search rather than labor (cf. Tsing 2015: 77–78). For the landfill workers, a mixture of hope and anticipation made their search for new finds enjoyable. They hoped they could find a real treasure, such as a bag full of money or golden jewelry. These dreams came up frequently during our discussions about the future, when the landfill would be shut down and the workers would be retired: it would be nice if something very precious and valuable would end up being discarded at the landfill. Hope as futural momentum compelled the workers to search even the loads of garbage that were not considered attractive. One never knows! Hope motivated searching that might actualize the potential of waste (cf. Bryant and Knight 2019: 157). Moreover, the joy from the search emerged for more down-to-earth reasons. Because of their extensive experience, the workers knew when the most interesting trucks with waste would come, and they prepared themselves for collecting in advance, in anticipation of new tools, clothes, food waste, or other goods. They were actively "pressing toward the future" (Bryant and Knight 2019: 27), which could, to a certain degree, be predicted but was still open to modification in the present. The affective dimension of scavenging indicates that joy is related to thrift not only as an experience that enables saving, as Miller (1998: 56) observed in shopping practices, but also as an experience that might (but does not have to) lead to saving. Searching for things in the landfill was exciting even if this activity did not result in saving money in the end.

As I have demonstrated, the workers' thriftiness had multiple layers of meaning. As Sosna, Brunclíková, and Galeta (2019: 320) argue elsewhere, thrift does not have to be understood as a unidimensional concept based on self-sacrifice to reach economic goals, or as a reaction to scarcity, or as a moral call to be good, or as the value of thrifty practices themselves. Landfill workers' understanding of thrift shows that it can be viewed as reducing household expenditure. At the same time, it is a kind of sociality that sustains relations among the workers, kin, friends, and acquaintances. The moral dimension grows from the pressing feeling that value should not be lost when one has an opportunity to save it. The activities themselves are also joyful because of the permanent anticipation and hope for unexpected new finds and their creative restoration, reuse, and exchange.

Who Cares? Wasting in the Landfill

While the previous section described various dimensions behind scavenging as thrifty activity that prevents the loss of resources, the workers did not always act as responsible guardians of value. As the opening vignette of this chapter showed, they sometimes appeared to be deliberately wasteful. After the event with the radio, I started paying more attention to various acts of wasting in the landfill. For Peter and other workers, it was normal to leave the radio or TV on when they left the container or trailer.[6] Sometimes they left the lights on for hours without feeling any guilt that electricity was being wasted. Also, I witnessed repeatedly that no one showed any concern that the tap was dripping, or that the engine of the front loader was left idling while the driver left the vehicle and started repairing something in the storage container. What seemed to me to be wasteful was considered normal behavior at work. It was so natural and ingrained in everyday practice over the years that my questions initially raised surprise or answers such as "who cares?" among the workers. These were subtle acts that were not supposed to be visible to others. Later, I discovered that there were at least two different notions of wasting, driven by different dynamics despite being similar in their appearance.

Wasting diesel fuel turned out to be an intentional strategy to outsmart the employer.[7] Two workers, Jindra and Petr, were also drivers of the two front loaders used in the landfill. The larger of the two loaders, a massive twenty-ton metal beast, had an engine that consumed about twenty liters of diesel fuel per hour.[8] Since the drivers reported the duration of the loaders' use in hours, it made perfect sense to let the engine idle. They received the amount of fuel estimated for the "working consumption" of the engine. Because idling consumed less fuel, extra idling enabled them to receive more fuel than was consumed, so they could keep the difference for themselves. This strategy was clearly calculative and took advantage of the formal employment arrangements. The workers explained the idling as a strategy to keep the front loader's cabin cool via air-conditioning during summer and warm via heating during winter, but the length of idling was often surprisingly long, which raised my suspicion about the validity of their explanation. I only once witnessed Jindra filling the extra canisters from a supply cistern truck. Since he behaved as though it had never happened, it took me a while to realize what really happened that day. It was part of an informal economy that even the workers considered a sensitive issue, in contrast to their scavenging, which was overt and was reflected in various narratives. The tactic to save extra fuel via idling was different. The workers were not willing to openly discuss the deliberate wasting of gas to outsmart the company and generate extra value for themselves. I can only speculate, but the main reason for such a silence could be that this behavior clashed with the values that the workers were otherwise using to describe themselves as good people. Obtaining extra fuel was beyond the usual informal tricks understood as justified. It was a contradiction that would force the drivers to be more self-reflexive and see the negative dimension of their practices. Also, a punishment from the company could be more severe for pilfering diesel than for the tricks with the unwanted waste matter.

To understand wasting electricity and water, from which the workers could not benefit, it is critical to explain the relationship to their company, Warm. They disliked Warm because they never felt respected for working in a dirty and dangerous environment[9] regardless of weather conditions and holidays. In addition to frequent complaints about the lack of interest from and experience of the Warm managers, a story about this troubled relationship reappeared several times over the years. It was as follows: The workers were invited downtown with other employees of their large company to celebrate an anniversary. When they arrived, all the chairs were occupied, so they could not sit down and have dinner with the others. The landfill manager did not take care of his subordinates and other managers never paid much attention to the laborers working in a distant landfill far away from the company's headquarters. They were left standing in the large hall while others were either staring or completely ignoring them. The workers felt as though they were being exposed in a medieval pillory. They just grabbed few schnitzels and decided to leave for a nearby pub, where they enjoyed a few beers on their own.

Although this story was told in slightly different versions by different landfill workers, a strong sense of humiliation was always present. On top of this, the frustration of being treated with disregard started reemerging from late 2015, when plans for the landfill's shutdown leaked from the headquarters. The shutdown was announced and postponed multiple times, thus creating a sense of uncertainty, which was frustrating given the years of previous stability. The workers were surprisingly passive in searching for more information or directly negotiating with the headquarters about their future. It was not an arena where they would have felt self-confident. Negotiating with the officers, writing letters, or filling out forms did not match the workers' capacities. Instead of resolving the uncertainty via direct action (e.g., negotiating with the employer, searching for a new job, etc.), they followed the strategy that they considered more natural and appropriate: everyday resistance. Interestingly, the acts of resistance were relevant at different scales. The workers felt mistreated not only by their manager, but also by more abstract entities, such as the company and "the politicians" who did not care about normal people.

The resistance consisted of various indirect complaints, deserting official tasks, or fulfilling their manager's orders extremely slowly (see Wilk, this volume). Wasting electricity and water was a part of this repertoire of acts that avoided any direct confrontation with the authority but was meant to hurt it (cf. Scott 1985: 29). These acts were not significant in terms of their effects, but hurting the company produced satisfaction because it was based on a conviction that such an approach was morally justifiable. Moreover, it was happening primarily in the interstices of social control, offstage (Scott 1985: 25), where the manager had limited capacity to exercise his power: he was rarely at the landfill full time because he had another office at the headquarters, and he divided his work time between the two places. Landfill workers' behavior is similar to what Rakowski (2016: 105–9) calls interior (internal) spectacles: the complaints and acts of destruction that generate satisfaction without being effective, because there is only a void at the other end of the communication channel. Such spectacles can serve to question and negotiate who the performers are and what their place in the world is (Rakowski 2017: 164, 175). In Rakowski's sense, it is more about potentiality and imagination than the direct effects of action. This fits the situation at Pureland landfill, as the workers attempted to understand what their position in the system and their ultimate "worth" was. The significance of these acts, however, did not lie in their visibility, but in their capacity to generate a contradiction, which could serve as a vehicle for moral reasoning (Alexander 2009b: 46). Their wastefulness was based on the direct reversal of the principle that made the most sense to their life at work: recovering value. It was a way to transform the experience of injustice and lack of respect into a paradox of guarding and wasting value. It expressed the clash between the workers' imagination of just relations with the manager, the company, and society as a whole and the real power imbalance that left them limited space for pursuing their vision of proper relationships.

Property Rights

The landfill workers' management of resources seems contradictory. On one hand, their overarching commitment lay in rescuing and recovering value. On the other hand, they wasted resources and did not express any moral remorse for their wastefulness. This paradox appears in a new light when one views it through the prism of property. Places of disposal are arenas where ownership is negotiated and contested (Lane 2011: 404). At the formal level of Czech legislation, a thing thrown into a bin or a waste container is owned by the sanitation company that collects the garbage. When the garbage truck deposits it at the landfill, it becomes the property of the company running the landfill.

Warm had the right to profit from the ownership of landfilled waste. In contrast to most kinds of things that stimulate a receiver to give something in exchange, waste often mobilizes the opposite logic. The donor must give something in addition to the waste itself if she wants to get rid of it. In the landfill, the managing company receives waste as well as payments for taking responsibility for the waste's future agency. Such agentic potential generates further profit when the company captures the landfill gas, transforms it into electricity in a cogeneration unit, and receives money in exchange. But the agentic potential foregrounds the other side of the coin: responsibility. The ownership of waste makes the company responsible for monitoring, draining, and neutralizing the landfill leachate, which is the most challenging entity because of its capacity to emerge in large quantities and leak through various barriers. Solid matter is less difficult to control, but the owner of the landfill must, by law, prevent any "undesirable degradation and theft" of garbage from the landfill.

The landfill workers' informal practices emerged from the interstices in property rights and the ambiguities associated with waste disposal imagined as a final act of closure (cf. Hetherington 2004: 159). They felt that Warm's formal property claims only related to where waste generated direct, measurable, and controllable financial value: waste disposal fees and production of electricity. Both relations were based on images of anonymous mass waste. Since individual pieces of garbage disappeared from the radar of both the company and the landfill manager, they were treated by the workers as a commons (Ostrom 1990), although only temporarily, accessible to anybody in the landfill: the landfill workers, truck drivers, sanitation workers, and other visitors. Naturally, the landfill workers had the most privileged access to these resources because of their proximity and exposure to "fresh waste." They were happy that their activities were undocumented and that only informal negotiation enabled exploitation of the commons. Because of the physical detachment and lack of care of the company and its representatives toward waste, the workers never felt any respect for the *de jure* property rights of their company toward waste. Similarly to Verdery's (1999: 70) villagers, the landfill workers' resistance to official property rights mobilized the notion of common good as a critical factor. Approaching property as being fuzzy enabled a wider range of actors who were in contact with the waste to salvage objects and recover value; this was seen as more just than allowing the company to have exclusive property rights. Moreover, the workers did not feel any obligation to respect formal rules concerning property rights when these abstract principles were created—in the workers' view—by lawmakers who had no experience in the real management of waste on the ground and were driven by their own interests in policy making (cf. Makovicky 2018: 503).

Instead of respecting formal property rights, the workers developed their own understanding of property relations based on recognition, proximity, and care. Property is not only contingent upon boundaries (Hirsch

2010: 356); a thing owned must be recognized in the first place. For the Warm Company management, components of mass waste were invisible, while the workers had the necessary experience and skill to recognize and claim what they originally considered a commons that was theirs. Workers' conviction about Warm's undeserved formal rights was also based on Warm's detachment and lack of care. When the owner does not care, others may claim a moral right to use the owner's property, as Faulk (2013: 82–83) demonstrated in the example of the employees of a previously bankrupted hotel who repaired it and fought for their right to operate it. They applied the Lockean understanding of property justified by the labor and care exerted. The landfill workers in the Pureland landfill felt they had moral rights to the landfill's waste material because of their experience and everyday labor expended in taking care of it. It was reinforced by their "seniority," because most of the workers were managing waste long before the company and its managers appeared on the scene. As Peter put it: "What are they going to tell us? They know nothing [*Ví prd*]." Also, past experience from socialist times shaped workers' perceptions of ownership at work, because all of them started working during socialism when a semi-joking motto suggested: "If you do not steal, you rob your family" (*kdo nekrade, okrádá vlastní rodinu*). Therefore, activity in the interstices of property rights was not only a matter of efficiency (see Hann 1993: 308), but also constituted an ability to undermine the official collective property claims of the state. There was an implicit notion of an amorphous and impersonal state that could be abused.

The workers claimed property rights in a portion of the mass waste through their labor of reclamation and repair. It was natural to be thrifty with respect to these resources. Electricity, water, and diesel fuel provided by the company for the workers to enable their work was perceived differently. Although it is challenging to delimit the property boundaries of electricity and water because of their fluidity and the nature of infrastructure that enables the flow, they were clearly perceived as company resources, or more specifically, resources paid for by the company. They were pure and ordered in contrast to the dirty mass of waste. But more significantly, there was limited potential to claim these resources in the same way that parts of mass waste could be. Transporting electricity out of the landfill could be potentially done only using batteries, and water was too cheap and heavy to be interesting enough. Therefore, the workers never saw the potential of these entities to become "theirs." They could, however, be exploited and wasted. Another traditional idiom, "Blood does not flow from the other" (*Z cizího krev neteče*),[10] underscored their activities. Indeed, the resources of "the other" could be wasted as a form of resistance to the unjust relations between the workers and their employer, as I argued earlier. Diesel fuel, however, was a different story. It was also fluid, but its distribution and storage were always linked to containers: the cistern, fuel tank, or canister. It was the container that facilitated the control because of its capacity to either enable or inhibit transaction (see Shryock and Smail 2017: 1). Interestingly, it did not prevent the workers from outsmarting the company via saving while wasting. This paradoxical tactic was so smart that it killed two birds with one stone: it simultaneously saved personal funds and hurt the company.

The paradox of being both thrifty and wasteful relates to materiality. Electricity and water do not have the thingliness (Gonzalez-Ruibal 2008: 251) typical of the discarded things in the landfill. Water is amorphous matter, while electricity is itself invisible—it is a property of matter rather than matter itself. Therefore, they are different from the tools, skis, or iron pipes that represent visible things with clear borders that can be touched, modified, stored, and exchanged. Despite the relational potential of things, they possess material properties and qualities that are critical for their engagement with the world (Ingold 2007: 3; Olsen 2010: 37). They have substance, surface, shape, color, and other potential qualities that can be perceived by various organisms, including humans. Such qualities contribute to the perception of value and make it easier or harder to witness its loss or engage with its recovery. As Jindra once told me: "Look at this snowboard. It's still nice, isn't it? Tell me, would you leave it in the landfill?" I had to admit that I would feel bad ignoring such a nice piece of sporting equipment. Weiner (1992: 59) argued a long time ago that the properties of objects might generate different kinds of relations and value associated with giving or keeping. In landfills, garbage items lure or discourage the engagement of workers, officers, managers, and truck drivers. Materiality plays its part in resource management because it generates different emotions in humans and enables different degrees of control. It is not a coincidence that the wasteful behavior of the landfill workers is directed toward resources with specific material properties.

Conclusion

Thrift is a rich and productive concept with which to think. Given its capacity to cross various physical, spatiotemporal, or imaginative boundaries, it is surprising that it has received limited attention in anthropological theorizing. This chapter builds upon those inspirations that have problematized the view of thrift as a monolith, a general and consistent tendency to save for future ends. Thrift is a slippery and multilayered concept with various meanings attached to it. It was my intention to explore its nature and richness in a special environment where abundant resources offer opportunities for value transformation and negotiation of property rights (see Alexander and Sosna this vol. to examine the link between thrift and abundance). When landfill workers salvage and recover value, it saves their funds, sustains social relations, generates profit, expresses moral commitment to prevent the loss of value, and generates enjoyment from the performance itself. It is impossible to point to the single most critical dimension of such thriftiness because they unfold together with varying degrees of prominence in different contexts. The diversity of meanings associated with thrift is its critical feature and may even be mobilized in a pursuit of the specific goals of the actors (Hájek, Kaderka, Nekvapil 2019: 28). Although the need to save, care, and recover was strong and ubiquitous among the landfill workers, it did not have a strong overt expression in a single term that was used by the workers themselves. It simply went without saying that saving resources and recovering value was good. As Bloch (1998: 7) argues, nonlinguistic knowledge can be critical for understanding others; this is exactly the case with the landfill workers, whose thrift unfolded in their everyday practices of scavenging and became prominent in the action itself. This tacit understanding emerged slowly over the four years of our interaction, and various linguistic expressions and stories served more as indirect tools for reinforcing this tacit knowledge and enriching its complexity.

Thrift embodies a vivid example of a relational concept. Rescuing bits and bobs from the landfill became meaningful when it was related to the different scales of relations created and reinforced via sharing, gift giving, and trading. It entailed individual variation in understanding and actions concerning thrift, interactions among the coworkers and with incoming truck drivers, and it also spread beyond the landfill to relations with household members, friends, acquaintances, and informal collaborators in the center for metal collection. In a more abstract sense, these acts unfolded in relation to public discourses on responsibility and consumption, as well as social inequality. The reversal of thrift, wasting, should be also understood through relations, however strange it may sound, as acts of saving or resistance that cross different scales, from opposing one's specific boss to resisting the more abstract state and its politicians. All this supports Alexander's (2012) argument that tiny, everyday actions of people who transform value via their creative acts become meaningful in relation to entities and processes at higher scalar levels. Therefore, using thrift as a vehicle for moving between the scales (see Alexander and Sosna, this vol.) along the pathways created by relations can be a productive strategy for understanding the ways value is saved and recovered.

The ethnography of waste scavenging shows that thrift does not preclude wasting. On the contrary, it demonstrates that they can go hand in hand.

The workers who devoted their time and energy to thrifty recovery of value from waste carelessly wasted the resources provided by their employer. It was either a tactic to save their own funds or resistance to asymmetrical power relations. Wasting diesel fuel at the landfill was almost a reversal of Miller's (1998) saving turned into spending during shopping: here, it was rather wasting turned into saving. Wasting electricity and water becomes meaningful when one considers property relations. In scavenging, the workers were taking advantage of ambiguous property rights to waste and using their labor to claim their rights to objects recovered from the heaps of garbage. The same approach could not be used in the cases of electricity and water, because their materiality and infrastructural conduits made similar claims unwieldy. Moreover, shapeless, amorphous, or invisible resources that lack thingliness did not mobilize passion for imagining value recovery, which was one of the important dimensions of thrifty scavenging. Moreover, water and electricity were linked to formal corporate ownership, the landfill manager who served the corporate owner, and the politicians who enabled the managers to treat their workers with little respect. All this made these resources a target for the subversive activities of workers bent on hurting via wasting. If we accept the view that thrift is multidimensional and can coexist with wasting, the challenge of promoting sustainable and less destructive ways of life becomes an even greater one, because it can hardly be promoted as "one size fits all." Instead, a critical reflection and more nuanced view on thrift and wasting would provide a better chance for us to get closer to understanding why human relationships to resources show paradoxes, and what sort of logic lurks behind.

Acknowledgments

I am grateful to Catherine Alexander for pushing me to rethink my material and for suggesting new ways to transform ideas into a text. Her work went beyond the usual level of a few comments from a colleague. Miguel Alexiades, Luděk Brož, David Henig, Paul Keil, Pavel Mašek, Barbora Stehlíková, Martin Tremčinský, participants of the thrift workshop in Pilsen, and two anonymous reviewers provided me with useful comments on various versions of this chapter and on my presentation of the material. Patty Gray kindly proofread the text and made several helpful comments. The work was supported by the Czech Science Foundation under grant GA20-06759S.

Daniel Sosna is a senior researcher in the Department of Ecological Anthropology, Institute of Ethnology, Czech Academy of Sciences. He received his PhD in anthropology from Florida State University, and his research resulted in the book *Social Differentiation in the Late Copper Age and the Early Bronze Age in South Moravia (Czech Republic)* (Archaeopress, 2009). Daniel is a specialist on ethnographic and archaeological research of waste regimes with a regional focus on Central Europe. He coedited the book *Archaeologies of Waste: Encounters with the Unwanted* (Oxbow Books, 2017).

Notes

1. Landfill leachate is a liquid formed in landfills via passing through or emerging from the disposed solid waste.
2. The workers purchased their own container for 30,000CZK [approx. 1,400USD] and brought this half-ton metal structure to the landfill to house their informal gadgetry and store their finds recovered from the landfill.
3. An interesting parallel about perceived abundance and the ability to live almost entirely from landfill resources comes from O'Hare's (2018: 35) research on waste pickers in Uruguay.
4. According to the Czech Republic's Act 185 of 15 May 2001, "On Waste and Amendments of Some Other Acts," Part 10, Title I, §66, (2)b, the organizations running landfills must prevent waste from "undesirable degradation, theft, or leakage." Therefore, taking waste that the workers formally do not own and transporting it out of the landfill is illegal unless the organization allows them to do so.
5. He meant landfill leachate.
6. Workers also had a TV in their official residential container at the gate.
7. I thank Martin Tremčinský for directing my attention to the tricks practiced by drivers of large vehicles.
8. In contrast to common notions of "mileage," the consumption of such heavy machinery is measured per unit of time, not distance.
9. Nagle (2013: 57) describes how dangerous the work with municipal waste might be.
10. This idiom means someone else's property does not require care, and its damage or loss does not hurt the ego.

References

Alexander, Catherine. 2009a. "Illusions of Freedom: Polanyi and Third Sector Recycling Schemes." In *Market and Society: The Great Transformation Today*, edited by Chris Hann and Keith Hart, 221–39. Cambridge, UK: Cambridge University Press.

———. 2009b. "Privatization: Jokes, Scandal, and Absurdity in a Time of Rapid Change." In *Ethnographies of Moral Reasoning: Living Paradoxes of Global Age*, edited by Karen Sykes, 43–65. New York: Palgrave.

———. 2012. "Remont: Work in Progress." In *Economies of Recycling: The Global Transformation of Materials, Values and Social Relations*, edited by Catherine Alexander and Joshua Reno, 255–75. London: Zed Books.

Alexander, Catherine, and Joshua Reno. 2012. "Introduction." In *Economies of Recycling: The Global Transformation of Materials, Values and Social Relations*, edited by Catherine Alexander and Joshua Reno, 1–32. London: Zed Books.
Alexander, Catherine, and Chris Smaje. 2008. "Surplus Retail Food Redistribution: An Analysis of a Third Sector Model." *Resources, Conservation and Recycling* 52(11): 1,290–98.
Alexander, Catherine, Chris Smaje, Rose Timlett, and Ian Williams. 2009. "Improving Social Technologies for Recycling." *Proceedings of the Institution of Civil Engineers–Waste and Resource Management* 162(1): 15–28.
Appadurai, Arjun. 1986. "Introduction: Commodities and the Politics of Value." In *The Social Life of Things: Commodities in Cultural Perspective*, edited by Arjun Appadurai, 3–63. Cambridge, UK: Cambridge University Press.
Bataille, Georges. 1985. *Visions of Excess: Selected Writings 1927–1939*. Manchester: Manchester University Press.
Bear, Laura. 2013. "The Antinomies of Audit: Opacity, Instability and Charisma in the Economic Governance of a Hooghly Shipyard." *Economy and Society* 42(3): 375–97.
Bloch, Maurice. 1998. *How We Think They Think: Anthropological Approaches to Cognition, Memory, and Literacy*. Boulder, CO: Westview Press.
Bryant, Rebecca, and Daniel M. Knight. 2019. *The Anthropology of the Future*. Cambridge, UK: Cambridge University Press.
Faulk, Karen Ann. 2013. *In the Wake of Neoliberalism: Citizenship and Human Rights in Argentina*. Stanford: Stanford University Press.
Geertz, Clifford. 1973. *The Interpretation of Cultures*. New York: Basic Books.
Gibson-Graham, Julie Katherine. 2014. "Rethinking the Economy with Thick Description and Weak Theory." *Current Anthropology* 55(S9): S147–53.
Gonzalez-Ruibal, Alfredo. 2008. "Time to Destroy: An Archaeology of Supermodernity." *Current Anthropology* 49(2): 247–79.
Gudeman, Stephen. 2012. "Vital Energy: The Current of Relations." *Social Analysis* 56(1): 57–73.
Gudeman, Stephen, and Chris Hann. 2015. *Oikos and Market: Explorations in Self-Sufficiency after Socialism*. New York: Berghahn Books.
Gudeman, Stephen, and Alberto Rivera. 1990. *Conversations in Colombia: The Domestic Economy in Life and Text*. Cambridge, UK: Cambridge University Press.
Hájek, Martin, Petr Kaderka, and Jiří Nekvapil. 2019. *Kdo šetří, má za tři? Diskurz šetrnosti v proměnách české společnosti* [A Penny Saved Is a Penny Earned? The Discourse of Thrift in a Changing Czech Society]. Praha: SLON.
Hann, Chris. 1993. "From Production to Property: Decollectivization and the Family-Land Relationship in Contemporary Hungary." *Man* 28(2): 299–320.
———. 2005. "Property." In *A Handbook of Economic Anthropology*, edited by James G. Carrier, 110–24. Cheltenham: Edward Elgar.
Henig, David, and Nicolette Makovicky, eds. 2017. *Economies of Favour After Socialism*. Oxford: Oxford University Press.
Hetherington, Kevin. 2004. "Secondhandedness: Consumption, Disposal, and Absent Presence." *Environment and Planning D: Society and Space* 22(1): 157–73.
Hirsch, Eric. 2010. "Property and Persons: New Forms and Contests in the Era of Neoliberalism." *Annual Review of Anthropology* 39: 347–60.

Ingold, Tim. 2007. "Materials against Materiality." *Archaeological Dialogues* 14(1): 1–16.

Kaneff, Deema. 2018. "Resources and Their Re/Valuation in Times of Political-Economic Reform." *Max Planck Institute for Social Anthropology Working Paper no. 189*. Halle/Saale: Max Planck Institute for Social Anthropology.

Lane, Ruth. 2011. "The Waste Commons in an Emerging Resource Recovery Waste Regime: Contesting Property and Value in Melbourne's Hard Rubbish Collections." *Geographical Research* 49(4): 395–407.

Lastovicka, John L., Lance A. Bettencourt, René S. Hughner, and Ronald J. Kuntze. 1999. "Lifestyle of the Tight and Frugal: Theory and Measurement." *Journal of Consumer Research* 26(1): 85–98.

Maine, Henry. 1861. *Ancient Law: Its Connection with the Early History of Society and Its Relation to Modern Ideas*. London: John Murray.

Makovicky, Nicolette. 2018. "*Kombinowanie*: Agency, Informality, and the Poetics of Self in Highland Poland." *Journal of the Royal Anthropological Institute* 24(3): 493–511.

Mauss, Marcel. 1990[1923–24]. *The Gift: The Form and Reason for Exchange in Archaic Societies*. London: Routledge.

Millar, Kathleen M. 2018. *Reclaiming the Discarded: Life and Labor on Rio's Garbage Dump*. Durham, NC: Duke University Press.

Miller, Daniel. 1998. *A Theory of Shopping*. Ithaca: Cornell University Press.

———. 2001. "Alienable Gifts and Inalienable Commodities." In *The Empire of Things: Regimes of Value and Material Culture*, edited by Fred R. Myers, 91–115. Santa Fe: School of American Research.

Nagle, Robin. 2013. *Picking Up: On the Streets and Behind the Trucks with the Sanitation Workers of New York City*. New York: Farrar, Straus and Giroux.

O'Hare, Patrick. 2018. "'The Landfill Has Always Borne Fruit': Precarity, Formalisation and Dispossession among Uruguay's Waste Pickers." *Dialectical Anthropology* 43(1): 31–44.

Olsen, Bjørnar. 2010. *In Defense of Things: Archaeology and the Ontology of Objects*. Lanham, MD: Rowman & Littlefield Publishers.

Ostrom, Elinor. 1990. *Governing the Commons: The Evolution of Institutions for Collective Action*. Cambridge, UK: Cambridge University Press.

Parry, Jonathan, and Maurice Bloch. 1989. "Introduction: Money and the Morality of Exchange." In *Money and the Morality of Exchange*, edited by Jonathan Parry and Maurice Bloch, 1–32. Cambridge, UK: Cambridge University Press.

Pawlik, Wojciech. 1992. "Intimate Commerce." In *The Unplanned Society: Poland during and after Communism*, edited by Janine R. Wedel, 78–94. New York: Columbia University Press.

Rakowski, Tomasz. 2016. *Hunters, Gatherers, and Practitioners of Powerlessness: An Ethnography of the Degraded in Postsocialist Poland*. New York: Berghahn Books.

———. 2017. "Interior Spectacles: The Art of the Informal among Bootleg Miners in Wałbrzych, Poland." In *Economies of Favour after Socialism*, edited by David Henig and Nicolette Makovicky, 161–80. Oxford: Oxford University Press.

Reno, Joshua. 2009. "Your Trash Is Someone's Treasure: The Politics of Value at a Michigan Landfill." *Journal of Material Culture* 14: 29–46.

———. 2015. "Waste and Waste Management." *Annual Review of Anthropology* 44(1): 557–72.

———. 2016. *Waste Away: Working and Living with a North American Landfill.* Oakland: University of California Press.
Richard, Analiese, and Daromir Rudnyckyj. 2009. "Economies of Affect." *Journal of the Royal Anthropological Institute* 15(1): 57–77.
Sanchez, Andrew. 2020. "Transformation and the Satisfaction of Work." *Social Analysis* 64(3): 68–94.
Scott, James C. 1985. *Weapons of the Weak: Everyday Forms of Peasant Resistance.* New Haven: Yale University Press.
Shryock, Andrew, and Daniel Lord Smail. 2017. "On Containers: A Forum. Introduction." *History and Anthropology* 29(1): 1–6.
Smiles, Samuel. 1876. *Thrift.* New York: Harper & Brothers.
Sosna, Daniel, Lenka Brunclíková, and Patrik Galeta. 2019. "Rescuing Things: Food Waste in the Rural Environment in the Czech Republic." *Journal of Cleaner Production* 214: 319–30.
Strathern, Marilyn. 2005. *Kinship, Law and the Unexpected: Relatives Are Always a Surprise.* Cambridge, UK: Cambridge University Press.
Tsing, Anna Lowenhaupt. 2015. *The Mushroom at the End of the World: On the Possibility of Life in Capitalist Ruins.* Princeton, NJ: Princeton University Press.
Verdery, Katherine. 1999. "Fuzzy Property: Rights, Power and Identity in Transylvania's Decollectivization." In *Uncertain Transition: Ethnographies of Change in the Postsocialist World*, edited by Michael Burawoy and Katherine Verdery, 53–81. Oxford: Rowman & Littlefield.
Wedel, Janine. 1992. *The Unplanned Society: Poland during and after Communism.* New York: Columbia University Press.
Weiner, Annette B. 1992. *Inalienable Possessions: The Paradox of Keeping-While-Giving.* Berkeley: University of California Press.
Widlok, Thomas. 2016. *Anthropology and the Economy of Sharing.* London: Taylor & Francis.
Wiessner, Polly. 2002. "The Vines of Complexity: Egalitarian Structures and the Institutionalization of Inequality among the Enga." *Current Anthropology* 43(2): 233–69.
Wilk, Richard. 2006. "Consumer Culture and Extractive Industry on the Margins of the World System." In *Consumer Cultures: Global Perspectives*, edited by John Brewer and Frank Trentmann, 123–44. Oxford: Berg.
Wolf, Eric R. 1966. *Peasants.* Englewood Cliffs, NJ: Prentice Hall.

8

Thrift and Its Opposites

RICHARD WILK

In this chapter I approach the question of thrift by looking at related concepts that have both similarities and crucial differences. My starting point is the concept of laziness—a topic that often arises when talking to people about issues of saving and spending—and the relationships between work and leisure. In the process of unpacking the many and various meanings of the word "laziness," I hope to reveal some of the close connections with the ontologies of time and temporality as matters of social and individual morality that both thrift and laziness share. I see both terms as related to the common discursive dichotomies of planning versus improvisation, present orientation versus thinking about the future, profligacy versus prudence and planning. Most of my discussion about thrift is limited to its meaning as frugality and saving toward the future, rather than the other meanings of the term discussed in the other chapters of this book (see the introduction to this vol.).

I also take this as an opportunity to finish an essay I began in 1990 when I was working in a Creole village in northern Belize. Laziness was a conspicuous part of daily conversation and was often mentioned in answering my questions about migration, employment, farming, village politics, kinship, interpersonal relationships, and rural versus urban life. Just like conservatives in the United States, villagers used laziness to explain inequalities, misfortunes, and what they saw as immoral behavior. The category of lazy people included the unemployed, those lacking ambition who exploited others, floated from one relationship to the next, ignored the needs of their family while focusing on immediate pleasures rather than their future responsibilities. Thrift came up constantly in my fieldwork, particularly in discussions of family problems, the difficulties of saving, holding property, starting a business, and honoring debts—the moral positives which were generally seen as lacking among lazy people.

It was jarring and difficult to hear villagers use a term that I associated with the worst of colonialism, chauvinism, ignorance, and privilege. In the colonial archives of British Honduras, British administrators and members of the mercantile elite constantly blamed the failure of development projects and the economic stagnation of the colony on the laziness of the natives, their lack of ambition or thought about the future. While I felt laziness discourse was certainly something worth documenting and discussing, I had trouble connecting it to anthropological theory, and the paper remained unfinished. I was also frustrated because writing about laziness in an ex-colony is ethically fraught and dangerous, because the term is so closely associated with colonialism and racist stereotypes.

In her research on Zulu ethnicity in South Africa, Jeske addresses laziness as a persistent myth, a narrative deployed against subordinate groups and individuals to explain and censure their behavior (2018, 2020). As she says, "This myth is a tool of the powerful, a means of morally justifying a system that benefits some to the detriment of others" (2020: 56). But the term was also used more widely: "I heard the word laziness again and again, by people of all racial, ethnic, class, age, and gender groups, nearly always to express the reasons why certain kinds of people—men, youth, Zulu people, and particularly black people—were not achieving something assumed to be the good life" (2020: 54). She also points out that the narrative of laziness has roots in scientific racism, since it was one of the criteria that Linnaeus used to define the subspecies of humans.

But here I want to approach laziness as more than a myth or a persistent narrative. I ask why accusations of laziness are so powerful, how laziness is connected with other forms of moral discourse, and why anthropology has so thoroughly ignored the term. I start by discussing the connections between laziness and thrift in historical social science and more specifically in anthropology. In the next section I focus on the history and context of laziness as discourse and behavior in Belize. I conclude that at their foundations, both thrift and laziness are closely connected forms of moral discourse, and both are at the intersection of culturally mediated perceptions of value and *time*. Talking about laziness is inevitably a statement about time, thinking ahead, and the morality of work and pleasure.

Laziness as Blaming the Victim

At one time I worked on the history of the European household and read the work of nineteenth-century conservative moralists. Frédéric Le Play, for example, saw industrialism and modernity destroying "the traditional stem family," producing an atomized class of workers who "lack judgement, are lazy and spendthrift, and are only worsened by philanthropy and assistance which . . . by exciting insatiable appetites, bring about the degradation of members of the working class" (Le Play 1871, in Zimmerman and Franklin 1936: 530). The close relationship between laziness and lack of thrift and forethought was further connected with dishonesty and self-delusion. Asking landlords in the American South why their tenants fed their children so badly when they knew better, two sociologists were told: "It is just like all people who are lazy, they are not going to be thrifty in anything. They all reason themselves out of things and find excuses for not doing things"(Cussler and De Give 1952: 142). This association between laziness and being a "spendthrift," someone foolish with money and unable to save it, is common in colonial-era comments about natives as well. Impoverished industrial working classes were often compared with "primitive" colonial natives. They were seen as infantile, uneducated, improvident, often foolish, and unruly. This kind of discourse gave legitimacy to aristocratic and authoritarian rule at home and provided a pretext and justification for the violence of slavery and forced labor in the colonies.

An important part of Le Play's argument is that giving aid or help to poor people, while a noble impulse, would do more harm than good by "exciting [their] insatiable appetites." This continues to be part of conservative dogma in the neoliberal United States, a justification for cutting welfare programs and subsidies for childcare, housing, healthy meals, and medical services. George Lakoff argues that the idea that helping people is actually harming them is based on an ideology of the family and parenting that he labels "strict father morality." Followers believe responsible adults must raise the children with clear rules and discipline, building self-reliance and the ability to survive life's challenges and harsh lessons (Lakoff 1996). Physically punishing children helps them in the long run, because facing hardships builds respect for patriarchal authority and quasi-military obedience to leaders and laws. Therefore, nurturant parents who try to help, understand, and communicate with their children, protecting them and easing their way in life, end up raising adults who are weak, lazy, dependent upon handouts and charity, improvident, and lacking in self-reliance and self-discipline.

Having no discipline, spoiled children cannot control their impulses, so they are sexually promiscuous (instead of saving virginity for marriage) and given to spending their earnings quickly on entertainment and other frivolous pastimes. They know that if they fail, someone will bail them out of trouble. These hedonists will not save for their children's education, a respectable house, or something else of lasting value, and instead demand handouts from governments and charities. When bad things happen and they have no savings, their pain and suffering should teach them a lesson. They are like Aesop's "grasshoppers" sailing through life without a care for the future, who must turn to disciplined and responsible "ants" in a predictable crisis (a pandemic for example).

Prominent conservative economists and political scientists often blame poverty and underdevelopment on weak governments that fail to plan and invest for the future, never enforcing laws that set clear moral boundaries on behavior. For example, pundits compare failed African regimes with the disciplined and forward thinking "Asian tigers" whose high savings rates provided the capital needed for industrial expansion (Harrison and Huntington 2000; Landes 1998). Lawrence Harrison specifically blames the poverty and failure of democracy in Latin America on Hispanic culture, particularly the lack of "emotional maturity" among men who are spoiled as children (which also explains the ethic of machismo and paternalist governance—1985: 80–83).[1] There is an entire conservative industry built on the criticism of liberal family values, blaming the evils of the world on weak parenting that fails to instill moral values and discipline (e.g., Bauer 1981; Dalrymple 2001, 2010; Sowell 2016). As P. T. Bauer says on his book jacket: "economic growth is possible under the right conditions. These include a certain amount of thrift and enterprise among the people, social mores and traditions which sustain them, and a firm but limited government" (1981). Some of these same writers accuse anthropologists of being weak minded liberals who are always finding excuses for dysfunctional behavior while refusing to make value judgments (unfamiliar with works work like Edgerton 1992 and Krech 1999). They find it particularly offensive that anthropologists' cultural relativism makes them unwilling to rank or judge different cultures or accept the superiority of modernity and civilization. Similarly, revisionist historians want us to admit that the Western countries really did bring civilization, Christian morality, and the benefits of science to ignorant savages, improving their lives in countless ways. They accuse liberal historians of blaming the West for colonialism and imperialism while ignoring the many benefits of European civilization (e.g., Ferguson 2004, 2011). Today we might view this as akin to pointing out the benefits of slavery.

Anthropological Contradictions

In the middle of the twentieth century, anthropology in the United States had an extended flirtation with psychology, explaining cultural traits and customs as the direct result of child rearing practices (see Manson 1988). This approach was popularized by Margaret Mead's work on Samoan adolescence, and it fueled a spate of writing on how "national character" could be explained by infant rearing practices such as swaddling, co-sleeping, or feeding on demand (Mead 1948; Whiting 1963).[2] Boasians like Ruth Benedict were comfortable seeing laziness or low work effort as a reflection of a general cultural ethos, a philosophy about life, and a set of cultural values (as in her distinction between Dionysian and Apollonian cultures, 1934). In *Peddlers and Princes,* Geertz built on this foundation when he explained that the differences between Hinduism and Islam explained divergent economic behavior and orientations to time in two Javanese towns (1968). This recalls Max Weber's contrast between the unmotivated and fatalistic Catholic peasant who responds to higher wages by working less, and the ambitious Protestant who works harder, while saving and deferring gratification (1930). For these Protestants, work should be valued in itself, which is why unemployment strikes at the very heart of identity (Wight 1993; Rudnyckyj this vol.).

A cultural approach to work effort also connects with substantivist economic anthropologists who argued that before capitalism and money, people were motivated by power or rank, goals set by transcendent cultural values. Following Polanyi, they argued that the desire for profit and wealth only dominates in market economies, which destroy previous social networks of reciprocity (see discussion in Wilk and Cliggett 2007).

A second anthropological approach explains low work effort and short-versus long-term decision making as rational responses to historical, environmental, and economic circumstances. For example, the mobile Ju/'hoansi bands in the Kalahari Desert described by Richard Lee did not need to work more than a few hours a day to feed themselves (1979). This mode of adaptation, what Sahlins called "the original affluent society," was based on a daily search for food and frequent moves, and therefore required few possessions (1972). According to Lee, these people valued their freedom and leisure more than possessions or social status. Binford related this foraging strategy to an environment where resources are widely scattered but seasonally abundant. He contrasts foraging with the collecting strategies of other hunter-gatherers who depend upon stored food for their security, who use more complex and specialized technology for gathering, transporting, processing, and ultimately storing food, what Binford called "logistical" organization (1980).

The original affluent society as depicted by Sahlins was made possible in an environment of abundance by networks of cooperation: strong but flexible social bonds that allowed people to be mobile but also secure. In a setting where security was based on social reciprocity, why bother working hard when you can gather enough to feed yourself and family in a couple of hours of work? Sahlins could ask this question because he implicitly accepted the universality of the *principle of least effort* (often called Zipf's law) according to which people always seek to spend the least possible amount of effort to achieve their goals. These foraging people were therefore not lazy; they were easily satisfied. An unspoken crux of his argument is that people can live happily with very limited wants and needs, which is undoubtedly true, particularly with egalitarian ideals and an economy of generalized reciprocity. Sahlins was also making an indirect attack on the sociology of leisure, which was established as an academic topic by Veblen's critique of modern consumer culture. While sociologists depicted the emergence of a modern "leisure class," Sahlins instead viewed modern society as fallen from an earlier state of leisure into an endless cycle of overwork and unneeded consumption.

As Lee described in a classic article, in the hunter-gatherer economy people cannot hold on to any valuable property, so they do not try (1969). But needs and wants are flexible: foraging peoples often proved vulnerable to the temptations of alcohol, adornments, metal tools, and weapons when they encountered Europeans (Salisbury 1962). Environmental anthropologists made an equally important argument when they pointed out how the pace of work is a product of seasonality and natural cycles. Farming people in particular often have seasons of extreme overwork balanced by slack periods when they might do maintenance or crafts around the home, celebrate, attend rituals, or rest (Netting 1993).

Twentieth-century anthropologists and sociologists also deployed the idea of reciprocity to explain laziness and improvidence among the poor in urban areas. In slums ridden with crime and offering few secure jobs or government services like healthcare or education, people could not plan for the future or build secure conjugal and corporate households (Lewis 1959). Instead, they used broad social networks of reciprocity to give them flexibility and allow mobility so they could take advantage of scattered opportunities and temporary resources, much like foraging hunters and gatherers. This so-called culture of poverty became a general explanation for how people could be trapped in dire circumstances, and it was widely used as a basis for welfare policies in developed countries (Moynihan 1969). In these urban circumstances of poverty, hard work would be irrational.

In retrospect, the idea has a certain liberal appeal because it accepts that the poor are thinking logically instead of being incapably stupid or lazy. But it also builds on the idea that modern capitalism is a meritocracy, where everyone could succeed if properly motivated. As Jeske points out, this kind of argument assumes that hard work is the determinant of success, that laziness is the reason people don't work hard, and that economic and social inequalities can be remedied by eradicating laziness (2020: 55–57).

This functional approach to laziness appears often in the ethnography of the Caribbean. For example, Nancie Gonzales argued that among the poor, any income is quickly dispersed through social networks through obligatory gifting and borrowing (1969). This offers men a practical form of long-term security, moving between households and building multiple sexual relationships, in contrast to women, who maintain "matrifocal" families of mothers, daughters, and grandchildren who pool resources. People survive by building alliances and extensive kin networks, which offer security in times of need while also preventing anyone from accumulating or saving. In Belize people call this way of life "catch and kill," taking opportunities when offered, improvising, and remaining mobile and uncommitted (in urban North America this way of life has been called "hustling"). It also prevents anyone from escaping poverty.

For many Belizeans, this lack of commitment and stability, the unwillingness to settle down and build a family around marriage, is associated with youth and particularly young men living in the violent and unpredictable world of gangs and drug dealing. Many Belizeans also see this way of life as the essence of laziness. Anthropologists of the Caribbean have called it a life based on values of "reputation" or "transience," contrasted with the values of "respectability" (Miller 1991; also discussion in Wilk 2006). The values of "reputation" also include the ability to speak well in all situations, persuade others, recognize opportunities, and exploit strangers, foreigners, and those of higher social status.

Laziness as Resistance and Transcendence

Slaves are almost proverbially lazy, implicitly because slavery gives them no motives for hard work (Rodriguez 1997). Descriptions of the work life of African origin slaves on plantations in the Caribbean and southern United States often depicts them "shirking" work through feigning illness or stupidity, and sabotaging production by damaging tools and theft (e.g., Follet 2005). The very same slaves could be seen working hard in their own provision gardens or fishing, hunting, and making things to sell on their own account in the market. These cases show that laziness can be a way to resist, or at least limit exploitation. "Slowdowns" ("Go Slow" in the UK) and "working to rule" are still common ways that workers and their unions protest inequity and exploitation. Laziness can be counted as one of the "weapons of the weak" enumerated by Scott (1985), not just as a means of shirking work but as a way to manage expectations. If the peasants can convince their masters that they are truly lazy, the masters will not expect them to act by their own volition; unless given specific work orders, they will sleep or wander off.

Day, Papataxiarchis, and Stewart bring together a number of case studies of social groups that pursue the short-term logic of "living for the moment" in their edited collection *Lilies of the Field* (1999). In their introduction they summarize the situation of groups as diverse as Romani, Greek gamblers, and Japanese day laborers as an inversion and refusal of the predictable life of wage earners. Rather than taking steady jobs and thinking for the future, people in these groups seek freedom and autonomy by occupying marginal situations and places, surviving by hunting, hustling, and living hand-to-mouth (1998: 2). In their words, "These are people who live resolutely in the short term and, in privileged moments, they transform this short term into a transcendent escape from time itself" (1988: 3) By resisting the demands of capitalist labor, they also refuse the commodification of time and work. Instead, labor is seen as a form of moral rectitude, a social obligation, and a means of personal expression.

Most of the case studies in Day, Papataxiarchis, and Stewart depict resistance from the margins as a practical response to prejudice and lack of opportunity. But there are also well-documented cases where avoiding work-life is a religious and philosophical practice of transcendence through renunciation. In India people and groups called Sadhus give up owning property, productive labor, and planning for the future, instead living by begging and charity. Many Sadhus consider the act of renunciation as their social and economic death (Openshaw 2007; Lorea 2014).

In this sense Sadhus are above the world, so giving charity and donations is a worshipful act that bring virtue to those living mundane working lives. When Sadhus get closer to God and achieve humility and clearer thinking by rejecting worldly distractions, living simply in the moment, they are seeking to completely transcend the needs of the body, tied to physical cycles of metabolism.[3] While the renunciation of the world was part of the earlier Christian and monastic traditions, under modern capitalist Christianity it has been supplanted by the virtues of prudence, hard work, saving for the future, and providing for descendants (see Rudnyckyj this vol.).

An economist reading *Lilies of the Field* would explain the cases of short-sightedness by saying that these people have a very high discount rate for the future. In other words, it would take a much larger reward in the future to make them forgo a reward in the present moment. Economic psychologists and anthropologists have collaborated on experiments that demonstrate that cultural differences in values have a strong effect on discount rates (Boyer, Lienard, and Xu 2012). They do not explain why.

Jane Guyer makes a similar point in a paper about the way economic monetarism and fundamentalist Christianity are changing Western perceptions of time: "the shift in temporal framing has involved a double move, towards both very short and very long-sightedness, with a symmetrical evacuation of the near past and the near future" (2007: 411). People may think about an ultimate state of grace, of redemption or rapture, but they do not or cannot plan for the next few years by saving or borrowing.

While Guyer embeds the loss of a predictable future in a global religious, intellectual, and economic milieu and new communication technologies, Day, Papataxiarchis, and Stewart focus on local history and the cultural specificity of colonialism and economic inequities. But both imply that people *choose* to live in the present because it offers more pleasures and satisfactions than working toward an indefinite future, though Guyer emphasizes compliance instead of resistance.

This particular disagreement is repeated over thousands of years of literature, history, and discourse. Are the poor to blame for their own situation, or are they victims of exploitation or dispossession (see Wilk 2019)? A closely related issue is whether poverty makes people miserable, or is it a kind of freedom that the hard-working bourgeois can only envy? A common ethical solution is to try to separate the deserving poor, those suffering from misfortune or accident beyond their control, from the undeserving poor. This dividing line is drawn differently depending on what we can reasonably expect from people. Can they anticipate the scarcity at the end of the dry season, so they should prudently put something aside for that future hunger? Should they be able to anticipate a flood every five years or so? What about a hundred-year flood, or a gradual rise in sea level over a millennium? Did they heed warnings by government experts to evacuate before a flood or fire? Or were they wise to ignore a government that has proven unreliable or oppressive? Is ignorance a source of peril or a form of bliss (or both)?

Laziness, History, and Self-Image

In a clear contradiction to Day, Papataxiarchis, and Stewart who see laziness as a functional form of resistance, or liberals who see it as a logical adaptation to poverty, most Belizeans treat it as a pathology of individuals, ethnic groups, and/or the country as a whole. Weaving through Belizean conversation, social and mass media, and publications are threads about laziness and development. This discourse about the "problems of Belize" is ubiquitous (and therefore impossible to catalog thoroughly in a short chapter), and it frames most discussions about laziness and improvidence. It also has a long history.

The European settlement of Belize began in the seventeenth century, a time when smuggling, privateering, and piracy were dominant across the

Caribbean and Central America (Linebaugh and Rediker 2000). The "Baymen" were typical of those unruly times. The Dutch buccaneer John Esquemeling visited "the Bay" in the late seventeenth century and reported: "whenever they have got hold of something they don't keep it for long. They are busy dicing, whoring, and drinking so long as they have anything to spend. Some of them will get through a good two or three thousand pieces of eight in a day—and next day not have a shirt to their back" (1985: 68).

Thirty years later Captain Nathaniel Uring, noting that the Baymen were of mixed and uncertain race, called them "a rude drunken crew, some of which have been pirates, and most of them sailors; their chief delight is in drinking; and when they broach a quarter cask or hogshead of wine, they seldom stir from it while there is a drop left. . . . they do most work when they have no strong drink, for while the liquor is moving they don't care to leave it" (1928: 241–42).

Remarkably, these stereotypes, and the moral approbation they elicit, persist to the present. Ethnic stereotyping was part of the colonial system of administration imposed by the British in the late nineteenth century. The colonial administrators incorporated their own assumptions about racial characteristics, including skin color and language, in law and everyday practice. They decided what kinds of work suited each "race" as defined by skin color and origin. People of different groups had characteristic jobs, which then reified the very boundaries that had been assumed.

The Garifuna (Afro-indigenes) were channeled toward teaching and nursing careers, while Afro-Caribbeans were the heirs of the Baymen's vices, given to hard work while living in the logging camps, but lazy by nature and improvident, spending their money quickly and recklessly on drink and luxury.[4] Official documents and studies of the British Honduran economy throughout the colonial era blamed the failure of plantations in the colony on the unwillingness of Creole Belizeans to do farm labor. They were also said to lack the "entrepreneurial spirit" needed to start and manage businesses (Bolland 1997; Sutherland 1998; Okeke 2016).

An argument that anticipates today's neoliberalism appears in a letter to the editor of a weekly newspaper in 1902. The writer says Belizeans are lazy and lack ambition "because the soil yields too well" (Clarion 1902: 2). With such abundance, there is no incentive to work or plan. A rejoinder in the next issue blames instead the lack of access to land, which was parceled out into giant estates, and points out that there are no roads or transport to get anything to market. One contemporary variation says people do not want to work hard because of the easy money from growing marijuana. As I was told, "Once they see how much they get from a lee [little] patch of ground, they never want to work hard again."

Similarly, Belizeans also accuse each other of a kind of complacency that prevents them from thinking ahead and planning to meet future threats or problems. In a village where people were getting good prices for their cashew nuts from wild trees a farmer explained: "right now they have a steady price and an easy market, and they are not looking to the future at all. Other villages are now planting cashew because they see this is a good money-making crop. And when they do, they will be willing to sell at a lower price—then [our village] people are going to lose out on the market. They are having an easy time of it now and are not really thinking about the future."

The idea that laziness is a vestige of slavery is a well-trodden folk theory in Belize, often linked with a lack of ambition or a willingness to take legal shortcuts to get ahead. A Creole village shopkeeper told me in 1990: "They were slaves and could not own anything. And they came to think 'why work for anything? I could never own that.' The master told them they could never have something nice. They saw how the master lived and decided that was too high to climb; so they would rather live in a hut because they don't think they could ever have a nice house. They are discouraged from even trying." As a consequence, he said, people have a "Father Christmas" attitude that their government should do everything for them: "depend on Massa to give everything." Instead of helping themselves and their community, they would rather wait and beg until they get what they want.

Many Belizeans also connect laziness with criminality. In 1989 I spoke with a teenager who had just had his expensive tennis shoes stolen from the front steps of his house. His comments reference the common belief in Belize of "crab catch crab": that everyone in a village will combine to pull down anyone who is escaping by "climbing" out. "Most people in the village are all right, but there are some guys who just teef [steal] everything. They don't wanna work, and it humbug [aggravate] them to see anyone else have something. If they have nothing, they want everyone else to have nothing."

This cynical autoethnography about motives plagues all kinds of social interaction. As one of my neighbors told me, "People always say they are going to help and work together, but when you actually get three people together to do some work, one of them is not going to carry his weight." This points to another supposed quality of lazy people in Belize, that they are "bad minded."

In contrast, new immigrants were often portrayed as the energetic and ambitious opposites of Belizeans. In the 1950s Mennonites from Mexico and Canada moved to Belize, bought huge tracts of land, and started colonies. By the twenty-first century Mennonites and their colonies could be found all over the country; they monopolized cash-crop agriculture for staple foods and controlled large portions of the hardware, poultry, furniture, and construction industries. Then in the 1980s there was a significant influx of Hispanic and indigenous refugees and migrants from war-torn and poverty-ridden neighboring countries. They have taken over menial and low-waged jobs on plantations and shrimp farms, and many have started successful small farms and businesses.

The mid-1990s brought an influx of Chinese, some fleeing Hong Kong reunification, and others fleeing rural poverty in the mainland. The number of new migrants quickly outnumbered the older Chinese community established in the nineteenth and early twentieth century. For a time Belize offered citizenship to Chinese immigrants with US$50,000 to invest. Initially many Chinese took Belizean citizenship so they could more easily get visas and green cards for the United States; but others invested in city real estate, building walled and gated communities, and then expanding to open restaurants and large retail shops in almost every part of the country. This prompted considerable hostility and accusations of unfair dealing, labor exploitation, and undermining the health of Belizeans by selling cheap fried food (Wilk 2012).[5]

Energetic and successful immigrants are often contrasted directly with native-born Belizeans. In 1991 a Belizean high school teacher stated a common opinion: "Belizeans don't think in the long term, they are not thinking about leaving something behind for their kids or the next generation. They just want to spend it and spend it now on things they want and partying. They see it in the shop window, and they buy it. It's not like the Chinese. They save and save and buy house and shop, while we just spend everything. That's why they own the whole city now."

While Belizeans are often critical of the "clannishness" of Chinese immigrants and their poor English, they still praise their long hours and hard work. While most Belizeans recognize that migrants from neighboring Hispanic republics are willing to work hard in the citrus and banana farms, they are also blamed for driving down wages.

Belizeans often say similar complementary things about the hard-working and frugal-living Mennonites. "Even when they get rich, they still working hard every day, riding tractor till sundown." In contrast, many people say Belizeans spend everything they make on foolish luxuries. In the 1980s, everyone pointed to expensive running shoes as an example. An Adventist preacher told me: "We Belizeans have big eyes. If you show a Belizean five big apples and five small apples, he will always take the five big apples, even if they are sour and the small ones are sweet." This echoes a Creole proverb about a man who needs shoes and sees that small ones and big ones cost the same, so he buys the big ones, even though they do not fit.

During the 1980s, I did a survey of the largest manufacturing businesses in Belize City, and managers consistently told me they would rather hire

Hispanic immigrants or Hispanic Belizeans over Creoles or Garifuna, because they were more "reliable." As the tourist industry has grown, so have hundreds of small service businesses owned by locals and expatriates. I cannot count the number of times expatriates and local managers have told me about their Belizean workers' laziness, unreliability, dishonesty, and "bad attitudes" toward work, often singling out urban Creoles. This discourse is clearly coded racism, akin to that of colonial times, though the consistently high crime rates in both urban and rural Belize provide plenty of incidents and examples that can be used as evidence. Of course, other expatriate retirees and business owners have strong relationships with local communities and express nothing but praise for Creole and other Belizean employees, and these people generally recognize that it takes many years to build relationships of mutual trust.

Another setting where I heard a lot of comments about laziness and improvidence was in 1990 interviews with returned migrants who had spent up to five years in the United States.[6] Most of them contrasted the "relaxed" or "slow pace" of life in Belize with the fast pace of life in the United States and Canada. In Belize, they said, people had time to stop and chat on the street, spend time with family and drop in on friends without calling ahead (the survey was done before cell phones). Some of the returned migrants connected this experience of time with the way appointments and meetings are always late in Belize, often jokingly called "on Belize Time." In colonial times it was called "Colored People Time" and was sometimes blamed for the poverty of the colony (Laing 1939). This is an important issue because it illustrates how racism was intertwined with the colonial ontology of time, which equated distance from civilization with backwardness, the primitive, and the infantile (Wilk 1994). A lazy person lives outside of regimented clock time and treats the present moment as far more important than the future. Thrift, as I define it in this chapter, is the exact opposite—investing in the future and foregoing the pleasures of the moment.

As an expression, Belize Time weaves across a border between Belizeans and strangers. When used between Belizeans or their trusted friends in an informal setting, it is a lighthearted and endearing affirmation of a common failing. Belizeans also talk among themselves about how other people are always late as a cultural or personal failing. It can also be used in anger by a Belizean or employer to criticize lateness, as in, "We not running on Belize Time here." When Belizeans accuse each other of a casual attitude toward time or laziness, it is an acceptable and often joking criticism. But coming from a foreigner or a rich person it is generally resented and seen as an example of racism.

The accusation of laziness can be used in exactly the same ways—as affirmation commiseration, accusation, or statement of solidarity. Laziness also has new uses as an incitement for tourism, a way of advertising Belize as a tourist destination. As an airline magazine advertisement says, "Belize offers visitors a contrast to the rat race of developed countries—a stress free and relaxed way of life."[7] The small island of Cay Caulker even has adopted "Go Slow" as its official slogan in tourist marketing (Gonzalez 2019). In this case laziness is about a change in the pace of time, providing the space for "doing nothing" (Lofgren and Ehn 2010), recovering from the recent past while purposively forgetting the future return to work.

Standard of Living as Indicator of Laziness

Comments about laziness are often prompted by poor neighborhoods, neglected housing, slums, favelas, refugee camps, and other settings where people live with few or no public services. This kind of environment is often disordered, littered with uncollected garbage, with rudimentary sanitation—unsightly and often smelly. The common explanations for these "eyesores" include laziness, unemployment, ignorance of proper hygiene and behavior, or perhaps the physical or psychological trauma of displacement or natural catastrophe. Governments often justify draconian measures to "clean up" slums on the grounds of public health, a move labeled "excremental colonialism" by Anderson (1995).

In Belize the settlements of migrant or temporary workers on citrus and banana plantations and shrimp farms (and sometimes on ranches and construction sites) are often described as filthy and squalid. Most of these workers migrate from neighboring republics, many illegally, and they take the lowest paid, most dangerous and arduous jobs in the country, which are still better than what they had at home. Belizeans are divided on whether these Hispanic migrants are taking jobs away from the native-born or are just filling the positions Belizeans will not tolerate. This is also a common issue in the United States and Europe, as they accommodate large numbers of migrants from poor countries.

The prevailing right-wing discourse in the United States and parts of Europe castigates migrants as lazy, ignorant, and criminal. But the argument can be reversed, to claim that native workers are too lazy to take these jobs and would rather collect welfare from the state. Belize is not a wealthy country, but even the poorest Belizeans reject the makeshift housing and poor services offered to migrant workers, as one farm owner told me, "the big problem with them is that they do not have the sense of hygiene that Belizeans have." The complex relationship between laziness and standard of living is revealed in this quote from the supervisor of a Belize banana plantation:

> Just like everywhere these days, we're looking for the cheapest labor possible.... They earn $15 a day and think they're in heaven. But then they turn around and say that Belizeans are too lazy to work in bananas. What they forget is that all of this was started by Belizeans. Belizeans cleared all of this bush, they planted the bananas and put up the cableways. It's not that Belizeans are lazy, but they want a good wage. They think that electricity and water are necessities, not luxuries. Well, these people are not used to the standards of living that Belizeans consider civilized, so we can work them for less. (quoted in Moberg 1997: 96)

The accusation of laziness can also come from Belizean farmers who voice the colonial-period belief that Afro-Belizeans will not do farm work.[8] This is particularly galling for many in the labor movement who remember that the owners of the banana plantations fired most of their Belizean workers when their union demanded higher wages. The immigrant workers were brought in as strikebreakers, just as Black migrant workers from the southern United States were pitted against White factory and coal workers in the middle of the twentieth century. As one union organizer said, "It is one thing when the management put us out of work. Did they then have to turn around and call us lazy too?" (Moberg 1997: 81).

Another theme running through the discourse of laziness in Belize is that people reject work because they want higher wages. These accusations connect with the economic elites' notion that people are "spoiled" by a soft and luxurious life and will never go back to hard work. Likewise, laziness is often a euphemism for "Black" in subtle and overt racism based on skin color that can be traced back to slavery (e.g., Okeke 2004: 44).

There is also a highly gendered aspect to accusations of laziness in Belize. Common wisdom blames Belizean men, particularly urban Creole men, for their failures to form permanent unions with women, accusing them of neglecting their children and their financial obligations. On the other hand, nutritionists and other medical authorities have been known to blame Belizean women's ignorance and laziness for high rates of malnutrition, stunting, and sickness among their babies and small children. In turn, villagers often accuse rural health workers and schoolteachers of laziness when they miss appointments or do not show up for work.

This in no way exhausts the rich set of cultural, political, economic, and historical meanings attached to laziness in Belize. I found many more definitions of laziness in my field notes and interview transcripts over more than forty years of fieldwork, including the phrases and quotes listed in Table 1. All are consonant with capitalist individualism; they normalize a disciplined and orderly society of respectable people engaged in productive labor, without reference to differences in power and privilege. They represent a kind of moral involution, where victims blame themselves and each other when they do not live up to the impossible demands of political and

Table 8.1. Components of laziness in Belize applied to individuals and groups.

1.	lacks ambition, has no goals or plans
2.	works slowly, requires constant supervision
3.	always tired and sleepy
4.	dishonest, lying, and thieving
5.	always late or misses appointments
6.	irresponsible, easily distracted, untrustworthy
7.	always in debt
8.	does not respond to incentives
9.	improvident, cannot save money for the future
10.	inflexible and stupid, cannot learn or change
11.	selfish and heedless of others
12.	addicted to drugs or alcohol, unable to stop
13.	short attention span, cannot concentrate
14.	demands unreasonable wages, expects more than they merit
15.	unwilling to do hard physical labor
16.	spoiled by easy money, handouts, inheritance
17.	works at their own pace
18.	gullible, impulse buyer
19.	willing to accept low living standards, poor hygiene

economic systems over which they have no control. The economy of Belize has always suffered periods of boom and bust, as a succession of capitalist schemes come and go. Without wealth, education, and positions of power, most Belizeans are blowing in the wind, subject to far-away events and decisions. How can we expect them to exercise all these bourgeois virtues? Why do they expect them of each other?

Laziness, Morality, and the Ontologies of Time

Laziness is an epithet often thrown at migrants and minority groups, at the unemployed as well as the super-rich. It was a staple of colonial discussions of the "natives," which often contrasted the hard-working ethnic groups from those considered spendthrift and difficult to motivate. In the age of conquest and imperialism, Europeans were often perplexed and vexed by conquered peoples' unwillingness to work on plantations, in mines, and other dangerous extractive industries. We often read some variation of "their wants are simple, and we could not induce them to work for us with promises of money." The consequences ranged from head taxes and forced labor to slavery, forced migration, and even extermination. Throughout the Caribbean the British brought poor laborers from China and India when slavery was abolished.

Is laziness a real phenomenon, a true quality of some individuals and part of the ideology and practice of some cultural groups? Thrift can be measured in various ways including savings rates and debt load, but laziness cannot (despite the efforts of many governments to separate the deserving poor from the lazy). But like thrift, laziness imputes a motive, a way of thinking about ethical economic and social behavior. Both laziness and thrift have deep connections to normative morality; they are ways of judging people and imputing their motives. They can only be seen as opposites in the moral frame of the "bourgeois virtues" defined by McCloskey (2007), where thrift is a virtue and laziness a sin. The peoples discussed in *Lilies of the Field* would fundamentally disagree, along with scholars who see laziness as a form of resistance to capitalism and exploitation, and those who view laziness as a path toward enlightenment.

Laziness and thrift also share an interesting moral quality in that both are values of moderation, of the "golden mean" (see Spalová this vol.). Many kinds of moral rules and norms demand absolutes, requirements, and the strictly forbidden. Laziness and thrift are part of a much smaller set of moral prescriptions that you could describe as two-tailed; at the extremes, both negative and positive are hazardous. You can be too thrifty or not thrifty enough, too lazy or overworked. They are opposite in the sense that being thrifty is generally given a positive value, while being lazy is generally used as a negative. This makes them more versatile as forms of social control and boundary making, always a debatable matter of degree rather than easily objective binary categories.

The broader lesson is that both laziness and thrift are ways of relating human life to the flow of time in ways that guide ethical and moral behavior. They are ontologies of time that reflect very different values of past, present, and future. Thrift is a form of time travel, displacing the labor of the present into the future, and in doing so, making the future seem more secure and predictable. Thrift requires faith in the future, a belief that our actions today will continue to have value, so thrift extends and projects the self into the unknown. Laziness denies that future, refusing time travel and the faith upon which it is based. Laziness is cynical and utilitarian, and it rejects the abstractions of the common good, of progress, growth, and modernity. Laziness is stubbornly lodged in the present, and in a warming world on the edge of disaster, it might be a reasonable option.

Perhaps the innovative appeal of the "slow food" and "slow city" movements is that they revalue experience and cast a slow life as both socially and environmentally responsible, *and* at the same time a source of pleasure, an escape from oppressive discipline. While the poor might be irresponsibly lazy consumers of fast food, the cultivated (and presumably well-to-do) consumer can take the time to appreciate inefficiently made artisanal products. These are exactly the same distinctions that have distinguished poverty from leisure over the centuries, making thrift and responsible labor the hallmarks of a long emergent middle-class.

Acknowledgments

I thank the editors of the volume for their constant encouragement and thoughtful comments and discussions, colleagues and students who provoke and inspire me, the Wenner-Gren Foundation and the Fulbright program that sponsored my research, and the many Belizeans who have patiently answered my questions for almost 50 years. I am especially grateful to my life partner Anne Pyburn, the least lazy person I know.

Richard Wilk is Distinguished Professor and Provost's Professor Emeritus at Indiana University. He has also taught at the University of California (Berkeley and Santa Cruz) and New Mexico State University and has held visiting positions in Sweden, France, Singapore, and the UK. His initial research on the cultural ecology of indigenous Mayan farming and family organization was followed by work on consumer culture and sustainable consumption, energy consumption, globalization, television, beauty pageants, and food. His most recent book is *Critical Approaches to Superfoods*, coedited with Emma McDonell.

Notes

1. Harrison has even more strident comments on the failure of Caribbean countries with sizable populations of the descendants of African slaves. About Haiti, he cites with approval Rotberg's argument that "Haitians seem to rear their children in a matter that is traumatic and conducive to later conflict. . . . Haitian children are highly indulged" (Rotberg 1971:19–22, cited in Harrison 1985: 85).
2. Swaddling restricts children's independence, while feeding on demand "spoils" them. Though widely rejected by contemporary anthropology (Montgomery 2008), this psychological approach has never disappeared. Reinvented by Harrison and Huntington (2000), it remains popular in cross-cultural marketing and psychology (Hofstede 1980).

3. Particularly in its early years, the Catholic church also hosted many prophets and holy men and women who achieved transcendent power through isolation, discomfort, and fasting.
4. I have written separately about this "binge economy." Almost all the evidence concerns the behavior of men and women, particularly those employed as servants, who were also stereotyped as lazy, pigheaded, and untrustworthy (Wilk 2014).
5. A Chinese restaurant owner who had lived in Belize for three years told me, "Belize is a country with good land, good soil, beautiful sea, but they remain poor because Belize people are lazy."
6. Most of the interviews were conducted by Melissa Johnson, then my research assistant, now a professor with a recent book about Belize Creole culture (Johnson 2018).
7. "Enjoy the slower pace of life in Belize. . . . What really transforms this Central American country into paradise . . . is what residents and visitors know as 'Belize time'" (Cobb 2016).
8. The idea that Creole Belizeans are averse to farm work has been debunked repeatedly by historians and anthropologists, including myself.

References

Anderson, Warwick. 1995. "Excremental Colonialism: Public Health and the Poetics of Pollution." *Critical Inquiry* 21: 640–69.

Babcock, Elizabeth, and Richard Wilk. 1998. "International Travel and Consumer Preferences among Secondary School Students in Belize, Central America." *Caribbean Geography* 8(1): 32–45.

Bauer, Peter T. 1981. *Equality, the Third World, and Economic Delusion*. Cambridge, MA: Harvard University Press.

Benedict, Ruth. 1934. *Patterns of Culture*. Boston: Houghton Mifflin Company.

Bernanke, Ben S. 1983. "Non-Monetary Effects of the Financial Crisis in the Propagation of the Great Depression." *The American Economic Review* 73(3): 257–76.

Binford, Lewis. 1980. "Willow Smoke and Dogs' Tails: Hunter-Gatherer Settlement Systems and Archaeological Site Formation." *American Antiquity* 45(1): 4–20.

Bolland, Nigel. 1997. *Struggles for Freedom: Essays on Slavery, Colonialism and Culture in the Caribbean and Central America*. Belize City: Angelus Press.

Boyer, Pascal, Pierre Lienard, and Jing Xu. 2012. "Cultural Differences in Investing in Others and in the Future: Why Measuring Trust Is Not Enough." *PLoS ONE* 7(7): e40,750. doi:10.1371/journal.pone.0040750.

Browne, Katherine E., and B. Lynne Milgram, eds. 2009. *Economics and Morality: Anthropological Approaches*. Walnut Creek: Altamira Press.

Clarion, The (Belize City), 1902. *Letter from "Admirer"*. Volume 8(256), April 10, 1902. Accessed at the Bancroft Library, UC Berkeley.

Cobb, Mike. 2016. "Enjoy the Slower Pace of Life in Belize." *Grand Baymen* (blog), 16 March. https://www.grandbaymen.com/blog/enjoy-the-slower-pace-of-life-in-belize.

Cussler, Margaret, and Mary De Give. 1952. *Twixt the Cup and the Lip: Psychological and Sociocultural Factors Affecting Food Habits*. New York: Twayne Publishers.

Dalrymple, Theodore. 2001. *Life at the Bottom: The Worldview That Makes the Underclass.* Chicago: Ivan R. Dee, Publisher.

———. 2010. *Spoilt Rotten: The Toxic Cult of Sentimentality.* London: Gibson Square Books Ltd.

Dampier, William. 1906. *Dampier's Voyages,* edited by John Mansfield. London: E. Grant Richards.

Day, Sophie, Akis Papataxiarchis, and Michael Stewart, eds. 1998. *Lilies of the Field: Marginal People Who Live for the Moment.* Boulder, CO: Westview Press.

Edgerton, Robert. 1992. *Sick Societies: Challenging the Myth of Primitive Harmony.* New York: The Free Press.

Esquemeling, John. (1685) 1987. *The Buccaneers of America,* edited by William Stallybrass. New York: Dorset Press.

Ferguson, Niall. 2004. *Empire: The Rise and Demise of the British World Order and the Lessons for Global Power.* New York: Basic Books.

———. 2011. *Civilization: The West and the Rest.* New York: The Penguin Press.

Follett, Richard. 2005. *The Sugar Masters: Planters and Slaves in Louisiana's Cane World, 1820—1860.* Baton Rouge: Louisiana State University Press.

Geertz, Clifford. 1968. *Peddlers and Princes: Social Development and Economic Change in Two Indonesian Towns.* Chicago: University of Chicago Press.

Gonzalez, Lorenzo. 2019. "Things You Might Not Know About Belize." *Belize Adventure* (blog), 2 May. https://www.belizeadventure.ca/things-about-belize/.

Gonzalez, Nancie. 1969. *Black Carib Household Structure: A Study of Migration and Modernization.* Seattle: University of Washington Press.

Graeber, David, and David Wengrow. 2018. "How to Change the Course of Human History." *Eurozine,* 2 March. https://www.eurozine.com/change-course-human-history/.

Gudeman, Stephen. 2012. "Vital Energy." *Social Analysis* 56(1): 57–73.

Guyer, Jane. 2007. "Prophecy and the Near Future: Thoughts on Macroeconomic, Evangelical, and Punctuated Time." *American Ethnologist* 34(3): 409–21.

Harrison, Lawrence. 1985. *Underdevelopment Is a State of Mind.* Lanham, MD: Madison Books.

Harrison, Lawrence E., and Samuel P. Huntington, eds. 2000. *Culture Matters: How Values Shape Human Progress.* New York: Basic Books.

Henne, Adam. 2015. *Environmentalism, Ethical Trade, and Commodification: Technologies of Value and the Forest Stewardship Council in Chile.* London: Routledge.

Hofmann, Wilhelm, Daniel Wisneski, Mark Brandt, and Linda Skitka. 2014. "Morality in Everyday Life." *Science* 345: 1,340–43.

Hofstede, Gert. 1980. *Culture's Consequences: International Differences in Work-Related Values.* Beverly Hills, CA: Sage.

Jeske, Christine. 2018. "Why Work? Do We Understand What Motivates Work-Related Decisions in South Africa?" *Journal of Southern African Studies* 44(1): 27–42.

———. 2020. *The Laziness Myth: Narratives of Work and the Good Life in South Africa.* Ithaca: Cornell University Press.

Johnson, Melissa A. 2018. *Becoming Creole: Nature and Race in Belize.* New Brunswick: Rutgers University Press.

Krech, Shepard. 1999. *The Ecological Indian: Myth and History*. New York: W. W. Norton & Co.

Kuldova, Tereza. 2016. "Fatalist Luxuries: of Inequality, Wasting, and the Anti-Work Ethic in India." *Cultural Politics* 12(1): 110–29.

Laing, E. A. 1939. *Hit or Miss*. The Daily Clarion (Belize), September 30, 1939. Archives of Belize.

Lakoff, George. 1996. *Moral Politics*. Chicago: University of Chicago Press.

Landes, David. 1998. *The Wealth and Poverty of Nations: Why Some Are So Rich and Some So Poor*. New York: W W Norton & Co Inc.

Lee, Richard Borshay. 1969. "Eating Christmas in the Kalahari." *Natural History* (Dec.): 60–64.

———. 1979. *The !Kung San: Men, Women, and Work in a Foraging Society*. Cambridge, UK: Cambridge University Press.

Lewis, Oscar. 1959. *Five Families: Mexican Case Studies in the Culture of Poverty*. New York: Basic Books.

———. 1969. "Culture of Poverty." In *On Understanding Poverty: Perspectives from the Social Sciences*, edited by Daniel P. Moynihan, 187–220. New York: Basic Books.

Linebaugh, Peter, and Marcus Rediker. 2000. *The Many-Headed Hydra*. Boston: Beacon Press.

Lofgren, Orvar, and Billy Ehn. 2010. *The Secret World of Doing Nothing*. Berkeley: University of California Press.

Lorea, Carola Erika. 2014. "Why Did You Go Swimming in the River Full of Algae? Conception and Contraception in Bauls' Songs and Oral Teachings." *Folklore and Folkloristics* 7(1): 9–45.

MacGaffey, Janet. 1991. *The Real Economy of Zaire: The Contribution of Smuggling and Other Unofficial Activities to National Wealth*. Philadelphia: University of Pennsylvania Press.

Manson, William. 1988. *The Psychodynamics of Culture: Abram Kardiner and Neo-Freudian Anthropology*. New York: Praeger.

McCloskey, Deirdre N. 2007. *The Bourgeois Virtues: Ethics for an Age of Commerce*. Chicago: University of Chicago Press.

Mead, Margaret. 1948. *Sex and Temperament in Three Primitive Societies*. London: Routledge and Kegan Paul.

Miller, Daniel. 1991. "Absolute Freedom in Trinidad." *Man* 26(2): 323–41.

———. 1998. *A Theory of Shopping*. Ithaca: Cornell University Press.

———. 2001.*The Dialectics of Shopping*. Chicago: University of Chicago Press.

Moberg, Mark. 1997. *Myths of Ethnicity and Nation: The Belize Banana Industry*. Nashville: University of Tennessee Press.

Monbiot, George. 2009. "We Cannot Change the World by Changing Our Buying Habits." *The Guardian*, 6 November. https://www.theguardian.com/environment/georgemonbiot/2009/nov/06/green-consumerism.

Montgomery, Heather. 2008. *An Introduction to Childhood: Anthropological Perspectives on Children's Lives*. New York: John Wiley & Sons.

Moynihan, Daniel P., ed. 1969. *On Understanding Poverty: Perspectives from the Social Sciences*. New York: Basic Books.

Nelson, Laura C. 2012. *Measured Excess: Status, Gender, and Consumer Nationalism in South Korea*. New York: Columbia University Press.
Netting, Robert. 1993. *Smallholders, Householders: Farm Families and the Ecology of Intensive, Sustainable Agriculture*. Stanford: Stanford University Press.
Okeke, Stephen. 2004. *Understanding the Problems of Belizean Youths: Positive Insights*. Belize City: Crossing Sign Publishers.
———. 2016. *The Psychology of the Belize Market Place: How to Succeed in Small Business in Belize*. Belize City: Crossing Sign Publisher.
Openshaw, Jeanne. 2007. "Renunciation Feminized? Joint Renunciation of Female-Male Pairs in Bengali Vaishnavism." *Religion* 37: 319–32.
Oxfeld, Ellen. 1993. *Blood, Sweat and Mahjong: Family and Enterprise in an Overseas Chinese Community*. Ithaca: Cornell University Press
Rodriguez, Junius P. 1997. *The Historical Encyclopedia of World Slavery*. Santa Barbara: ABC-CLIO.
Sahlins, Marshall. 1972. *Stone Age Economics*. Chicago: Aldine.
Salisbury, Richard. 1962. *From Stone to Steel*. Cambridge, UK: Cambridge University Press.
Scott, James. 1979. *The Moral Economy of the Peasant: Rebellion and Subsistence in Southeast Asia*. New Haven: Yale University Press.
———. 1985. *Weapons of the Weak: Everyday Forms of Peasant Resistance*. New Haven: Yale University Press.
Shove, Elizabeth, Frank Trentmann, and Richard Wilk. 2009. "Introduction." In *Time, Consumption and Everyday Life: Practice, Materiality and Culture*, edited by Elizabeth Shove, Frank Trentmann, and Richard Wilk, 1–16. Oxford: Berg Publishers.
Sowell, Thomas. 2016. *Wealth, Poverty and Politics*. New York: Basic Books.
Sutherland, Anne. 1998. *The Making of Belize*. Westport, CT: Bergin & Garvey.
Uring, Nathaniel. 1928. T*he voyages and travels of Captain Nathaniel Uring, with introduction and notes by Captain Alfred Dewar*. London: Cassell and Company.
Weber, Max. 1930. *The Protestant Ethic and the Spirit of Capitalism*. Translated by T. Parsons. London: George Allen & Unwin Ltd.
White, David Gordon. 1998. *The Alchemical Body: Siddha Traditions in Medieval India*. Chicago: University of Chicago Press.
Whiting, Beatrice, ed. 1963. *Six Cultures: Studies of Child Rearing*. New York: John Wiley & Sons.
Wight, Daniel. 1993. *Workers Not Wasters: Masculine Respectability, Consumption and Employment in Central Scotland*. Edinburgh: University of Edinburgh Press.
Wilk, Richard. 1994. "Colonial Time and TV Time." *Visual Anthropology Review* 10(1): 94–102.
———. 2006. *Home Cooking in the Global Village*. Oxford: Berg Publishers.
———. 2012. "Loving People, Hating What They Eat: Marginal Foods and Social Boundaries." In *Reimagining Marginalized Foods: Global Processes, Local Places*, edited by Elizabeth Finnis, 15–33. Tucson: University of Arizona Press.
———. 2014. "Poverty and Excess in Binge Economies." *Economic Anthropology* 1(1): 66–79.
———. 2018. "Is Time Really like Money? Binge Consumption, Temporality, and the Value of Money." Academia, 23 September. https://www.academia.edu/37461979.

———. 2019. "Rethinking the Relationships between Scarcity, Poverty and Hunger—an Anthropological Perspective." In *Scarcity in the Modern World, 1800–2015*, edited by John Brewer, Neil Fromer, Fredrik Albritton Jonsson, and Frank Trentmann, 221–28. London: Bloomsbury Academic.

Wilk, Richard R., and Lisa C. Cliggett. 2007. *Economies and Cultures: Foundations of, Economic Anthropology*. New York: Routledge.

Wilson, Peter. 1973. *Crab Antics*. New Haven: Yale University Press.

Zhong, Chen-Bo, Gillian Ku, Robert B. Lount Jr., and J. Keith Murnighan. 2010. "Compensatory Ethics" *Journal of Business Ethics* 92: 323–39.

Zimmerman, Merle, and Carl Frampton. 1936. *Family and Society: A Study of the Sociology of Reconstruction*. London: Williams and Norgate.

Afterword

Chris Hann

I must have been quite small when the word "thrift" entered my vocabulary. Perhaps I was practicing it even earlier: eking out my pocket money to buy sweets and the next Beatles record. Yet the connotations of the word were not contemporary. Thrift was exemplified by an elderly widow, Auntie Cis who lived nearby and sometimes babysat for my family. When we called on her to extend Christmas greetings, my parents would politely decline the ritualized offer of a glass of sherry. The level of Harveys Bristol Cream in the bottle that stood on the dresser in the living room of Auntie Cis' never seemed to alter. She might not have been strictly teetotal, but she was definitely abstemious and thrifty. Many years later I understood that her family was quite representative of Chapel Protestants in industrial South Wales. The contrast between this moral climate and the hedonism of British youth in the 1960s could hardly have been greater.

In the 1970s as a student of economics I learned to make further distinctions. Thrift was not a virtue in Keynesian macroeconomics. On the contrary, deficit spending was the only way to revive a capitalist economy mired in depression. Budget deficits, however, appeared to lead to inflation, unemployment, declining profit rates, and financialization that served the interests of a plutocracy. This debate continues in the twenty-first century. Global financial crisis and the impact of the Covid-19 pandemic demand Keynesian pump-priming. In the other camp, German politicians preach austerity to southern Europeans. They argue that careful housekeeping is as essential at the level of the state as it is for every household.

This volume contains rich ethnographic explorations of the economic and ethical paradoxes of thrift around the globe. The authors' multiscalar investigations prompt the reader to reflect on how a private virtue became a key factor in the rise of capitalism before morphing intermittently into a public vice. They raise many deeper questions: Is it virtuous to sanction the behavior of those who take what powerful others consider to be undue pleasure in the present? Are the concept and the practice of thrift a waste of the human spirit, a peculiarly European impoverishment of our impulse to enjoy and be generous? Or is the spirit of thrift the last hope for responsible planetary housekeeping in the Anthropocene?

At the end of his contribution, Stephen Gudeman (Chapter 1) quotes and modifies Keynes: the most powerful ideas of renowned European scholars originate with the people in what Gudeman calls the "house model" of economy. This was the dominant model from Aristotle's *oeconomia* to Max Weber's concept of *haushalten*. The aim is secure, solid management, not monetary gain (profit). Thrift in the everyday sense of the Colombian peasant, Gudeman shows us, is about muddling through and making ends meet, not the accumulation of capital.

This focus on the household has a long tradition in economic anthropology. Early evolutionist schemas posited "closed household economy" as a higher stage that followed the egoistic needs-satisfaction of primitive man (see Spittler 2008, particularly his discussion of the contributions of Karl Bücher). Technologies of storage opened up new temporalities and possibilities for both exchange and thrift. One of the most important results of the early ethnographers (notably Malinowski in the Trobriands Islands) was the demonstration that goods circulate, not only between households but also between larger "tribal" units (Malinowski 1921). The notion of closure was clearly misleading. But it was not wrong, as Gudeman explains, to distinguish the goals of good household management from those of capitalist profit-maximization.

If the theoreticians of "tribal economy" a century ago expanded the scale of economic organization significantly beyond the household, the task facing contemporary economic anthropologists is more complex. Thrift, understood as more or less calculated, future-oriented economic management, is illustrated by contributors to this volume in a great variety of settings. The concept is stretched far beyond the bourgeois moral compass. It encompasses collective stewardship for a territorially bounded (home) region in the cases of Mongolian (ex-)pastoralists (Rakowski, Chapter 4) and Czech monks (Spalová, Chapter 5). My Auntie Cis would probably find more recognizable forms of thrift in the housebuilding strategies of the Guarani in Argentina (Diz, Chapter 3) and even in the recycling activities of Czech waste workers (Sosna, Chapter 7). She would, however, criticize the wastage of fuel that Sosna interprets as a form of resistance to uncaring management, just as she would deplore indolent Belizeans who resist by rejecting "respectability" (Wilk, Chapter 8). Were she alive today, my Auntie Cis would be shocked to learn that, for many poor citizens of South Africa in receipt of state benefits, thrift means the juggling of debts to other individuals and organizations (James, Neves, and Torkelson, Chapter 2). But she might appreciate the motivations behind these calculations, not only in South Africa but also in the Argentinian case presented by Diz, where new state benefits have strengthened the position of women as household managers better able to make responsible long-term plans. Although it is pure speculation on my part, I think Auntie Cis would empathize warmly with the emotional rewards of parsimony as described by Sosna (including the "affect of discovery" in the landfill, regardless of whether the item in question has utilitarian value).

In all these contemporary case-studies, the economic anthropologist must investigate the impact of capitalist political economy. A "market model" has become dominant, from Mongolia to Latin America, from Central Europe to South Africa, from the Caribbean to Indonesia. Yet this model never entirely breaks down the resilience of older forms of domestic and community organization. Scalability applies in politics as well as in economy: the house model has a political dimension in the form of patriarchal power. Polish peasants have long imagined their polity in terms of the responsibilities of the head of the household to provide for all its members (Malewska-Szałygin 2017). Beyond political economy, several chapters raise the moral or ethical dimensions of thrift explicitly. Thrift is a value as well as a management strategy. It is usually associated with frugality, sometimes asceticism, and perhaps even transcendence. Daromir Rudnyckyj rehearses the Weberian argument that an ethos of "hard frugality," in particular strands of Protestantism, played a critical role in the transition to a new era of political economy. Some external forms of thrift might persist unchanged, but the stakes were different when the goal became profit, rather than muddling through. The state-owned Indonesian steel plant in which Rudnyckyj did his field research was formerly a "moral economy" characterized by over-staffing, patron–client relations (also discussed by Diz), and corruption. To maintain competitiveness, management has brought in a charismatic consultant who preaches a transparent "spiritual economy" grounded in the precepts of Islam.

The context could hardly differ more from that of Weber's industrious Calvinists: the state corporation needs docile workers, not dynamic entrepreneurs. The analogy with the Protestant ethic hinges on workers and management alike internalizing new norms of hard work, individual responsibility, and self-improvement. Previous leaders could rely on state subsidies and had no hard budget constraints (the work of the late János Kornai on this point is discussed in the editors' Introduction). By the standards of neoliberal global capitalism, their "hoarding" of surplus labor was inefficient. Yet the proliferation of jobs was the key to a "social mission" that has apparently vanished in the new century, as employment has contracted and become more precarious. This example of a spiritual economy appears to have unwelcome consequences. Is the grounding in Islam sufficient to render the "pure business" model more ethical than the "fatalistic" moral economy of Indonesia's developmentalist phase? As in Europe several centuries ago, it seems that religious doctrines are legitimating new forms of economy and domination. The beliefs and values are absorbed not just by the elites who profit from them but by much broader social strata (the family of my Auntie Cis in Wales was barely middle class).

We are on more comfortable ethical-moral ground in Barbora Spalová's fine chapter, in which she investigates "spiritual discernment" and the "moral standard of living" in two significantly different postsocialist monasteries in the Czech Republic. We learn that the Czech word for frugality, *střídmost*, is etymologically connected to "middle." Benedictine norms emphasize the "golden mean": neither intemperance nor extremes of frugality. Wilk makes a similar argument in his discussion of Belizean "laziness." I am reminded of the emphasis on *moderation* (*mérsékeltség*) in Hungarian peasant society (Fél and Hofer 1969, 1972) and, more distantly, of Gregory Bateson's Balinese who combined thrift ("penny-wise") and extravagance ("pound-foolish") within an overarching "steady state" ethos (Bateson 1949). I doubt whether Auntie Cis was capable of being "pound-foolish," but generalized household thrift is not inconsistent with exuberant hospitality to kin and other households when warranted on special occasions, such as a wedding (cf. the sponsored feast discussed by Rakowski in Chapter 4 as an example of generous "social thriftiness" in Mongolia). If Czech monks prefer to recite their prayers in a building heated to 16 degrees, that is no problem for their accountants. There is much individual variation, since only God is the ultimate arbiter of one's "spiritual growth." Ambiguities are bound to arise, if only because these monasteries are simultaneously complex economic organizations that supply goods and services in markets. Thriftiness must be carefully negotiated and planned. Should the monks aim to increase revenue in the market to be able to ratchet up their charitable redistribution outside it? Can an ascetic order justify the expenditure of large sums on the renovation of ornate baroque heritage when local Roma are living in poverty? Spalová tells us that it is considered immoral/unethical to be stingy in glorifying God, or in receiving guests. In practice, the monks somehow manage to reconcile many competing desiderata. Thrift must be relativized and its limits embraced.

I think Auntie Cis would grasp this. Much has changed in global (non-)scalability, transforming human beings and states alike, since her passing a few decades ago. Control over large swathes of public spending in our native Wales is no longer exercised from London but from a parliament in Cardiff. A rather more powerful parliament in London has taken the British state outside the aegis of Brussels, but without fundamentally altering the connectivities of international political economy. Diverse forms of state compete and struggle to regulate and tax diverse forms of corporation. The upshot of this anarchy, which transcends both the Keynesian scale of economic management and the ambivalences of household thrift cross-culturally, is the lack of any authority capable of halting ecological destruction. How long must it take before this planet is managed according to the thrift principles of the postsocialist Cistercian monastery at Vyšší Brod?

Chris Hann is an economic anthropologist who has carried out fieldwork in Eastern Europe (Hungary and Poland), Turkey, and China (Xinjiang Uyghur Autonomous Region). He is a Founding Director of the Max Planck Institute for Social Anthropology and a Fellow of Corpus Christi College, Cambridge. Recent publications include *Repatriating Polanyi: Market Society in the Visegrád States* (Central European University Press, 2019) and *The Great Dispossession: Uyghurs between Civilizations* (LIT Verlag, 2020, with Ildikó Bellér-Hann).

References

Bateson, Gregory. 1949. "The Value System of a Steady State." pp. 35-43 in Meyer Fortes (ed), *Social Structure. Studies Presented to A. R. Radcliffe-Brown*. Oxford: Clarendon Press.

Fél, Edit, and Tamás Hofer. 1969. *Proper Peasants: Traditional Life in a Hungarian Village*. Chicago: Aldine.

———. 1972. *Bäuerliche Denkweise in Wirtschaft und Haushalt; eine ethnographische Untersuchung über das ungarische Dorf Átány*. Göttingen: Schwartz.

Malewska-Szałygin, Anna. 2017. *Social Imaginaries of the State and Central Authority in Polish Highland Villages, 1999–2005*. Newcastle: Cambridge Scholars Publishing.

Malinowski, Bronislaw. 1921. "The Primitive Economics of the Trobriand Islanders." *The Economic Journal* 31(121): 1–16.

Spittler, Gerd. 2008. *Founders of the Anthropology of Work: German Social Scientists of the 19th and Early 20th Centuries and the First Ethnographers*. Berlin: LIT.

Index

Note: Pages noted with an *f* are figures.

www.ingramcontent.com/pod-product-compliance
Ingram Content Group UK Ltd.
Pitfield, Milton Keynes, MK11 3LW, UK
UKHW020726230926
8686IPUK00002BB/6